29.95
60B

D1249303

THE HUMAN
AND
THE HOLY

THE HUMAN AND THE HOLY

The Spirituality of
ABRAHAM JOSHUA HESCHEL

DONALD J. MOORE, S.J.

Fordham University Press
New York
1989

© Copyright 1989 by Fordham University
All rights reserved.
LC 89–80461
ISBN 0–8232–1235–1

Printed in the United States of America

296.3
MB21h

255276

TO ALL OF THOSE,
FAMILY AND FRIENDS, COMPANIONS AND COLLEAGUES,
STUDENTS AND STRANGERS,
OF VARIOUS FAITHS AND OF NO FAITH,
WHOSE HUMANNESS HAS IMAGED GOD'S HOLINESS
IN OUR WORLD

ACKNOWLEDGMENTS

I should like to express a word of profound gratitude to:

–the late Rev. William F. Lynch, s.j., singled out as one among many whose critique of this manuscript in the early stages provided a constant source of encouragement;

–Sylvia Heschel, whose advice, suggestions, and insights were of enormous assistance, and who shared with me, as did Rev. Daniel Berrigan, s.j., many personal anecdotes about Heschel;

–Rabbi Marc Tanenbaum and the American Jewish Committee for permission to use unpublished or archival materials cited in the Introduction of this work;

–Dr. Mary Beatrice Schulte, who patiently and painstakingly edited the final copy for Fordham University Press.

CONTENTS

INTRODUCTION

FEW JEWS OF THIS OR ANY AGE have so profoundly influenced relations between Christians and Jews, and more specifically between Catholics and Jews, than Rabbi Abraham Joshua Heschel. In the view of a former student and colleague of his, one need only record, not embellish, the accomplishments of Heschel's life because his "contributions and achievements—intellectual, theological, and, above all, the impact of his person—were so singular, profound, varied and lasting. . . ." The facts alone present a "monumental statement."[1]

Less than three months after his death on December 23, 1972, *America*, the Jesuit weekly and one of the leading Catholic journals in the United States, devoted an entire issue (March 10, 1973) to an assessment of Heschel's life, thought, and influence upon Christians and Jews in this country and throughout the world. Donald Campion, editor of *America* at the time, noted that this was probably the first time that a Christian journal had devoted an entire issue to a contemporary Jewish religious figure. Heschel merited such a testimony because he was an enormously energetic person "both intellectually and spiritually." Just as we Christians often point to the life of an authentic Christian as the best way of learning about Christianity, so we may point to the life and example of a Jew like Heschel as the best mode of instruction concerning "the continuing vitality and richness of the Judaic tradition in which we providentially share." To encounter Abraham Heschel is to encounter "the living tradition of Judaism in all its energy, holiness and compassion."[2]

Much has also been made of Pope Paul VI's remark on January 31, 1973, when he told his listeners in a general audience: "Even before we have moved in search of God, God has come in search of us." These words are a clear reference to one of the great central themes in Heschel's writings and are actually taken from the French translation of Heschel's masterpiece, *God in Search of Man*.[3] Rarely had any pope ever made public reference to the writings of a non-Christian, yet Heschel was well known to Paul VI not only through his writings, but, more important, through their meetings, conversations, and growing friendship over the previous decade, especially during the crucial months prior to the promulgation on October 28, 1965, of Vatican II's *Nostra Aetate*, the Council's "Declaration on the Relation of the Church to Non-Christian Religions."

Who was Abraham Joshua Heschel, and what led to his prominent role in the Second Vatican Council? I can sketch only a brief response to these questions, and I might begin by citing an incident toward the close of Heschel's life. He suffered a near-fatal heart attack in the late 1960s. On his first day out of bed following the attack, he received a visit from his good friend Rabbi Samuel Dresner. A weak and pale Heschel spoke to his visitor in a barely audible whisper. "'Sam, when I regained consciousness, my first feeling was not of despair or anger. I felt only gratitude to God for my life, for every moment I had lived. I was ready to depart. "Take me, O Lord," I thought, "I have seen so many miracles in my lifetime."'" Heschel then referred to a line he had once written: "'I did not ask for success; I asked for wonder. And You gave it to me.'"[4]

Few anecdotes capture so well the person of Abraham Heschel as he was known to his friends, colleagues, and readers. For Heschel, the authentic human life is a life lived in response to the wonder of God's creation. One's whole life becomes an answer to God's gift, a service of creation and a service of the Creator. Knowing that one's destiny is to serve is the very core of wisdom; this makes death a "homecoming," a gift to God in return for His gift of life. As Heschel once wrote: "For the pious man it is a privilege to die."[5] Clearly, Heschel's was an authentic human life, and he well deserved the accolade of the "pious man." As Rabbi Dresner commented, "Reading Heschel is to peer into the heart of the rarest of human phenomena, the holy man. . . . He wrote what he thought and lived what he wrote."[6]

Heschel was born in Warsaw in 1907, a direct descendant of a distinguished line of Hasidic rabbis, the most famous of whom was his grandfather and namesake, Abraham Joshua Heschel, known as the "Apter Rav" and held by some followers to be the incarnation of the spirit of the founder of the Hasidic movement, the Baal Shem Tov.[7] Even as a child Heschel became the source of great hopes and expectations for the Hasidic community. Some Hasidic leaders saw in him the one who would bring about renewed vigor to their whole movement. Heschel was aware of these hopes and of the responsibility and dignity conferred by them. Nevertheless he felt compelled to extend himself beyond the confines of the Hasidic world and to pursue a course of secular studies. And so in his late teens he left Warsaw for Vilna and then went on to the university in Berlin where he earned his doctorate in 1933. Two years later his study on Maimonides was published, establishing a solid basis for Heschel's scholarly reputation. The following year his dissertation on the prophets of Israel was published in Berlin; this was the basis for a more extensive work in English, *The Prophets*, published a quarter of a century later and recognized as Heschel's most important contribution to the field of biblical studies. After a year of teaching as Martin Buber's successor at the Jewish *Lehrhaus* in Frankfurt, he was forced by the Nazis to return to Poland in 1938. In the spring of 1939 Heschel received an invitation to teach at The Hebrew Union College in Cincinnati; thus he left Poland in the summer of 1939, just six weeks before the Nazi invasion. He would later describe himself as "a brand plucked from the fire,"[8] a fire that destroyed his family, his community, and so much of Jewish culture and piety in Eastern Europe. The Holocaust placed upon Heschel an awesome responsibility as one of the few who could preserve this tradition both for Jews and for non-Jews. Part of this responsibility was met through the appearance of his first major work in English, *The Earth Is the Lord's: The Inner World of the Jew in Eastern Europe.* Reinhold Niebuhr's review of this book hailed it as "'a spiritual treasure snatched from the smoldering embers of Nazi Germany.'"[9]

Heschel took up his post at The Hebrew Union College in 1940, and five years later he accepted a professorship at the Jewish Theological Seminary of America in New York City where he remained until his death. It was during his tenure at Jewish Theological Seminary that Heschel would achieve his greatest fame. In 1946 he married Sylvia Strauss, a noted concert pianist from Cleveland. Some ten years later, in an address on "The Vocation of the Cantor," Heschel would describe himself, perhaps in an oblique and humorous reference to his wife, "as a person who has been smitten by music, as a person who has never recovered from the blows of music."[10] (But Sylvia Heschel also assured me, in conversations of June 1987,

that her husband's interest in music long antedated their acquaint-
anceship and marriage!)

Heschel's reputation at Jewish Theological Seminary grew not
only through his writings but also through his contributions to such
national gatherings as the White House Conference on Children
and Youth in 1960, the White House Conference on Aging in
1961, and the National Conference on Religion and Race in 1963.
In 1965–1966 Heschel served as the first Harry Emerson Fosdick
Visiting Lecturer at Union Theological Seminary in New York City.
Both in his writings and in his addresses Heschel strove to underscore the relevance of his Jewish tradition to our contemporary world,
and in a more direct way to contemporary Christianity. Robert
McAfee Brown wrote that "Heschel's contribution to Christians
consisted in his being such a good Jew. . . . for when I have been in
his presence and have talked with him and have heard him pray, I
have been moved to ask myself, 'What have I got to tell this man
about God?' and thus far I have never found an answer."[11] And in
the words of John C. Bennett, former president of Union Theological Seminary:

> He was profoundly Jewish in his spiritual and cultural roots, in his
> closeness to Jewish suffering, in his religious commitment, in his
> love for the nation and land of Israel, and in the quality of his pro-
> phetic presence. And yet he was a religious inspiration to Christians
> and to many searching people beyond the familiar religious bounda-
> ries. Christians are nourished in their own faith by his vision and
> his words.[12]

Heschel's growing reputation among Christians and Jews made
him the logical choice of the American Jewish Committee in its
efforts relating to the Second Vatican Council. He became for the
AJC a valuable collaborator and frequent spokesperson. As such,
Heschel was often in contact with Augustin Cardinal Bea, who
headed the Secretariat for Promoting Christian Unity, which was
assigned the task of drafting the Council's statement on Catholic–Jewish relations.

The initial steps taken in this area were in response to a request by
Cardinal Bea. The American Jewish Committee, in collaboration
with Heschel and other Jewish leaders, submitted two memoranda
to the Secretariat for Christian Unity, "The Image of the Jew in
Catholic Teaching" in July 1961 and "Anti-Jewish Elements in

Catholic Liturgy" in November 1961. These memoranda were a constructive attempt to examine sources that could lead to misunderstanding and hostility between Catholics and Jews. After the second memorandum was submitted, Rabbi Heschel and representatives of the AJC met with Cardinal Bea in the Vatican, and the Cardinal asked them to recommend a set of positive suggestions for the betterment of Catholic–Jewish relations.

In February 1962, perhaps as a partial response to Bea's request, three of Heschel's books, *God in Search of Man, Man Is Not Alone,* and *The Sabbath,* were sent to the cardinal, who later acknowledged them as representative of "'the strong common spiritual bond between us.'"[13] In any event, a third memorandum, "On Improving Catholic–Jewish Relations," was prepared by Rabbi Heschel in cooperation with the AJC and submitted by Heschel to Bea in May 1962. Marc Tanenbaum describes this thirteen-page memorandum as "pure Heschel, flaming with his Jewish spirituality and his prophetic passion against injustice."[14] The memorandum was accompanied by a letter of Heschel's to Cardinal Bea which is indicative of the strong personal bond between these two key figures of the Catholic–Jewish dialogue. The letter is dated May 22, 1962.

> Your Eminence,
>
> . . . I am still under the spell of our conversation of last November. Since then I have been living with the feeling of the overwhelming importance of the theme which we touched upon and of the sacred seriousness of our undertaking. I am deeply grateful that Providence has permitted me to serve this noble undertaking, and I fervently beseech God that in His mercy He may make it possible for you to fulfill this mighty task, the hope of so many centuries and so much in accord with the prophetic vision. . . .
>
> The idea for composing this memorandum I owe to the inspiration which has come to me through your encouraging words so rich in understanding and through the depth of your own piety and wisdom. . . .
>
> The fraternal directives concerning the importance of improving Catholic–Jewish relations, which have come from Pope John XXIII and from Your Eminence, have filled Jews throughout the entire world with hope and longing for the monumental steps to be taken by the upcoming Vatican Council.
>
> May I close this note with my heartfelt good wishes for your personal well being. . . .[15]

The opening sentences of the memorandum express so well Heschel's approach to the task at hand: "With humility and in the spirit of commitment to the living message of the prophets of Israel, let us consider the grave problems that confront us all as the children of God." Both Judaism and Christianity, Heschel adds, share the certainty "that mankind is in need of ultimate redemption, that God is involved in human history, that in relations between man and man God is at stake. . . ." Our common task lies in history; God calls for mercy and righteousness but only in history can this demand be satisfied. "It is within the realm of history that man has to carry out God's mission."[16]

Heschel, as he does so often in his writings, then appeals to the prophets:

> This is the outstanding characteristic of the prophets: openness to the historical situation, to the divine call and its demands. In their eyes the human situation may be a divine emergency.
>
> It is such a situation that we face today when the survival of mankind, including its sacred legacy, is in balance. One wave of hatred, prejudice or contempt may begin in its wake the destruction of all mankind.[17]

The memorandum proceeds to set forth four proposals with the hope that they might improve the mutually fruitful relationship between the Roman Catholic Church and the Jewish community; Heschel recognizes that the Church represents "a rock of solidarity, belief and morality" in a world where so many moral and religious values have foundered.

The first proposal expresses the wish that the Church would reaffirm its opposition to all persecution and bigotry, and in particular to anti-Semitism. "We would hope that the Ecumenical Council will issue a strong declaration stressing the grave nature of the sin of anti-Semitism as incompatible with Catholicism and, in general, with all morality." It asks that the Council condemn those who assert that Jews as a people are responsible for the crucifixion of Jesus and that thus they "are accursed and condemned to suffer dispersion and deprivation throughout the ages. . . ."[18]

The second proposal expresses Heschel's distress at the failure of the Church to acknowledge the holiness of the Jews as Jews in their loyalty to the Torah.

Through the centuries our people have paid such a high price in suffering and martyrdom for preserving the Covenant and the legacy of holiness in faith and devotion. To this day our people labor devotedly and with commitment to educate their children in the ways of the Torah. Genuine love implies that Jews be accepted as Jews.

Thus, it is our sincere hope that the Ecumenical Council would acknowledge the integrity and permanent preciousness of Jews and Judaism.[19]

This leads to Heschel's third proposal: namely, that the Council would assert the need of Catholics "to seek mutual understanding of Jews and their tradition" because ignorance easily breeds suspicion and distortion. Catholics and Jews are called to love one another, and love implies transferring "the center of one's inner life from the ego to the object of one's love." However, we cannot love those whom we do not know. "Knowledge and charity are interrelated." Thus Heschel expresses the hope that the Church would disseminate positive information about Jews and Judaism, promoting "mutual understanding and a greater mutual comprehension of the issues between us and also of the richness of each other's heritage." He calls for joint research and publication projects by Jewish and Christian scholars, as well as cooperation in working together in civic affairs and in combating social problems. Such cooperation in a labor of love for others would add "considerably and decisively to the purification of the souls and the creation of a climate of mutual respect."[20]

Perhaps nowhere in this memorandum do the power and passion of Heschel's eloquence appear so clearly as in the opening paragraphs of his fourth proposal:

The prophets' preoccupation with justice and righteousness has its roots in a powerful *awareness of injustice*, a sense for the monstrosity of injustice. Moralists of all ages have been eloquent in singing the praises of virtue. The distinction of the prophets was in their remorseless unveiling of injustice and oppression, in their comprehension of social, political and religious evils.

Justice is precious, injustice exceedingly common. One of the troubles seems to be that we have delegated the concern for justice to the judges, as if justice were a matter for a few specialists. The prophets insist that justice must be the supreme and active concern of every man. It was not to the judges but to every member of the people that the words of the Lord are directed: "Seek justice, correct oppression, defend the fatherless, plead for the widow."

There is an evil which most of us condone and are even guilty of: *indifference to evil.* We remain neutral, impartial, and not easily moved by the wrongs done unto other people. Indifference to evil is more insidious than evil itself; it is more universal, more contagious, more dangerous. A silent justification, it makes possible an evil erupting as an exception becoming the rule and being in turn accepted.

. . . The great contribution [of the prophets] to humanity was their discovery of the *evil of indifference.* One may be decent and sinister, pious and sinful. I am my brother's keeper. The prophet is a person who suffers the harm done unto others. Wherever a crime is committed, it is as if the prophet were the victim and the prey.[21]

The memorandum then expresses both gratitude for the sacrifices of so many Catholics on behalf of persecuted Jews and dismay at the indifference of vast numbers of Catholics to the fate of the Jewish community, at their failure to condemn anti-Jewish atrocities especially during the Nazi era. The hope is expressed, therefore, that a permanent commission be established at the Vatican for the purpose of eliminating prejudice and of overseeing Jewish–Christian relations everywhere and that a similar commission be established in each diocese in order to further the demands of justice and love. Heschel's memorandum concludes: "It is our faith in the magnificent blessings which the spirit of God bestows upon those who are dedicated to Him that gives us the courage to pray that in this grave hour of history His children may be granted the wisdom and the power by which obstacles can be overcome."[22]

Anyone familiar with the course of Catholic–Jewish relations will recognize the remarkable coincidence between the four proposals set forth in this memorandum and what has actually taken place within the Roman Catholic Church in its teachings and structures over the past quarter of a century.[23] With good reason one might argue that no single document has had such a profound influence in bringing about what in retrospect Jan Cardinal Willebrands, head of the Vatican's Commission for Religious Relations with the Jews, has called "'a real, almost miraculous conversion in the attitudes of the Church and Catholics toward the Jewish people.'"[24]

However, many obstacles remained as the Council opened its deliberations in September 1962. A few bishops opposed any statement on the Jews; rumors were spread that reprisals might be taken against the Church in some Arab countries. Because so much time had been given over to procedural matters, consideration of the statement was postponed until the second session scheduled for September 1963.

In the early spring of that year Cardinal Bea visited the United States, a visit which included an interfaith dinner held in New York City on April 1, 1963, at which Heschel delivered the keynote address. The day before this dinner Cardinal Bea, along with two of his staff members including the then Msgr. Jan Willebrands, met with a select group of Jewish leaders at the offices of the American Jewish Committee in New York City. Rabbi Heschel was chosen to chair this gathering. In his opening remarks Heschel spoke of the ecumenical spirit which was permeating the Catholic world, due in no small part to Pope John XXIII and to Cardinal Bea; for Heschel this was "an event of historic significance," representing a "breakthrough toward the Divine message in accordance with Holy Writ." [25] Cardinal Bea then responded to a series of questions which had been submitted to him three weeks earlier for his consideration at this meeting and which to a large extent paralleled the four proposals of Heschel's memorandum of May 1962. [26]

The cardinal's response to these questions began with a general refutation of the charge of deicide, using the framework of established Catholic dogma, and he concluded: "[F]rom what we have said, it is sufficiently clear how unjust it is to accuse the Jewish people *as such* of having rendered themselves guilty of deicide and that their dispersion among all peoples is in close connection with this curse." He pointed out that it would be "neither necessary nor wise" to refute this accusation by attacking either the claim of Jesus' divinity or the credibility of the Gospels, for here one would come into direct conflict with fundamental Christian beliefs. All such fundamental religious beliefs, whatever they might be, must be treated "with respect and veneration." Then addressing the questions submitted to him, Bea assured the assembled scholars that rejection of the charge of deicide and of the Jews as an accursed people was a primary target of the statement being drafted by his Secretariat. He expected that the statement would also affirm the integrity and preciousness of Judaism as a living religion in its own right. On other points Bea hoped that the Council would stress the fundamental obligations of justice, truth, and love especially toward Jews, but specific regulations or practical applications would have to come from the Church's ordinary teaching, preaching, and practice rather than from specific actions by the more than two thousand bishops gathered at the Council. [27]

In his concluding remarks Heschel told Cardinal Bea: "I believe I speak for all those present when I say that the discussion we have held has been most meaningful and encouraging and of historical significance. May our Father in Heaven bless this work that is so deep a concern of us all." [28] Clearly, it was the hope of all at this meeting that the cardinal's remarks contained what would be the core of the forthcoming statement by the Council.

On the following evening in his address at the dinner honoring Cardinal Bea, Heschel spoke of the proclamation of the prophets that although humankind professes so many varied conceptions of God, men and women are really worshipping one and the same God, despite their ignorance of this fact. Yet intolerance so often plays a disruptive role.

> This is the agony of history: bigotry, the failure to respect each other's commitment, each other's faith. We must insist upon loyalty to the unique and holy treasures of our own tradition and at the same time acknowledge that in this aeon religious diversity may be the providence of God.
>
> Respect for each other's commitment, respect for each other's faith, is more than a political and social imperative. It is born of the insight that God is greater than religion, that faith is deeper than dogma, that theology has its roots in depth theology.
>
> The ecumenical perspective is the realization that . . . religion involves the total situation of man, his attitudes and deeds, and must therefore never be kept in isolation. [29]

Two months later, on June 4, 1963, Pope John XXIII died. Pope Paul VI vowed to continue in the spirit of his predecessor, yet unforeseen obstacles began to appear. Upon the opening of the Council's second session in September 1963 it became evident that, despite earlier hopes, definitive action on the statement on the Jews would be slow in coming. The contents of the proposed draft, closely following the themes outlined by Heschel and Bea, became

public knowledge through media reports. On learning of the proposed statement, Heschel issued his own personal response:

> The report about a Declaration to be introduced to the Ecumenical
> Council fills me with a sense of intense gratification. Such a Decla-
> ration will, should it be adopted, open new sources of spiritual in-
> sight for the Western world. It is an expression of the integrity and
> ultimate earnestness of those who are inspired by the consciousness
> of living in the presence of God, the Lord and Judge of history. May
> the spirit of God guide the work of the Council.[30]

Despite objections from some sources, the proposed draft was for-
mally brought before the Council on November 18; it was the object
of an enthusiastic welcome. Cardinal Bea told the assembled bishops that the document was drafted at the wishes of the late Pope
John and that the Holocaust perpetrated on European Jewry during
the Nazi era made imperative this statement by the Council. Although its passage seemed assured, the statement was never brought
to a vote. Suddenly the favorable tide began to turn. Some bishops
objected to combining a statement on Jews with a schema on Christian ecumenism; others opposed the statement as a way of voicing
their objections to a draft on religious liberty being considered at the
same time. There were efforts by some to pry the statement on the
Jews away from Cardinal Bea's Secretariat for Christian Unity and
transfer it to a new Secretariat for Non-Christian Religions.[31]

Heschel wrote to Cardinal Bea on November 22, 1963, expressing his deep concern about rumored proposals that would lead to a
general weakening of the text and especially about the prospect that
the theme of conversion of the Jews was being introduced into a revised text. A week later while in Rome he voiced these same concerns in a meeting with Msgr. Willebrands. Pressures from those
opposing the original text had become so strong that Cardinal Bea
believed it would not be politically wise for him to meet with Rabbi
Heschel. Willebrands listened carefully to Heschel's objections and
promised to bring them to Cardinal Bea and the Secretariat. While
many observers expressed support for Heschel's position, they were
not able to stem the negative tide. By the summer of 1964 the opti-
mism of the preceding fall had faded into disappointment and consternation among those who supported the original text.[32]

In early September 1964 the new text of the statement on the
Jews was made public through the media. It had weakened a num-

ber of the points that Cardinal Bea had originally espoused and that had been suggested in Heschel's memorandum of May 1962. Of greatest disappointment to many Jewish leaders was the hope it expressed for the eventual union of Jews with the Church. The American Jewish Committee issued a statement acknowledging the Church's right to hope for the Christianization of humankind, yet added: "'Any declaration, no matter how well intended, whose effect would mean . . . the elimination of Judaism as a religion would be received with resentment.'"[33]

Heschel issued his own strong response to the revised text in a three-page statement dated September 3, 1964. He asserted that the "omissions, attenuations and additions" were so serious that they amounted to a clear repudiation of what had been termed the desire "to right the wrongs of a thousand years." His major criticism was aimed at what he believed to be the contradiction between the document's call for "reciprocal understanding and appreciation" between Jews and Catholics and at the same time its expression of the Church's unshakable faith in, and ardent desire for, "the union of the Jewish people with the Church." Rabbi Heschel labeled this faith and desire of the Church as "*spiritual fratricide*," scarcely the basis for achieving "fraternal discussion" or "reciprocal understanding." He then explained in detail the reasons for his profound disappointment:

A message that regards the Jew as a candidate for conversion and proclaims that the destiny of Judaism is to disappear will be abhorred by the Jews all over the world and is bound to foster reciprocal distrust as well as bitterness and resentment.

Throughout the centuries our people have paid such a high price in suffering and martyrdom for preserving the Covenant and the legacy of holiness, faith and devotion to the sacred Jewish tradition. To this day we labor devotedly to educate our children in the ways of the Torah.

As I have repeatedly stated to leading personalities of the Vatican, I am ready to go to Auschwitz any time, if faced with the alternative of conversion or death.

Jews throughout the world will be dismayed by a call from the Vatican to abandon their faith in a generation which witnessed the massacre of six million Jews and the destruction of thousands of synagogues on a continent where the dominant religion was not Islam, Buddhism or Shintoism.

It is noteworthy that the Vatican document on Mohammedans makes no reference to the expectation of the Church for their conversion to the Christian faith. Is one to deduce from that that Islam offers a more acceptable way to salvation than Judaism?

Heschel recalled the marvelous inspiration that touched so many hearts because of the ecumenical spirit of Pope John XXIII and his reverence for the humanity of each person. He concluded by expressing his profound hope that the overwhelming majority of the bishops who expressed their desire to eradicate the sources of tension between Catholics and Jews "will have an opportunity to vote on a statement which will express this sacred aspiration."[34]

So crucial were the negotiations at this point that Heschel left for Rome for an audience with Pope Paul VI, held on September 14, 1964, the very eve of Yom Kippur. He repeated his objections to the current text, emphasizing especially his opposition to the expressed hope for the conversion of the Jews. The audience was described as friendly and cordial, lasting over half an hour. Heschel left an eighteen-page memorandum with Paul VI, who promised to submit it to Cardinal Bea's Commission. In this document Heschel wrote: "'Are we Jews in need of recognition? God himself has recognized us as a people. . . . It is not gratitude that we ask for; it is the cure of a disease affecting so many minds that we pray for.'"[35]

When the third session of the Council opened on September 16, 1964, it was evident that the weakened statement had evoked widespread opposition. When the text was debated before the Council, an overwhelming majority asked that it be strengthened. Following this debate a new and stronger version of the statement was drafted and given a resounding approval on the final day of the third session.

Various pressures were exerted through the early months of 1965 and into the opening days of the Council's fourth session, which began on September 16. Further debate followed the release in late September of the final version of the draft by the Secretariat for Promoting Christian Unity. On October 28 what is now known as *Nostra Aetate* was approved by the Council Fathers by the overwhelming majority of 2,221 in favor and 88 opposed.

Clearly Rabbi Heschel was a central, if often hidden, figure in bringing about the final version of the Council's statement on the Jews. Marc Tanenbaum remarked that during these years Heschel gave of himself so "freely, abundantly, even sacrificially," that what-

ever progress is made in the Jewish–Christian dialogue in the generations to come will be "immeasurably indebted to my beloved men-
tor, friend and inspiration, Rabbi Abraham Joshua Heschel."[36]

During a conversation taped for television seven years after the
close of the Council, Heschel gives us a rare personal reflection on
his efforts at that time:

> I was the major Jewish consultant to Cardinal Bea. . . . And it's no
> secret any more . . . that one of the issues I fought for in the prepara-
> tion of the schema about the Jews was to eliminate once and for all
> the idea of mission to the Jews. . . . I have great reverence for many
> Christians, but I also have to remind them that my being Jewish is so
> sacred to me that I am ready to die for it. And when a statement
> came out from the Ecumenical Council expressing the hope that
> Jews would eventually join the Church, I came out with a very
> strong rebuke. I said "I'd rather go to Auschwitz than give up my
> religion."
>
> And I succeeded in persuading even the Pope. . . . [H]e person-
> ally crossed out a paragraph in which there was reference to conver-
> sion or mission to the Jews. The Pope himself. . . . This great, old,
> wise Church in Rome realizes that the existence of Jews as Jews is so
> holy and so precious that the Church would collapse if the Jewish
> people would cease to exist.[37]

It must also be mentioned that just as Heschel greatly influenced
the deliberations of the Council Fathers on *Nostra Aetate*, so also
did the Council greatly influence Heschel's view of the Catholic
Church. Emigrating from Poland in 1939 as "a brand plucked from
the fire," Heschel was keenly aware of the relative silence of the
Church during the ascendancy of the Nazi Party in Germany, of
the passivity or complicity of so many Catholics during the period
of the Holocaust, of those officers and workers at the death camps
who were also communicants at their local churches. His association with so many bishops and theologians during the years of the
Vatican Council and his experience of the Catholic Church in the
United States, especially in the post–Vatican II years, gave him
fresh and deeper insights into the meaning of the Catholic Church
and of Christianity in general. One might say that the Catholic
Church was reborn for Heschel; he saw it in an entirely different
light because of his involvement.[38] Rev. Daniel Berrigan, S.J., a
close friend of Heschel's from the mid-1960s when they collabo-

rated in opposing the war in Viet Nam, recalls an evening in the summer of 1972 when he and Heschel were walking along Broadway in New York City, not far from Heschel's home. Rabbi Heschel was visibly upset because of a book he had recently read by a noted American Catholic writer which was strongly and negatively critical of the Catholic Church in the United States and of the direction it was taking in the years following the Council. He considered the work defamatory and slanderous of the Church. Heschel turned suddenly to Berrigan: "You and I must write a book that will refute these charges!" Heschel did not live to carry out this project, but the story reveals his growing care, understanding, and respect for Catholics and their Church.[39]

When Heschel was lecturing in Italy in 1971, he and his wife were invited to a private audience with Pope Paul VI. Heschel was deeply impressed by the friendly and cordial atmosphere of the visit. The leader of the world's Roman Catholics and this great spokesman for world Jewry recognized how much they had in common. Pope Paul, who had read several of Heschel's books, told Heschel how much he admired his work, and to Heschel's surprise he added: "Everyone should read your books." To the mind of Paul VI the wisdom of Heschel clearly reached far beyond the boundaries of his Jewish faith. Finally, both these leaders expressed a concern and a compassion for the youth of the world. Paul VI believed that Heschel had a message that was especially relevant to young people, and indeed one of Heschel's last public messages was addressed directly to the youth of this country.[40]

Catholics, and all who are involved with or interested in the dialogue between Jews and Christians, owe an immeasurable debt to Abraham Joshua Heschel. Heschel's adamant affirmation of his Jewish faith, "I'd rather go to Auschwitz than give up my religion," should give the reader pause, particularly the Christian reader. Judaism should not be viewed merely as a preamble to Christianity. Heschel worked diligently to combat this notion. The whole thrust of his teaching, his writing, his prayer, his social involvement was aimed at demonstrating the relevance of his Jewish faith and its traditions for our contemporary world. This was corroborated by the person he was. It was not my privilege to have known Rabbi Heschel personally, but there is an extraordinary and widespread consensus dealing with the impact of his person upon those who were his friends, his students, his colleagues, his adversaries, his admirers. In addition, Heschel's writings give us a deep insight into the person he was. His daughter, Susannah, put it so well: "'My father was the kind of man he wrote about.'"[41] I hope this analysis of his spirituality will help the reader recognize the kind of man Heschel wrote about and hence the kind of man he was.

In presenting here one understanding of the spirituality of Rabbi Heschel, one written from a Christian perspective, I have tried to let those writings of Heschel's available to the English reader speak for themselves so that they may address us wherever we stand in our pilgrimage through life. We make this pilgrimage in a world that so often appears to be unhinged from its foundations, closed to values of ultimate significance, devoid of any real sense of the human or the holy. It is a world in need of healing and compassion, of vision and hope. Heschel helps to meet this need. Quite obviously there are a depth and a richness in Heschel's thought that I am unable to plumb. Nevertheless, I hope that this study will convey to its readers a deeper understanding of Heschel and of Judaism as a whole. For Christian readers such a deeper understanding would lead to a clearer recognition of all they share with Jews on a religious, personal, and social dimension, and shed greater light on the roots and meaning and challenge of their own tradition. For Jewish readers the wisdom and insights of Heschel can only enhance their grasp of the faith, teachings, and tradition they share with him.

In the special issue of *America* dedicated to the memory of Rabbi Heschel, the editors note: "No Christian who ever entered into conversation with Professor Heschel came away without having been spiritually enriched and strengthened."[42] The same may be said of those who enter into dialogue with him through his writings. The following pages are an effort to continue this conversation with Abraham Joshua Heschel in the hope that through him we all may be spiritually enriched and strengthened.

NOTES

1. Marc Tanenbaum, "Heschel and Vatican II—Jewish–Christian Relations," unpublished lecture delivered at The Jewish Theological Seminary of America, February 1, 1983, p. 1. I am most grateful to Rabbi Tanenbaum for providing the transcript of this lecture.

2. "Of Many Things," *America*, 128, No. 9 (March 10, 1973), 200.

3. Cf. "Contemporary Judaism and the Christian," ibid., 202.

4. Cited in Samuel H. Dresner, "Remembering Abraham Heschel," ibid., 146, No. 21 (May 29, 1982), 414.

5. *Man Is Not Alone: A Philosophy of Religion* (New York: Farrar, Straus, and Young, 1951; repr. New York: Farrar, Straus & Giroux, 1977), p. 296.

6. "Remembering Abraham Heschel," 415.

7. *A Passion for Truth* (New York: Farrar, Straus & Giroux, 1973), p. xiii. For more detailed biographical data, see Samuel H. Dresner, "Heschel the Man," in *Abraham Joshua Heschel: Exploring His Life and Thought*, ed. John C. Merkle (New York: Macmillan, 1985), pp. 3–27, and John C. Merkel, *The Genesis of Faith: The Depth Theology of Abraham Joshua Heschel* (New York: Macmillan, 1985), chap. 1.

8. "No Religion Is an Island," *Union Seminary Quarterly Review*, 21, No. 2 (January 1966), 117.

9. Cited in Tanenbaum, "Heschel and Vatican II," p. 3.

10. *The Insecurity of Freedom: Essays on Human Existence* (New York: Schocken, 1972), p. 246.

11. "Abraham Heschel: A Passion for Sincerity," *Christianity and Crisis*, 33, No. 21 (December 10, 1973), 257.

12. "Agent of God's Compassion," *America*, 128, No. 9 (March 10, 1973), 205.

13. Cited in Tanenbaum, "Heschel and Vatican II," p. 9.

14. Ibid., p. 8.

15. This letter, which I have translated from the original German, is in the archives of the American Jewish Committee in New York City.

16. "On Improving Catholic–Jewish Relations," memorandum submitted to Cardinal Bea, May 22, 1962, in the archives of the American Jewish Committee, New York City, p. 1.

17. Ibid., p. 3.

18. Ibid., pp. 5–6.

19. Ibid., p. 7.

20. Ibid., pp. 8–10.

21. Ibid., pp. 11–12.

22. Ibid., p. 13.

23. Regarding Heschel's first proposal, *Nostra Aetate* states that, concerning the death of Christ, "neither all Jews indiscriminately at that time, nor Jews today, can be charged with the crimes committed during his passion," that "Jews should not be spoken of as rejected or accursed," that the Church "reproves every form of persecution against whomever it may be directed," and that she "deplores all hatreds, persecutions, displays of anti-

semitism leveled at any time or from any source against the Jews" ("Declaration on the Relation of the Church to Non-Christian Religions [*Nostra Aetate,* October 28, 1965]," in *Vatican Council II: The Conciliar and Post Conciliar Documents,* ed. Austin Flannery, o. p. [Collegeville, Minn.: Liturgical Press, 1975], p. 741).

Nostra Aetate also points out that the Church continues to draw "nourishment from that good olive tree onto which the wild olive branches of the Gentiles have been grafted," reminding Catholics that "Jews remain very dear to God, for the sake of the patriarchs, since God does not take back the gifts he bestowed or the choice he made" (ibid., pp. 740–41). This is at least a partial response to Heschel's second proposal.

The Council's acceptance of Heschel's third proposal can be found in these words of *Nostra Aetate:* "Since Christians and Jews have such a common spiritual heritage, this sacred Council wishes to encourage and further mutual understanding and appreciation. This can be obtained, especially, by way of biblical and theological enquiry and through friendly discussions" (ibid., p. 741). Furthermore, the 1975 "Guidelines" of the Holy See's Commission for Religious Relations with the Jews reaffirms the need for "better mutual understanding and renewed mutual esteem" between Catholics and Jews pointing to the role of joint social action and cooperation between Catholics and Jews on the local, national, and international levels as a way of fostering this mutual understanding and esteem (Vatican Commission for Religious Relations with the Jews, "Guidelines and Suggestions for Implementing the Conciliar Declaration *Nostra Aetate* [n. 4]," in *Stepping Stones to Further Jewish–Christian Relations,* ed. Helga Croner [New York: Stimulus, 1977], pp. 11, 15).

Heschel's final proposal was implemented through the establishment of the Vatican Office for Catholic–Jewish Relations following the Council and by the upgrading of this Office in October 1974 to the Vatican Commission for Religious Relations with the Jews. In addition, the 1975 "Guidelines" urges bishops to "create some suitable commissions or secretariats on a national or regional level" in order to carry through the directives of *Nostra Aetate* and of other Vatican documents on Jewish–Catholic relations (ibid., p. 16).

24. Cited in Thomas Stransky, "The Catholic–Jewish Dialogue: Twenty Years After *Nostra Aetate,*" *America,* 154, No. 5 (February 8, 1986), 93.

25. English translation of the minutes of the meeting with Cardinal Bea on March 31, 1963, in the archives of the American Jewish Committee, New York City, p. 6.

26. "Questions to Be Submitted to Cardinal Bea at the Meeting with Jewish Scholars," dated March 7, 1963, in the archives of the American Jewish Committee, New York City.

27. "Conversation of Cardinal Bea with Jewish Scholars and Theologians," dated March 31, 1963, in the archives of the American Jewish Committee, New York City. Cf. also Tanenbaum, "Heschel and Vatican II," p. 11.

28. From the English translation of the minutes of the meeting with Cardinal Bea on March 31, 1963, in the archives of the American Jewish Committee, New York City, p. 10.

29. "The Ecumenical Movement," *Insecurity of Freedom*, p. 181.

30. Cited in Tanenbaum, "Heschel and Vatican II," p. 12.

31. Ibid., p. 13.

32. Ibid., pp. 13–14.

33. Cited in ibid., p. 15.

34. Statement of September 3, 1964, in the archives of the American Jewish Committee, New York City.

35. Cited in Tanenbaum, "Heschel and Vatican II," p. 17.

36. Ibid., p. 21.

37. "A Conversation with Doctor Abraham Joshua Heschel," December 20, 1972, National Broadcasting Company transcript, pp. 12–13.

38. This was brought to my attention in a conversation with Rev. Daniel Berrigan, s.j., in June 1987 and confirmed in a conversation with Sylvia Heschel that same month.

39. Conversation with Father Berrigan in June 1987.

40. Conversation with Sylvia Heschel in June 1987. Cf. "Conversation with Doctor Abraham Joshua Heschel," p. 21.

41. Cited in Dresner, "Heschel the Man," p. 4.

42. "Contemporary Judaism and the Christian," 202.

1

The Quest for Being Human

ANY APPROACH TO A MEANINGFUL SPIRITUALITY must be rooted in an understanding of the human person. So it must be in this study of the spirituality of Abraham Joshua Heschel. God's grace complements our humanity; it never substitutes for our humanity.

Yet as we near the end of this twentieth century, we realize it is becoming more and more difficult to live a life that is authentically human. Every age has presented obstacles to those who sought to live truly human lives. Such obstacles have always been able to be overcome, but progressively they loom ever larger. For Abraham Heschel ours is an age that is tragically losing any understanding of what it means to be human, an age in which one is ashamed to be human; ours is an age that has forgotten how to pray, how to think, how to cry, how to resist the lures of the many hidden persuaders in our midst; ours is an age that has exchanged "holiness for convenience, loyalty for success, love for power, wisdom for information, tradition for fashion."[1] The spirit of this age is one of instrumentalization of the world around us, of the people in that world, of all values. On the one hand, this is an age obsessed with power, an obsession that has stunted our sensitivity to beauty and grandeur; on the other, we are mired in helplessness, misery, even agony. We have easy access to pleasure; entertainment is in abundance. Yet we have forgotten the meaning of joy, and we have lost the ability to celebrate.

This is an age that has gone mad. We legislate against homicide and murder, yet we wage wars with ferocity and slaughter whole peoples. We refuse to acknowledge the impotence of force. History is scarred by a succession of wars, victories, and more wars, with so many dead and so many tears. In a world drenched in blood and endless with guilt, may one dare to continue to hope? We look to the sword as our primary source of security; it serves as the symbol of honor and the measure of manhood because we remain blindly convinced that history is ultimately determined on fields of battle. What is the ultimate harvest of all the wars, the arms, the victories? "Destruction, agony, death. . . ." There is no hope for the survival of humanity unless we recognize the absurdity of this false sense of sovereignty and the fallacy of absolute expediency, an arrogance that can fill the world only with terror.[2]

HUMANITY ON TRIAL

Other ages and cultures have suffered degradation from poverty; today we are threatened with degradation from power. Western society tends to look upon nature almost exclusively in terms of usefulness. The achievement of power, the accumulation of wealth, and the attainment of comfort are the primary goals of life. The spirit of this age makes it difficult for a person to understand Heschel when he speaks of time as the border of eternity, or when he urges us to live this single moment as if the fate of all time were totally dependent on it; we are deaf to his teaching that the essence of existence lies in compliance, agreement, obedience. The spirit of this age is opposed to his view that all existence stands in the dimension of the holy, that all existence stands before God "here and everywhere, now and at all times." Humankind can never separate itself from the holy, not by sin, apostasy, stupidity, or ignorance. There is no escape from God, for we cannot exist apart from God. Human life is holy, a holiness that comes as God's gift, not by our achievement. The human is the borderline of the divine, and life is lived in the proximity of the sacred, a proximity that endows human existence with ultimate significance.[3] But the spirit of this age dims our understanding of what Heschel is trying to tell us.

The struggle to be human is always on trial; it is full of risk, for one is always in danger of forfeiting one's humanity. To be human is to place oneself in a precarious position. It is like a "whisper calling in the wilderness." It demands that one resist temptation, that one be strong in the face of frustration, that one refuse the craving for immediate satisfaction. And it is something, unfortunately, that can be discarded at any time with the greatest of ease.[4]

Clearly, then, to be human is to be a problem. We all have at least an inkling of what we ought to be and of how we ought to act. We also recognize a gap between what we are and what is expected of us. We know so little about the meaning of humanity; there is something so important at stake in being human, yet it is obscured in our day-to-day living. Is it not conceivable, asks Heschel, that the entire structure of our civilization may be built upon a misinterpretation of what a human person is? The failure to identify human being, to know what is authentic human existence, leads one to pretend to be what one is unable to be or to deny what is at the very root of one's being. "Ignorance about man is not lack of knowledge, but false knowledge."[5]

Self-knowledge is an important aspect of my being. Any conception about what I am going to do with myself presupposes some sort of self-image. The image I have of myself affects what I am because it enters my consciousness, determines my self-understanding, and thus modifies my very existence. This self-understanding would be dangerously incomplete if I dwelt exclusively on the facts of human existence and disregarded what is at stake in human existence. The chief problem, then, is not so much my nature as such as what I do with my nature.[6]

All too often we treat ourselves as if we were created in the likeness of a machine rather than in the likeness of God. Having lost an awareness of our sacred image, we have become deaf to its challenge, namely, to live in a way that is compatible with this image. God has a stake in the life of a person, of every person. This idea cannot be imposed from without; it must be discovered from within. It cannot be preached; it can only be experienced. Part of the genius of Heschel is that he helps us to come to this discovery and to reach this experience.

We must begin by recognizing that authentic humanity, our being human, is a goal to be accomplished, an ideal to be striven for, not a fact given with human existence. There is a difference between saying "I am a human being" and saying "I am being human." I am born a human being; what I have to reach is being human. Human being demands being human. A prolonged failure to be human implies a brutalization of the individual.

We cannot say with certainty that every human being reaches the level of being human; nor may any of us claim that in all we do we are truly being human. Our being human is an opportunity, an achievement. It is indeed an undertaking that is precarious and full of risk, one that must constantly be rescued from chaos and extinction. To assume otherwise would be a "fatal illusion."[7]

Authentic Humanity

Heschel's approach to an understanding of the human person is for the most part concrete, direct, practical. He avoids theoretical solutions just as he avoids utopian ideals. His concern is not "how to worship in the catacombs but rather how to remain human in the skyscrapers."[8] In almost all his major works he touches to some degree upon his understanding of authentic humanity, of being human, but it was in his 1963 Raymond West Memorial Lectures at Stanford University (later published as *Who Is Man?*) that Heschel summarizes so thoroughly his thought on this point.

There are certain qualities, he argues, that belong necessarily to the experience of being human. The first of these springs from the contrast between the person as seen from without by society and as seen from within through self-reflection. Seen from without, I am average, ordinary; from within, I see myself as unique, precious, unprecedented; I am not to be exchanged for anything else. Beyond all agony and anxiety lies this most important aspect of self-reflection; I am of great moment. The problem comes in trying to actualize this "quiet eminence" of my being. My existence is so exceedingly precious that I reject the thought of "gambling away" its meaning. My existence is an original, not a copy. Each person is unique; no two are alike. Thus each person has something to say, something to think, something to do, that is entirely unprecedented. Every human being is "a disclosure, an example of exclusiveness." What I recognize of myself, then, I must recognize of others: that each has a task to carry out, a task so great that "its fulfillment may epitomize the meaning of all humanity."[9]

Conformity to the crowd and mere repetition of the past tend to obscure one's uniqueness and to lead to drudgery and inner devastation. For Heschel there is no such thing as the "typical" person. The average man is the creation of statistics. In real life the average person is non-existent unless one allow oneself to be "drowned in indifference and commonness." Such spiritual suicide, unfortunately, is within the reach of every person.[10]

Closely allied to this sense of uniqueness is the sense of surprise that is found in being human. Life is unpredictable; no one can write his autobiography in advance. I am a complex of opportunities as well as a bundle of facts. Finality and humanity appear to be mutually exclusive. The great enigma of human being lies, not in what one is, but in what one is able to be. Even if we were able to describe what humanity is, it would always be beyond our power to grasp what humanity is capable of becoming. The being of a person is never complete or finalized. Each person is in a *status nascendi*, a state of being born. We are being called upon constantly to be more than we are. There is no standing still for humanity. Being human means "being on the way, striving, waiting, hoping."[11]

This implies, in Heschel's terms, that being human is not a process but a sequence of events. A process is what happens regularly; it is continuous, ordinary, typical; it follows more or less a permanent pattern. An event is what happens suddenly; it is unique, unprecedented, extraordinary. I live not only in an order of process, but in an order of events. Being human implies moments of insight, of decision, of prayer; these are events that help put life into focus.

Life lived as an event is a drama, while life lived as a process becomes static and stale. Indeed, to be human is to take part in a cosmic drama. One's awareness of life as a drama comes about as a result of recognizing the self as unprecedented and of refusing to consider existence as a waste.[12]

Essential to one's being human is the ability to stand alone. For the one who seeks to be authentically human, what other resource is there than the occasional withdrawal from the world's glaring and deceitful eyes? Proximity to the crowd spells the death of creativity and uniqueness. Solitude implies a period of rest and recovery from the incursion of society's hysteria. I have to withdraw into stillness in order to be able to listen and to discover there a distilling of humanity, not a discarding of it. Genuine solitude is in reality a search for genuine solidarity, for I am never alone, even in seclusion. I live and suffer and rejoice with all my contemporaries. In my very being I am directed to the community of humankind. For the human person "*to be* means *to be with* other human beings. . . . existence *is* coexistence." I can never attain fulfillment except through sharing with other human beings. Any analysis of the human situation which disregards social involvement and human interdependence will miss the meaning of being human.[13]

The true dignity of human existence lies in one's power of reciprocity. For Heschel "I become a person when I begin to reciprocate." To be human means to offer in return, to reciprocate for what one has been given. We are receiving continually; our very being is gift, and every breath of fresh air is an "inhalation of grace." For each new insight we must pay a deed. Knowledge is not private property, but a debt that makes new demands upon us. Life itself is not my property; what I have is mine, but what I am is not mine.[14]

Reciprocation implies appreciation, sensitivity, compassion. The degree to which I am responsive to the suffering and humanity of others becomes the index of my own humanity. One can achieve the fullness of being human only in fellowship and in care for others. Just as the true standard by which to measure a culture is the extent to which reverence and compassion and justice are to be found in the lives of a people, so is it true in measuring each individual. The degree of my being human stands in direct proportion to the degree to which I care for others. Heschel makes it quite clear that in his mind the essence of being human lies in this intense care and concern. There is no quality of human existence on which he places greater emphasis; he turns to it again and again in his writings.[15] The child becomes human by becoming sensitive to the interests and need of other selves. The ability to be concerned for others is at the heart of human personhood. "Human is he who is concerned with other selves."[16] One cannot hold onto life if one is entirely unconcerned with self; but one who is exclusively concerned with self is a beast. The failure to acknowledge the humanity of another, the failure to be sensitive to the needs of another, denotes the failure to be human.

The human person alone recognizes that it is insufficient merely to be, to exist, to live; rather the problem is *how* to be and *how* to live. What do I do with this gift of life? How do I give shape and form to my being? Our ability to give form to the being that is ours depends upon our understanding of the uniqueness and singularity of human living. We are constantly being challenged not to surrender to mere being. There is an innate discontent with mere being, with just being in the world. Mere being is to be surpassed by living. There is no guarantee or assurance of attaining true personhood. "It is a mistake to assume that significant being is attained unwittingly." Human living is a struggle for meaning that may be lost or won, totally or partially. What is at stake may be gambled away, for a meaningful life is not given with existence; it must be achieved by each individual.[17]

THE STRUGGLE FOR MEANING

The key to Heschel's understanding of personhood is found in this search for significant being, this struggle for meaning, in which all humanity is engaged. Human being is always involved in one way or another with meaning; the dimension of meaning is indigenous to my being human. What I do may be creative of meaning or destructive of meaning; I may be coming into meaning or betraying it; but I cannot live outside of it. For anyone who is sensitive to the human situation the overriding problem is that of meaning. It would be disastrous for a person to try to live without inner meaning or identity. There can be no order, direction, or significance to one's life without the attempt to identify the meaning of being a person. Anguish and boredom are occasioned more by the experience or fear of meaninglessness, of meaningless events, than by anything else. I want to know who I am, and in relation to whom I live, and how to live my life so that it would deservingly evoke an "eternal Amen." I want to know how to answer the one question that underlies all other questions: What am I here for? Human anguish is rooted in the fear of finding oneself cut off from ultimate meaning, and this anguish can be quelled only by a sense of significant being.[18]

In all that we do or think or plan we raise a claim to significant meaning. The trees we plant, the meals we prepare, the books we read, the tools we invent—these are all answers to a need of a purpose. This is not to say that we confer meaning upon all reality, as though the world were chaotic or bare of significance until we approach it with the magic of our minds and hands. The essence of meaning lies more in discovery than in invention. Reality may appear to the ordinary person with only a minimum of significance, while to the artist or the saint it overflows with meaning. Reality conveys to the creative mind more significance than it is able to absorb. The artist or the scientist or the saint merely lends categories of expression to a meaning that is already there. Expectedness of meaning, the certainty that whatever exists must somehow be worthwhile, is the basis of all human living. We are convinced that the hidden and the unknown will never turn out to be absurd or meaningless. The world is resplendent with a transcendent preciousness that surpasses our power of appreciation. We sense this wherever we turn. We stake our very lives on the certainty of ultimate meaning. In each judgment we make, in each act we perform, there is the assumption that the world is meaningful. Life would be absolute chaos if we truly acted as though there were no ultimate meaning.[19]

It is possible to disregard this ultimate dimension of human existence, to avoid asking the ultimate questions, as long as we can occupy ourselves with immediate goals and objectives. But when tragedy strikes, when our small world collapses, when joy deserts us, the discovery of our evasion becomes a nightmare. Our fear lest in winning small prizes we may have lost the ultimate prize of meaning opens our being to questions we have long been trying to avoid.[20]

Granted the claim to meaning in all that *I do*, is there also meaning in what *I am*? This is the way Heschel so often begins his probing for ultimate meaning. The world may look upon me as average or ordinary, but I see my life as something precious. Is it precious to me alone, or is someone else in need of my life? Imbedded in the mind is the certainty that life ought to be meaningful. In spite of failures and frustrations this irrepressible quest continues to haunt us. We cannot accept the idea that life is hollow, that it is incompatible with meaning. There is always the urge for "significant being," for a meaning which transcends the individual and which, therefore, the self cannot furnish; it is an urge for the ultimate relevance of humanity. Significant being is not achieved by the satisfaction of needs and desires, or even by the realization of one's capacities; it reaches out beyond these toward beauty, justice, goodness, truth, love. Significant being confronts the question posed by Heschel: "*After satisfaction, what?*" It breaks out of the narrow circle of need and satisfaction, desire and pleasure. Needs demand satisfaction, but being human demands appreciation, the beginning of a thirst that knows no satisfaction. To be human is to pledge one's total existence to the truth that "the quest for significant being is the heart of existence."[21]

Significant being demands that one rise above the level of being satisfied to that of being able to satisfy, to rise above the level of having needs to that of being a need for another. "Personal needs come and go, but one anxiety remains: Am I needed?" Every human being has been moved by that anxiety to a greater or lesser degree.[22]

No person is self-sufficient because no person can furnish his or her own meaning. Human life is not meaningful unless it is serving an end *beyond itself*, unless it is of value to someone else. To hoard the self, to center existence on the self, is to pave the way for an overwhelming feeling for the futility of living. Sophisticated thinking may at times enable one to feign being self-sufficient, but such illusions eventually lead to the feeling of being useless, of not being needed in the world. Heschel is correct in saying this is probably the most common cause of psychoneurosis. The only way to avoid such despair is to see oneself as a need for another rather than as an end for self. Human happiness is found in the certainty of being needed by another. But, asks Heschel, who is in need of *me*?[23]

Does the individual person find his or her purpose in the service of society or of humanity? Is the ultimate worth of the human person determined by that person's usefulness to others? Such a solution would be of little consolation to the aged, the incurably ill, the severely handicapped. If society rejects this service, does one's life become useless or meaningless? Moreover, such service cannot claim the whole of one's life. There are vast areas where one walks alone, areas that are hidden from the public eye. Thus, service to society cannot answer the quest for the meaning of human existence. A person usually has much more to give than what others are able or willing to accept.

Is nature in need of humankind? Nature can get along quite well, in some cases better, without the help of the human race. Nature has the ability to satisfy all our needs except the one that is central: "the need of being needed." This is a need unlike all other needs. It is a striving to give satisfaction rather than obtain it.[24]

All other needs are temporary. Once the need is fulfilled, once the desire is satisfied, it dissolves. My being needed, however, is lasting. Each human being comes to the realization that life is futile unless there is something about it that is permanent and lasting, even though the meaning of the lasting may often be misunderstood. We are all caught up in the search for something that makes the toil of living worthwhile, "something that outlasts life, strife and agony." The quest for meaning, then, is a quest for abidingness. Human life is often experienced as a race against time, attempting to perpetuate significant moments, or to establish relations that, one hopes, will perdure. This quest is not a product of whim or fancy, but an essential element of human nature. There is nothing, says Heschel, that we esteem more than abidingness. It is not the hope that my self and all that is contained therein may last, but rather that all that I stand for may last.[25]

All other needs are one-sided. When hungry, I am in need of food; when thirsty, I am in need of drink; when homeless, I am in need of shelter. But food and drink and shelter are not in need of me. My being needed, however, or ultimate meaning, is two-sided. Not only does it imply the satisfaction of my need, but it points to the fulfillment of the need of another. It implies not only that I am tolerated, but that I am needed, I am precious, I am indispensable. Life is indeed precious to each person; is it precious to that person alone?

We can reflect on other beings without regard to meaning, but it is impossible to reflect on human being without concern for its meaning. We can think of human being only in terms of meaning, for each person is a fountain of immense meaning, not merely a drop in the ocean of being. This care for ultimate meaning, for significant being, is inherent in being human. It dwells in every heart, a care that is "strong, elementary, provocative." This care or quest is a response to a requirement of existence; it is something that is constitutive of the very nature of being human. Surely, if the anxiety about ultimate significance should be considered an absurdity, then "to be human would mean to be mad." We cannot prove ultimate significance; we can only be a manifestation of ultimate significance.[26] "The secret of being human is care for meaning. Man is not his own meaning, and if the essence of being human is concern for transcendent meaning, then man's secret lies in openness to transcendence. Existence is interspersed with suggestions of transcendence, and openness to transcendence is a constitutive element of being human."[27] In other words, the cry for ultimate significance is a cry for a referent that transcends personal existence. Clearly, for Heschel, this concern is what constitutes the truth of being human. To consider human being devoid of the possibility of meaning is to confront "an absurdity, or worse, a nightmare." And if one should give up the care and anxiety for meaning, one would simply cease to be human.

The quest for meaning, then, is the attempt to understand oneself, as well as the whole of humanity, in terms larger than the self. It is an attempt to grasp the ultimate relevance of human existence. The goal of each person is not the mere acceptance of being, but the relating of being to meaning, the searching for the way or ways of coming into meaning. For to be human is to become involved, "to act and react, to wonder and to respond." The quest for meaning is the quest for relationship to what is beyond being.[28]

It is roughly at this point in his various analyses of the human situation that Heschel introduces the distinction between the biblical and the ontological, or the Hebraic and the Hellenic, modes of thinking. Ontological thought seeks to relate humanity to a transcendence called being as such; biblical thought seeks to relate humanity to a transcendence called the living God. The underlying difference between these two approaches is that the former accepts being as that which is ultimately real, while the latter points to living as that which is ultimately real. In other words, what really counts from the biblical perspective is not being as such, but what one does with being. The Bible begins, not with being, but with the surprise of being, with being as a divine act, with being as creation.[29]

The human person is more than intellect, and so ultimate meaning must be more than an idea if it is to be a response to human anxiety. Our quest for meaning is a quest for ultimate relationship and belonging, a quest in which all our masks are put aside and all pretensions dropped. We have in common a terrible loneliness. Repeatedly the question forces itself upon our minds: Are we alone in this maze of the self, alone in this wilderness of time, alone in this silent universe, of which we are a part and yet in which we so often feel like strangers? Is there no one to collect the tears, soothe the pain, understand the agony of the innocent, the poor, the sorrowing? Is there no Presence worth living for, no Presence worth dying for, no way of living compatible with this Presence? My ultimate meaning cannot be derived from being as such. Being as such is devoid of personal relationships, and unless meaning is personally related to me, it is not meaningful *for me* as a person. If ultimate meaning is not in need of me, I cannot relate myself to it, and thus ultimate meaning would be meaningless for me. The need to be needed cannot be fulfilled by a one-sided relationship. Food and drink and shelter may not be in need of me, but that which is the source of ultimate meaning *must* be in need of me.[30]

The search for meaning as formulated in Hellenistic terms might be expressed as humankind in search of a thought; the search for meaning formulated in biblical terms could be expressed as God in search of humankind. The meaning of our existence depends on whether or not we respond to God who is in search of us. We are engaged in a search for meaning because there is a meaning that is first in search of us. Our anxiety about meaning is not a question, but an answer, a response to a challenge. In the biblical framework, humankind is concerned about meaning because God is first concerned about humankind.[31]

The question about God is in reality the question of God. When Heschel uses the phrase, as he so often does, "God in search of man," he means that human life, as a gift from God, is also a question from God, a question that requires an answer on our part. If God did not ask the question, our effort to deal with it would be in vain. We are constantly being called upon, comforted, challenged; human history can be viewed as a probing, a questioning, a testing.

In the biblical view meaning lies beyond all mystery. God is not simply meaning, but meaning that transcends mystery, meaning to which mystery alludes, meaning that speaks to us out of mystery. The meaning seeks to come to expression through us. It is our destiny to articulate what is concealed in mystery; the divine seeks disclosure through the human.

We become aware of this transcendent meaning through the experience of the ineffable, in moments of awe and wonder. It is a meaning we cannot comprehend; it is a meaning we encounter, not an object like a self-subsisting or timeless idea, but a Presence. Thus transcendent meaning can never be a possession; it must not be reduced to an object I acknowledge, my assent to an idea. Rather, the experience of meaning is an experience of "vital involvement," of sharing a dimension that is open to everyone. We come together in the "stillness of significance," sharing a fellowship of being related to a common concern for meaning. The longing for such vital involvement is part of our vocation as human beings. Ultimate meaning is not something grasped once for all, like a changeless idea;

rather, it is a Presence that we confront in moments of encounter, an intimation that comes and goes. It leaves behind a memory and our commitment to that memory. It implies that I stand in a relationship to God that I may betray but never sever, a relationship that constitutes the essential meaning of my life.[32] This relationship constitutes life's essential meaning because it is one through which constant demands are made upon the individual.

THE CHALLENGE OF LIVING

The need to be needed corresponds to a fact: something is asked of every person. Being human is a fact as well as a demand, a condition as well as an expectation; it can be understood only in relation to a challenge. The crisis of humankind results from a failure to accept that challenge or to acknowledge it as the central problem of human living. The widespread despair that affects so many, especially the young, comes from the inability to hear "deeply and personally" the challenge that confronts us.

The world we confront is a problem, a task, an expectation. We discover meaning by recognizing our role in this task. We are never left alone; rather we are constantly being called upon, judged, challenged, cross-examined, required to answer. If we eliminate the challenge and the struggle, we would be deprived of our humanity. Being challenged is an essential aspect of being human. There is no escape from this world, which forces itself upon us, demanding and challenging. Human living implies "being-challenged-in-the-world," with the consequent awareness of a task-to-be-done. If I have no awareness of this task waiting for me, then I feel like an outcast, an alien; there is no belonging. The *content* of this task remains to be found, but the search for the task comes with consciousness.[33]

My being-challenged-in-the-world may be expressed in terms of demand and expectation. This sense of "requiredness" is essential to being human; my life takes on significance through the attempt to adjust to what is expected and demanded of me. Being human, then, implies not only concern for meaning, but also sensitivity to a demand; my response to this demand is indeed my responsibility.

Once again it is important to differentiate between the Hellenic and the Hebraic modes of thinking, between the Greek understanding of person as a rational being and the biblical understanding of person as a commanded being. The central problem for human inquiry is not "What is being?" but rather "What is required of me?" This indeed is the question posed by the heart of each person, the basic, fundamental question around which one focuses one's life: What is required of me? Heschel elaborates this point in a particularly eloquent passage:

> Over and above personal problems, there is an objective challenge to overcome inequity, injustice, helplessness, suffering, carelessness, oppression. Over and above the din of desires, there is a calling, a demanding, a waiting, an expectation. There is a question that follows me wherever I turn. What is expected of me? What is demanded of me? . . . Over and above all things is a sublime expectation, a waiting for. With every child born a new expectation enters the world.

The process of creation is by no means complete; its goals are not yet attained. There is a cry for justice that only we can answer; there is a need for gentleness, for compassion, for understanding that only we can satisfy.[34]

The most important experience in life, which everyone senses at one time or another, is this "mysterious waiting," that something is being asked of me. Meaning in life is found by experiencing this demand and by responding to it. Our consciousness of this demand is no guarantee that the particular ways in which we strive to attain these goals are valid. Our conception of these goals is subject to change; our being committed to them endures forever. For example, we may fail to find adequate ways to implement justice; even our understanding of justice is subject to change. Yet we know that justice is a standard to which our laws and actions ought to conform. Our basic concern is to fulfill what is being demanded of us.

The awareness of being asked is so easily suppressed, but it cannot remain forever subdued. We cannot survive without knowing what is asked of us. There is a challenge that I cannot evade, indeed that I must not evade. It is there in moments of triumph as well as in moments of failure. I am being inescapably challenged on every level of existence. It is precisely in my being challenged that I discover my authentic self in all my uniqueness and preciousness.[35]

Indebtedness and obedience are other ways of expressing this challenge or task in life. Indebtedness is given with our very being. I cannot think of myself as a human person without being conscious of my indebtedness. It implies that I have a call, a task to perform; it is gratitude for a gift received, an experience of life as receiving and not merely as taking. Indebtedness is expressive of my concern for being human, for meaning; it is awareness of the self as committed. It is also a constitutive aspect of being human; to eradicate it would be destructive of our humanity. This sense of indebtedness may be expressed in terms of duty, conscience, obligation, sacrifice, and the like. What really counts is that I arrive at the point of realizing that I must transcend myself, my interests, my needs, if I am to have any kind of authentic human existence.[36]

Indebtedness is part of our very being, because our being is not simply being; our being is being created. That means our being is obedience; it is response to a command. I have not brought myself into existence; nor was I merely thrown into existence. My being is the result of the biblical command "Let there be!" To be is thus to obey this command of creation. All that exists obeys because all that exists endures as a response to a command. My being endures as a response to God's command. One of the reasons we have lost an understanding of the significance of life is that we have lost an understanding of this commandment of being. Human existence is a compliance, an agreement. In being and in living we obey. I am because I am called upon to be. I am because I am commanded. God's word is at stake in my being. The central problem of being could well be called a problem of reconciliation: how to shape one's total existence, how to fashion a lifestyle for oneself, in relation to all that is.

Thus, there is a given sense of indebtedness in the consciousness of the human person, an awareness of gratitude, an awareness of being called upon in moments of stillness to reciprocate and to answer by living, as Heschel so often states, in a way "compatible with the grandeur and mystery" of being human. The reality of being human depends upon my sense of indebtedness as a response to a transcendent demand. Failure to understand that we are commanded, that something is being demanded of us, is a source of grave anxiety. The acceptance of this existential debt is the prerequisite for sanity.[37]

If there is no sense of indebtedness, no awareness of transcendent demand, one reason may well be that we live in a society centered upon a "Yes" education. There is very little training in the art of saying "No" to oneself. Our society is accustomed to associate knowledge with power, and civilization with comfort, whereas we ought to have insisted that more knowledge means more reverence, and more civilization means more gentleness and compassion. One of the great failures of our society is that it demands too little of the individual, offering comfort in abundance and asking very little in return.

We should not be surprised, then, at the lack of embarrassment that one finds, a quality that Heschel esteems so highly. How embarrassing to be the greatest of miracles and not to understand it, to live in the shadow of greatness and yet to ignore it, to be a contemporary of God and yet not to sense it. Embarrassment comes with the discovery that by our lives we are either fulfilling or frustrating a wondrous expectation, that we may have wasted the grandeur of existence, that we may have missed so many unique, never-to-be-recovered moments. Embarrassment is our protection against pride, arrogance, self-righteousness. The end of embarrassment would be the brutalization of humanity. "I am afraid," writes Heschel, "of people who are never embarrassed at their own pettiness, prejudices, envy and conceit, never embarrassed at the profanation of life. A world full of grandeur has been converted into a carnival." While disease and starvation afflict two-thirds of the human race, we build more luxury hotels, more massage parlors, more gambling casinos. How are we to deal with people who are always certain of their wisdom, in whose minds problems are solved with absolute clarity, who never experience doubt or uncertainty? Clearly, the world needs a sense of embarrassment. We have to acknowledge our failures, our inadequacies, our shortcomings; we are guilty of misunderstanding the meaning of existence and of misrepresenting the goals for which we should be striving.[38]

How do we recover a sense of embarrassment? How do we come to this awareness of indebtedness, of challenge, of demand? The power of being human is so easily submerged in triviality. Lost in routine we begin to treat all hours alike. Each moment comes, stillborn and stale; we are overwhelmed by boredom, anonymity, indifference; and there follow upon this the disenchantment and disintegration of being human. We thrive on inertia; we rely on past perceptions; we delight in being entertained. In all this we shun the strain of insight.

Our basic fault here is the failure to be alive to the grandeur of the moment; we sense neither the marvel and the mystery of being nor the possibility of wonder and of quiet exaltation. Every moment is a new arrival, a new opportunity. Heschel cites the biblical commentary on the creation of heaven and earth—"And God saw that it was good"—as words of appreciation. Our responsibility is to reconcile God's view with our experience. The truth of being human is gratitude; what is required is appreciation, a sense of awe and wonder. This indeed is the secret of experiencing embarrassment, indebtedness, challenge—a sense of awe and wonder, even amazement, that springs from our encounter with the world in which we live.[39]

Wonder, Awe, and Amazement

Awe begins when I stand before sheer being, facing the marvel of the moment. When I confront reality face to face, there is a sense of awe and radical amazement before a mystery that staggers my ability to grasp it. Awe is an intuition for the dignity and preciousness of all things; it is a way of understanding, an act of insight into a meaning greater than ourselves, namely, that all things stand in a relationship to their Creator. Through awe one is brought into rapport with the mystery that underlies all reality. When truly present to a flower or a work of art or another human being, one perceives that every being is an expression of divine care and concern. Awe is the realization not only that things are what they are, but also that they stand, even if remotely, for something absolute, for something sacred. Awe is an opening to transcendence, a sense for the allusion that is everywhere to the One who is beyond all things. Awe is the attitude that helps us to perceive in the world around us intimations of the divine, to see in the simple and ordinary things of life the beginnings of immense significance, to sense in the passing rush of time the "stillness of the eternal."[40]

Awe implies furthermore a "spiritual suggestiveness" present in reality, an awareness of, and allusiveness to, transcendent meaning. There is no acknowledgment of transcendent meaning that is not rooted in wonder and awe. Wonder, or radical amazement, is a way of going beyond the given; it refuses to take anything for granted or to regard anything as final. Wonder is our honest reponse to the grandeur and mystery of reality. Wonder is the basis for awe, just as awe is the basis for wisdom.

We are able to relate to the world with two faculties: reason and wonder. Through reason we try to explain the world or adapt it to our concepts; through wonder we try to adapt our minds to the world. As concern for reality, wonder is at the root of knowledge, and yet at the same time it goes beyond knowledge. Where the faculty of wonder is at work, nothing is taken for granted; everything is a surprise; being itself is unbelievable. We are amazed not only at particular things and events, but also at the "unexpectedness of being as such," at the fact that there is any being at all.[41]

Awe is more than a feeling or an emotion. It is the sense of wonder and humility that is inspired by the sublime or that is felt in the presence of mystery. It is the answer of my heart and mind to the presence of this mystery in all things. It draws me toward the awe-inspiring object. It is an intuition for that meaning that lies beyond mystery, an awareness of the ultimate value of the universe. The mystery and grandeur I face are overwhelmingly real. What things stand for is so sublime that it staggers my ability of expression. There is so much more meaning in reality than my mind and heart can absorb.

If we forfeit our sense of awe, if we let conceit and possessiveness supplant the faculty of reverence, then the universe and all its grandeur become simply a marketplace. The loss of awe is an obstacle to insight, and it may even imply the deliberate avoidance of insight. A recovery of awe and reverence is the first prerequisite for the revival of wisdom, for the discovery that the world is indeed an allusion to God. Our greatest insights happen to us in moments of awe.[42]

Before we even begin to conceptualize what we perceive, we are first amazed beyond words. We may doubt everything except the fact that we are struck with amazement. We ask questions when we are in doubt, but we do not even know how to ask a question when we are lost in wonder. We may resolve our doubts, but radical amazement can never be resolved; there are no answers in the world for it. Beyond all our scientific theories and explanations lies the profound experience of radical amazement.

Radical amazement has a wider scope than any other human act; it refers to the whole of reality, not only to what we see, but to the very fact that we do see and to the very self that sees. We must strive to keep this radical amazement alive within us. If we fail to do this, then we will fail in our quest for insight. Sometimes we may wish that the world would cry out and explain what it is that has made it so filled with awe-inspiring grandeur. Sometimes we may wish that our own hearts would explain that which makes them heavy with wonder. By such yearnings is the spirit of amazement kept alive. Yet there is no answer in the world for our ultimate wonder at the world, just as there is no answer in the self for our ultimate wonder at the self. The world and the self are mysterious; they are questions, not answers.[43]

Endless wonder unlocks an inborn sense of indebtedness, a recognition of being a recipient of something precious and of holding it in trust. The world consists not of things, but of tasks; wonder is the state of our being asked. When our mind is aglow with wonder, we do not ask "Where is God?" for this would imply that we are present while He is absent. Rather we can only exclaim "Where is He not?"

This sensitivity to the mystery of living is the essence of our human dignity. It is the soil from which our consciousness springs and from which a sense of meaning is derived. We cannot live by exclamations alone; we need a sense of wonder and mystery. Without it there is no religion, no morality, no sacrifice, no creativity. Indeed, without it there is no being human. Yet, as Heschel reminds us, because we have learned how to replace the kerosene lamp, we have concluded that we can also replace the mystery of existence. As a result, the delicate balance of mystery and meaning, of reverence and action, is at a perilous tilt.[44]

The awareness of grandeur and wonder has all but disappeared in the present age. Our educational system stresses the importance of controlling and exploiting reality, of deriving power from knowledge, but there is little education for wonder, for the sublime. We carefully teach children how to measure and weigh and spell, but we fail to teach them how to revere, how to admire, how to appreciate. The sense of wonder and awe, the sense for the sublime, is such a rare gift; without it the world becomes flat and the human person hollow. It is not necessarily related to the vast and the staggering in size. Every grain of sand, every drop of water, every summer flower, every winter snowflake may arouse within us a sense of wonder to the mystery that surrounds us. In this regard Heschel cites the words of William Wordsworth:

> To me the meanest flower that blows can give
> Thoughts that do often lie too deep for tears.

Even more appropriate might be these lines from William Blake:

> To see a World in a Grain of Sand
> And a Heaven in a Wild Flower
> Hold Infinity in the palm of your hand
> And eternity in an Hour.[45]

Yet we have become indifferent to the sublime wonder of living, and this perhaps is the root of all human failings. We have fallen into the trap of believing that everything can eventually be explained, and that life consists basically in the organizing and mastering of reality; all enigmas can be solved, and wonder is simply the effect of primordial ignorance. Wonder is thus cast aside. Yet to dim our sense of wonder is a personal tragedy. Life becomes routine, and routine is the great obstacle to wonder. Wonders surround us, they are with us daily, yet we do not recognize that in the midst of which we stand. The Baal Shem Tov, founder of the eighteenth-century Hasidic movement in Eastern Europe, warns us: "Replete is the world with a spiritual radiance, replete with sublime and marvelous secrets. But a small hand held against the eye hides it all."

How long shall we hide from ourselves the wonders of our world? How long shall we refuse to acknowledge what is beyond our sight, satisfied with converting reality into concepts and mystery into dogma? To some, explanations and answers are tokens of the loss of wonder, like a curfew tolling the end of discovery. But there are others for whom reality is more than information; and life, more than concepts and explanations. They are never deluded into believing that what they know and perceive is the whole of reality. Poetry, art, and religion begin through an encounter with an aspect of reality that eludes the grasp of reason and the power of language.

Yet, as civilization advances, this sense of wonder unfortunately declines. This is an alarming symptom, for the beginning of our happiness lies in the understanding that life without wonder is not worth living. Wonder, or radical amazement, is a prerequisite for a genuine awareness of that which is. We must not be deceived by the limited splendor of theories that answer some of our questions, but respond to none of the most vital problems and only ridicule the inborn drive to ask the most urgent question: What is the secret of existence? Why and for whose sake are we living? Only those who have tasted neither the terror of life nor the sublime wonder of life, only those who identify the goal of life with pleasure and who claim that more and more pleasure must be provided for future generations, can deny the necessity of asking: Wherefore? For whose sake? Life without a sense of awe, wonder, or amazement is life without ultimate questioning, without indebtedness, without challenge. Such a life cannot be an authentically human life.[46]

MANIPULATION AND APPRECIATION

The ability to sense the wonder of the world, to experience awe and amazement at the "sublime and marvelous secrets" of life, depends upon the way we approach this world in which we live. One's life-style affects one's way of thinking. Our thought sums up the truth of our living, just as contemplation is the distillation of a person's entire existence. My thinking is an echo of my total relationship to the world.

Heschel points to two opposing ways in which we relate ourselves to reality. His clearest analysis of these two ways is found in the aforementioned Raymond West Memorial Lectures. Here the dichotomy is one of manipulating the world as opposed to appreciating the world. In an earlier work, *The Sabbath*, published in 1951, he expresses similar thoughts in terms of space and time. Technical civilization represents our conquest of space; gaining power and control over the world of space is one of our tasks as human beings. The danger comes when we become so enamored with our control of space that we forgo all aspirations in the realm of time. Yet time is at the heart of existence. Our goal in the realm of time is not to have but to be, not to possess but to give, not to control but to share, not to subdue but to face.

When the acquisition and conquest of space become our sole concern, then we lose focus on the meaning of life. We heed only what our senses spell out for us, what our eyes perceive, what our fingers touch. Reality is reduced to things and objects that occupy space. Even God becomes simply an object in that realm of space over which we seek control. As a result we are blind to all reality that fails to allow itself to be classified as a thing or object or fact in our world of space. Thus we suffer from an overwhelming dread of time, frightened when compelled to look into its face.

In the world of time we deal not with things but with presence; we seek not to amass a wealth of information but to face sacred moments. Our human and spiritual lives begin to disintegrate when we fail to sense the grandeur of what is eternal in time. This is not to denigrate the world of space, for time and space are interrelated. To overlook either of them is to miss a dimension of reality. What we must beware of is the unconditional surrender to the world of space and our enslavement to things.

We are proud of our conquests of space, proud of the comforts and commodities we have been able to produce. Yet these victories may soon become defeats, for we are in danger of falling victim to the work of our hands. The forces we have conquered now seem to be conquering us. It is in this light, following the theme of this earlier work, that Heschel points to the Sabbath as the great bulwark of humankind against the encroachment of the world of space. It represents neither a rejection of space nor a condemnation of civilization, but a way of surpassing civilization and all its accutrements. The Sabbath is a sanctuary we build in time, helping us to be independent of the world of space and technology. It represents a time of freedom, a time to be ourselves, a time of detachment from the vulgar idols of technology, a time of truce in our economic struggles with nature and with one another. By focusing our attention on the world of time, the Sabbath helps us overcome the attractions and seductions of the world of space. It is one thing to have power and control over the world of space that surrounds us; it is another thing altogether to stand still and "to embrace the presence of an eternal moment."[47]

In dealing with this problem in *Who Is Man?*, rather than speaking of *two worlds* of reality, space and time, Heschel stresses *two attitudes* the individual can take toward the world in which he is living: manipulation and appreciation. The way one relates to the world is the primary factor in determining whether a human being actually achieves being human. In manipulation a person sees the world basically as something to be used, to be handled, to be possessed. In appreciation one recognizes the world as something to be admired, to be revered, to be understood, to be shared.

Manipulation is the attitude that brings about separation and alienation. I am apart from the objects that clutter my life; the things that I appropriate remain at a distance from my being; I am alone. Manipulation gives a distorted view of the world; reality is equated with use or availability, so that what I manipulate is, and what I do not or cannot manipulate is not. A life of manipulation cuts one off from transcendence; a life given exclusively to manipulation implies the death of all awareness of transcendence. Even more basically, such a life implies the death of one's own humanity.

When one lets the drive for power and appropriation dominate existence, then one is certain to lose a sense of the reverence due to creation; the sense of the sacred vanishes. Heschel relates the story of a young father who never had the opportunity to visit his first-born in the hospital. Only when the infant was brought home and placed in a crib was the father able to see his child for the first time. As he looked down on the infant, his first remark was: "How can they make such a fine crib for only $29.50?" How easily manipulation can destroy that which is most precious in a human being.

In the biblical narrative of creation, mankind is given mastery over nature, but this mastery is a privilege that is all too quickly abused and misunderstood. The world becomes a utensil, an object to be used. It is no longer that which is, but merely that which is available. As one's status is reduced to that of the user and consumer, so also is one's very humanity diminished. One sees only the availability of things, with no thought of what lies beyond availability. Even though we are well aware that the world does not exist for our sake or simply to please our ego, nevertheless when we are caught up in manipulation, we feel, act, and think as if the principal purpose of the universe were to satisfy our needs. Dominated by the desire to appropriate and own, we grasp at everything, never asking whether this may be a type of robbery. Oil refineries, factories, strip mines, department stores—all are reminders of how we appropriate nature for our benefit.[48]

The manipulators do not know how to be still, how to appreciate a moment or an event for its own sake. When confronted with a beautiful view, they take a picture; when hearing a lovely sound, they tape it; instead of facing the grandeur of the universe, they explain it away. They cannot quietly behold; they cannot attentively listen; they never understand what truly confronts them. They lock themselves out of reality by reducing the world to mere objects; all relationships become possessive; they destroy for themselves all sense of transcendence. Transcendence is not a dogma of faith; rather it is that which is experienced when we confront reality face to face, something which the manipulator assiduously avoids.

That world that we seek to exploit and manipulate is not the whole of reality. What we perceive of things is not the whole of reality. Manipulation merely touches the surface; the depth of reality is immune to our exploration. We can describe or define a tree, a flower, a sunset, another human being, but in moments of stillness we know such definitions or descriptions fall far short of encompassing the fullness of their being. What is apparent to our senses and intelligible to our minds is but a thin layer covering the profoundly undisclosed.[49]

Appreciation, on the other hand, is the source of fellowship and communion. It implies acceptance of reality, meeting the world with openness, standing "face to face" with that which confronts us. We are struck by the immense preciousness of being, a preciousness that is a cause of wonder. It is inexplicable and cannot be put into any of our categories; nonetheless it is real. Any conceptual formulation of this preciousness would appear to be a diminution of reality. We cannot communicate it to others; we cannot receive it from others; we must discover it for ourselves.

In appreciation one turns to the world not like the hunter seeking a prey, but like a friend extending the hand in a state of fellowship that embraces oneself and all of creation. Such appreciation is a fundamental prerequisite for survival; it is the secret of existence. We will certainly not die from lack of information, but we may well perish for lack of appreciation. There is needed in our lives a spirit of gentleness, of stillness, of openness, of reverence, if we are to grow in appreciation of the reality that confronts us everywhere.[50]

However, we have such a strong inclination to equate existence with expediency; our needs and interests become the ultimate norm for what is right and wrong. Every human being is a cluster of needs; many are authentic, indigenous to our humanity; many others are fictitious, induced and expanded constantly by advertising, by fashion, by a desire for social acceptability. This unchecked expansion of needs could become a torrent capable of sweeping away civilization itself, Heschel warned in 1951. The pressure of needs turns into aggressive desire and becomes a constant cause of unrest, civil strife, violence, wars. This pressure seems to increase in direct proportion to our technical progress. Needs become our gods; we fail to discern the authentic from the inauthentic; we toil and spare no effort in order to satisfy them. Thus we move so easily from need to greed and become the prisoners of our own shortsightedness.[51]

Our age, wrote Heschel again in the mid-1950s, is one that looks upon nature primarily for its usefulness in satisfying our needs. Our chief purpose is to achieve power and control over nature's resources for the sake of our self-fulfillment; we consider ourselves sovereigns of our destiny. We are indeed tool-making animals, with the world a gigantic tool box for our use and satisfaction. We study and learn in order to use and to appropriate. We do not even know how to justify any value except in terms of expediency. Value is simply that which avails. We have supreme faith in statistics and ridicule the idea of mystery. Life guided by expediency easily becomes a dead end, with no sense of exaltation and no awareness of the sacred; arrogance, pride, and self-contentment are its marks. Leading, as it does, to a denial of transcendence, it is a life that contradicts the essential truth of being human.

We must recognize the error of absolute expediency and cultivate a sense for what is above expediency. The human person is too great to live by expediency alone. Happiness does not come from self-satisfaction or complacency. Self-satisfaction is the "opiate of fools" and breeds nothing but futility and despair. All that is creative in a person grows from the seed of endless discontent; by overcoming self-satisfaction we open the way to new insights. This demands the maintenance and strengthening of a basic discontent, of a craving that would know no satisfaction. To the point are the words of Oscar Wilde cited by Heschel: "'In this world there are only two tragedies. One is not getting what one wants, and the other is getting it. The last is the real tragedy.'"[52]

In other words, what is required is a relationship of appreciation and reverence for the world around us; the world is too sublime to be simply our tool. From appreciation and reverence come wonder and awe, a sense of indebtedness, an awareness of a challenge and demand that can know no satisfaction in this life, and the response to which confers upon us a realization of meaning and fulfillment. True, we are caught in a vicious circle: discontent is a feeling that by nature we seek to overcome, yet if we do not foster a truly human discontent, we turn ourselves into automatons.

Our concern with the world should not be reduced to what can be used and exploited. The more we attempt this, the more we reduce ourselves to mere instruments of utilization. Even despite our efforts in this direction, the world remains essentially evasive in its mysterious otherness. It will continue to present itself to us in two ways: as a thing I own, control, and manipulate, or as a mystery I confront, reverence, and appreciate. What I owe is a mere trifle, but what I confront and reverence is sublime. Just as we are careful not to waste what we own, so we must learn not to miss what we face.

To be human involves this ability to appreciate, as well as the ability somehow to give expression to that appreciation. Until recent generations it was relatively easy to balance both manipulation and appreciation, both utilization and celebration. Today the situation is different. To be alive is commonplace; the sense of awe and wonder is gone; the world is all too familiar, and familiarity breeds neither appreciation nor exultation. Celebration is the expression of appreciation, but we are losing the power to celebrate, and we seek instead amusement and entertainment. Entertainment is a diversion, a distraction from the preoccupation of daily living, while celebration is a confrontation, giving attention to the precious moments of living and expressing a deep inward appreciation. We must once more let our lives be a form of celebration, and we must teach the world how to celebrate. Indeed, the very meaning of existence is experienced in moments of exultation and celebration. Perhaps this is one of the rewards of the struggle to be human: quiet exultation and a capacity for celebration.[53]

Abraham Heschel presents us with a beautiful ideal of humanity, a lofty ideal, but one for which we *must strive*. The security of our human existence lies in its exaltation; we have to struggle to reach the summit merely in order to survive on the ground. This analysis has raised a number of questions which have been left unanswered, or to which only partial answers have been given. How do we know there is a Presence worth living and dying for? Whence comes this challenge and demand upon my life? To whom are we indebted? How do I know specifically what is required of me? The response to such questions comes to a great extent from the rich faith of Heschel, from his understanding of God, of religion, and of Judaism in particular. It is to these aspects of his thought that we turn in the following chapters.

NOTES

1. *Man's Quest for God: Studies in Prayer and Symbolism* (New York: Scribner's, 1954), p. 150.

2. *The Prophets*, 2 vols. (Philadelphia: Jewish Publication Society of America; New York: Harper & Row, 1962; repr. Harper Torchbooks, 1969, 1971), I 160–61; *Insecurity of Freedom*, pp. 164–65.

3. *Man Is Not Alone*, pp. 205, 237–38, 265; *Man's Quest for God*, p. 124.

4. *Insecurity of Freedom*, p. 27; *Who Is Man?* (Stanford: Stanford University Press, 1965), pp. 100–101.

5. *Who Is Man?* pp. 3–4.

6. Ibid., pp. 7–10.

7. *Insecurity of Freedom*, pp. 12–13, 185; *Who Is Man?* pp. 29, 41–42.

8. *Insecurity of Freedom*, p. 23.

9. *Who Is Man?* pp. 34–37; *Insecurity of Freedom*, p. 13.

10. *Who Is Man?* pp. 38–39.

11. Ibid., pp. 39–41; *Man Is Not Alone*, p. 207.

12. *Who Is Man?* pp. 42–44, 68.

13. Ibid., pp. 44–45; *Passion for Truth*, p. 215.

14. *Who Is Man?* pp. 46, 48; *Man Is Not Alone*, p. 48.

15. Cf. *Who Is Man?* pp. 46–47; *Insecurity of Freedom*, pp. 26, 70ff.; *Man Is Not Alone*, pp. 136–38.

16. *Man Is Not Alone*, p. 138.

17. *Who Is Man?* p. 95; *Man Is Not Alone*, p. 191.

18. *Who Is Man?* pp. 51–53; *Insecurity of Freedom*, p. 77.

19. *Man Is Not Alone*, pp. 28–29; *God in Search of Man: A Philosophy of Judaism* (New York: Farrar, Straus and Cudahy, 1955; repr. New York: Farrar, Straus & Giroux, 1977), p. 147.

20. *Who Is Man?* p. 53.

21. Ibid., pp. 54–57; cf. also *Man Is Not Alone*, pp. 191ff.; *Insecurity of Freedom*, pp. 77ff.

22. *Man Is Not Alone*, p. 193; *Who Is Man?* p. 57.

23. *Who Is Man?* p. 58; *Man Is Not Alone*, pp. 194–95.

24. *Who Is Man?* p. 60; *Man Is Not Alone*, pp. 195, 213–14.

25. *Man Is Not Alone*, pp. 198–205.

26. Ibid., pp. 206, 214; *Who Is Man?* pp. 61–65.

27. *Who Is Man?* p. 66.

28. Ibid., pp. 66–68; *Insecurity of Freedom*, p. 77.

29. *Who Is Man?* pp. 69–72. For Heschel creation is an essential truth. It is the source of what was mentioned above, p. 23, about living in God's image, and it leads to a corollary that will be developed at several points in this study: to live is to obey.

30. Ibid., pp. 72–73; *God in Search of Man*, p. 101.

31. *Who Is Man?* p. 74; *Insecurity of Freedom*, p. 163. The New Testament expresses the same thought: we love God because He has first loved us (1 Jn 4:19).

32. *Who Is Man?* pp. 74–80; *Man Is Not Alone*, p. 211.

33. *Who Is Man?* pp. 103–105.

34. Ibid., pp. 107–108; *Insecurity of Freedom*, p. 49.

35. *Who Is Man?* pp. 108, 111; *Man Is Not Alone*, pp. 223–26.

36. *Passion for Truth*, pp. 259–60; *Who Is Man?* pp. 108–109.

37. *Who Is Man?* pp. 97–98; *Man Is Not Alone*, p. 203.

38. *Who Is Man?* pp. 100, 112–13, 115.

39. Ibid., pp. 114–15. These three terms are difficult to distinguish in Heschel's writings, if indeed they should be distinguished. At times he seems to be describing a hierarchy of experiences, as though one proceeds from wonder to awe to amazement; e.g., he speaks of wonder as the beginning of awe (ibid., p. 88; *God in Search of Man*, p. 74). Elsewhere he identifies the terms; e.g., wonder is the same as radical amazement (*Who Is Man?* p. 78). John Merkle, in *The Genesis of Faith*, argues well for a real distinction between wonder and awe in Heschel's writings. Nevertheless, while at times Heschel sees these terms as distinct, his use of them tends to obliterate any distinction.

40. *God in Search of Man*, pp. 74–75.

41. *Man Is Not Alone*, pp. 11–12; *Who Is Man?* pp. 78–79.

42. *God in Search of Man*, pp. 76–78, 106–107; *Who Is Man?* p. 90.

43. *Man Is Not Alone*, pp. 13–16.

44. *Insecurity of Freedom*, pp. 123–24; *Man Is Not Alone*, pp. 68,70.

45. *God in Search of Man*, pp. 36, 39.

46. Ibid., pp. 43, 46, 85; *Man Is Not Alone*, pp. 35–37, 40.

47. *The Sabbath: Its Meaning for Modern Man* (New York: Farrar, Straus and Young, 1951; rev. ed. New York: Farrar, Straus and Co., 1963; repr. New York: Farrar, Straus & Giroux, 1979), pp. 3–6, 27–29. In another book published in 1951, *Man Is Not Alone*, Heschel speaks of looking at the world through two faculties, reason and wonder, and of our

being citizens of two realms: in one we sense the ineffable; in the other we name and exploit reality (pp. 8–11, 36). This may be a step closer to what he says in *Who Is Man?* but it lacks the precision and clarity of the latter. The terms of manipulation and appreciation help to clarify, and in turn are clarified by, the remarks of Heschel in these earlier works.

48. *Who Is Man?* pp. 81–84; *Man Is Not Alone*, p. 290. Anyone familiar with the writings of Martin Buber will see a strong similarity between Heschel's twofold approach to the world, detailed in *Who Is Man?*, with the twofold approach of Buber in his classic *I and Thou*. Heschel's "manipulation" is almost identical with Buber's I–It, and much of what I–Thou stands for is reflected in Heschel's "appreciation." Unfortunately, Heschel does not acknowledge any debt to Buber's thought, so it is difficult to ascertain how much Buber actually influenced Heschel on this point.

49. *Insecurity of Freedom*, pp. 19–20; *Who Is Man?* pp. 84–85.

50. *God in Search of Man*, p. 106; *Who Is Man?* pp. 82–83.

51. *Man Is Not Alone*, pp. 182–88; cf. *Insecurity of Freedom*, pp. 5–7.

52. *Who Is Man?* pp. 85–87; *God in Search of Man*, p. 30.

53. *Who Is Man?* pp. 87–88, 117–18.

2

Faith: The Flowering of the Human

ABRAHAM HESCHEL HAS BEQUEATHED TO US a profound and meaningful spirituality embodied both in his writings and in his person. It is a spirituality that developed from his scholarly research in biblical and rabbinic thought, from the strong attachment to his Hasidic heritage, from his sensitivity to the human situation, but above all from the depth of his faith as a believing Jew.

The treatment of faith in the writings of Heschel is rich and many-sided. He touched upon the subject frequently; he speaks of it in many different terms, often in a repetitious manner, yet he brings to it a simplicity and familiarity that can come only from lived experience.

Today so many have lost faith in faith itself, in the value and meaning of faith. We look at this world in which we live, and we are filled with a sense of horror at what we have done to it. We are afraid of our own power and terrified at our mindless greed, our selfishness, our callousness. What meaning can faith have in a value system that equates knowledge with power, and morality with satisfaction of needs? It is so much easier to permit ourselves to be swept along in a torrent of guilt and misery, drowning in the depths of discouragement and despair.

That is why, if we are ever to know the meaning of faith, we must study it as found in the lives of men and women of faith, that is, we must study it from a situational, not merely a conceptual, standpoint. This was the premiss under which Heschel wrote about faith, and it is the premiss within which I shall attempt to expound his understanding of faith.

Heschel's most extensive treatments of faith are found in his *Man*

Is Not Alone, published in 1951, and its companion volume published four years later, *God in Search of Man*. In these works he is concerned not so much with the *content* of believing as with the *act* of believing, not with dogma, doctrine, and creed, but rather with what it means to believe, with what happens within a person to bring about faith. Thus his primary concern is not to analyze concepts but to expose situations; he seeks to explore the depths of faith, the substratum from which belief arises.[1] His approach to the affirmation of God's existence moves from the unknown to the known, from the ontological to the logical and conceptual, from the reality of being overwhelmed by the divine Presence to the knowledge of that Presence. It will be helpful to study his approach more in detail.

THE GENESIS OF FAITH

There are three primary ways by which humanity is led to an awareness of God's presence: by the world, by revelation (which for Heschel consists primarily in the Jewish Bible), and by sacred deeds. The history of Israel is testimony that these three ways are really one way, for the God of nature is the Lord of history and the way to know Him is to accomplish His will. At this point we are interested for the most part in the first way, the awareness of God's presence in the world, and to a lesser extent in the awareness of God's presence in revelation. The latter, along with the third of Heschel's ways, the awareness of God's presence in sacred deeds, will be treated more fully in the following chapters.

It is the beauty and grandeur of the world, and consequently our sense of appreciation and awe, that lead us to an awareness of what Heschel calls the "sublime" or the "ineffable." The ineffable inhabits the great and the small, the magnificent and the common aspects of reality. When we stand face to face with the world, we often sense a quality that exceeds our ability to comprehend. The world at such moments is simply too much for us; it is filled with marvel. Some people sense this quality only rarely, in extraordinary events; others experience the ineffable day after day, even in the most ordinary events—a piece of paper, a morsel of bread, the glance of a stranger. If we could part company with our expectations, our desires, our greed, and look upon the world as though for the first time (a capacity which is innate to the child and reacquired by the creative person), we would quickly abandon the pretense of routine acquaintance with the world around us.

Thought and knowledge may maintain this pretense by hindering our perception. Thought deals with "posthumous" objects; it has only memories at its disposal; its object is a matter of the past, so near and yet so far away. Knowledge, then, can be considered to be a set of reminiscences. We see the present only in the light of what we already know. Knowledge is expressed in words and names that describe only what things have in common; what is individual and unique in reality is not captured by names. We are unable to express what it is that we miss.

Thus the awareness of the unknown precedes the awareness of the known. Knowledge springs forth from the soil of mystery, the nameless, the unknown. Our thought and concepts are the ways and means by which we try to "alleviate our amazement." It is with this awareness of the nameless, the sublime, the ineffable that Heschel begins his approach to the affirmation of the reality of God. [2]

By the ineffable or sublime Heschel means that which we are able to sense but are unable to convey. It is that aspect of reality that by its very nature lies beyond our comprehension and is acknowledged to be beyond the scope of the mind. The ineffable is never an ultimate aspect of reality; it always represents something greater than itself; it is an allusion to transcendent meaning, a meaning we are unable to express. We do not become aware of the ineffable by analogy or inference. Rather it is sensed as something immediately given by way of insight, an insight that is unending and spontaneous. Each person is endowed with the ability to sense the ineffable. It is that which our words, our concepts, our categories can never encompass. Works of art, systems of philosophy, theories of science—all are unable to express that depth of meaning and that boundless reality in the sight of which artists and saints and philosophers live. [3]

Those who avoid the widespread error of assuming as known a world that is unknown realize quite well that the growing abundance of human knowledge can never displace the world of the ineffable. The ineffable is not something that we have created; it is something that we encounter. The beauty and grandeur of creation, the impact of a work of art, the mystery of birth and death—these are realities we discover, not invent. We are overwhelmed by the awareness of the immense preciousness of being. It cannot be specified or categorized or explained. It gives us a certainty without knowledge; it is real even though inexpressible. One has to discover it for oneself, for it cannot be communicated to others. In those moments when we sense the ineffable, we are also certain of the value of the world around us. There must be a value underlying the world's existence, for the preciousness of its being is beyond question.

One attitude that would be alien to our finding God's presence in nature is indifference, our taking things for granted. Finding an approximate explanation for things or events is no answer to a sense of wonder. Wonder is an act that goes beyond knowledge; it is an attitude that never ceases. It is not the known as such, or the unknown as such, that causes a response of awe or reverence. Rather we revere that which is extremely precious; reverence is our response to the presence of mystery; we respond by our stillness and quiet, hoping that the moment may last.

Grandeur or mystery is something that confronts us everywhere and at all times. Mystery reigns within reasoning, within perception, within explanation. Science does not curtail the mystery; instead it extends the scope of the ineffable. Radical amazement is deepened rather than eclipsed as our knowledge advances. Mystery is not a synonym for the unknown; it denotes rather a meaning that stands in relation to God.[4]

Awareness of the divine begins with wonder; the way of faith leads through wonder and radical amazement; the insights of wonder must be constantly kept alive. Every being we encounter may be seen as representative of something more than itself; to be implies to stand for; the seen and the known stand for the unseen and the unknown. At whatever stage of knowledge we arrive, we confront transcendent significance.

Admittedly, there are some for whom mystery does not exist and who insist that mystery connotes simply something which we do not yet understand but for which we will some day have an explanation. Yet to imply that the most sensitive minds of our human past were the victims of an illusion and that poetry, art, and religion are the result of self-deception is itself too unreasonable to accept. Certainly one can point to countless examples of religious idols and symbols that were meaningful for some, but meaningless for others. The idol-worshippers err when they try to give expression to the mystery they encounter. Conventional needs and desires cloud their understanding. Motives come into play that have little or nothing to do with the original insight, and expediency begins to exert its influence. Such idol-worshippers have yet to hear the command "You shall not make unto yourself a graven image."[5]

As long as we are not overwhelmed by the concept of God, as long as we can speak of a First Cause or a Supreme Designer and still say "So what?" then it is not God we are talking about. The idea of a Supreme Designer or a First Cause may serve as a source of intellectual security in our quest for the reasonableness and order of the universe. But are these matters of supreme concern? Are these the answers to the ultimate questions that have never ceased to stir humankind? Science cannot silence these questions for they are concerned with a truth that goes beyond science and the world with which science is concerned. The problem of God is not a scientific problem; the scientific method is obviously incapable of solving it. It is a fallacy to treat the problem of God and the problem of faith as if they belonged within the order of nature.

This does not imply that the problem of God and of faith must be detached from everyday living. On the contrary it is centered in the concrete events, experiences, and insights of actual life. It comes to light in those moments when one's being is shaken with relentless concern about the meaning of all meanings, and about the ultimate direction and goal of one's existence. It comes to light in those moments when all one's presumptions and conclusions are overturned, when all the enticing distractions are suspended, when one's being is starved for a glimpse of eternal reality.

There is much we can achieve in a quest for God by applying rational methods, but reason is not the sole source of certainty, and it can never be the source of certainty for religious faith. Religious faith demands the acceptance of the ineffable, of that which lies beyond reason. When the basic religious issues of faith—God, prayer, revelation, and worship—are deprived of supreme relevance and fitted into our preconceived categories, they become almost meaningless. The categories of religious thought are unique, and they represent a level of thought deeper than the level of concepts and symbols. In teaching religion we often attempt to express our insights in terms of concepts, dogma, and creed. Yet these utterances must be recognized as pointers or indicators, as attempts to convey what cannot be adequately expressed. Otherwise they would stand in the way of authentic faith. It is in the realm of the ineffable that the basic religious issues are born. For the mind that is unbiased by what it already knows, unhindered by dogmas, unrestricted by laws and codes, there is only wonder, the realization that the world is too incredible, too meaningful for us. When we begin without presuppositions, without doctrines, without prejudices, we are free to confront the ineffable.[6]

This is the initiation of the faith process for Heschel. Faced with the awesome grandeur of the universe, we are forced to admit that there is a reality that discredits our wisdom and shatters our concepts, that there is a meaning greater than the whole of humankind, that the universe is full of a glory that surpasses our comprehension. The reality of this undisclosed meaning is beyond argument. Its guarantee is the imperative of awe that we all experience, not because we seek it, but because we are stunned and cannot do otherwise. There is much more meaning in reality than we can encompass; in moments of sensing the ineffable we are as certain of the value of the world as we are of its existence. Those for whom this awareness of the ineffable is a constant state of mind know that mystery is an aura that lies beyond all being, a spiritual dimension of all existence; there is a holiness that hovers over everything. Through the ineffable we are introduced to a reality more precious to us than our own existence. The thought of it is too powerful to be ignored.

There is no voice, no speech, no word; the mystery remains silent. Yet each of us is endowed with a "preconceptual faculty" that somehow senses the presence of the divine. The God, whose presence in the world we sense, is anonymous and mysterious; we have only an awareness of something that can be neither conceptualized nor symbolized.

If we take the world for granted, then our problem is to know its cause; if we confront the world as mystery, then the most pressing problem is: What does the world stand for, what is its meaning? So also, if God is merely a speculative concern, the problem that confronts us is whether or not there is a God. If God is a religious concern, then the problem that confronts us is our personal response to all that is addressed to us through the world and through our experience. This ultimate problem gives us no rest; each is called upon to answer.

For the speculative mind the world presents itself as an enigma; for the religious mind the world presents itself as a challenge. The speculative concern seeks an answer to the question about the cause of being; the religious concern seeks an answer to the question about what is demanded of us. We do not conjecture or theorize about the meaning of God as though in a vacuum; it is not nothingness we confront, but the sublime, the ineffable, the mystery, the challenge.[7]

Thus faith is not so much the product of our efforts to search and find as the answer to a challenge that at some time or other each of us must confront. Faith is our response to God's question, a question imbedded in the very heart of nature, a question posed for us whenever we turn to the world in a spirit of appreciation and reverence. That awareness of the divine, which begins first with a sense of wonder, silently grows until it overwhelms us with a feeling of concern, forcing us to care for things we ordinarily would not care about and for goals which go beyond our self-interest. What is the nature of this enforced concern that extends beyond self-interest? It is a pressure that weighs upon each of us, asking, calling, demanding. It plants a question that resounds in our hearts "as if it were the only sound in endless stillness and we the only ones to answer it." It is a question that demands the whole of our being in response. We would not even hear the question if we did not have the ability to surpass the self and to know that our most important concern must go beyond self-concern. Our thoughts, our possessions, our achievements no longer suffice; our concern is how to open our hearts to Him who calls upon us to live in a way compatible with the dignity and preciousness of our humanity.

This is the basis for Heschel's insistence on the need to experience awe and wonder in our lives. This is essential not only to our being human but also to our being religious, to our being men and women of faith. Only in moments of awe is God sensed as a personal issue. In moments of apathy and arrogance God may be a concept but never a concern. It is only *concern* that puts one on the path toward faith and inaugurates religious thinking. Religion comes about as a result of what one does with ultimate wonder. It is not awe or wonder or amazement as such that is the root of religion, but rather the question of what one does with the sense of awe, wonder, and amazement that kindles within us the experience of indebtedness. Wonder above all is "the state of our being asked."

Obviously, if awe is rare and wonder dead, then the question of what to do with one's sense of awe, wonder, and amazement has no relevance; one simply has no awareness of being asked. But this emptiness cannot remain forever. We are unable to survive unless we know what is asked of us. To whom do we owe anything? To whom are we accountable? How do we go from intimations of the divine to a certainty of the reality of God? Heschel is concerned with the question not of whether or not there is a God, but rather whether *we know* that there is a God. It is a question not of whether or not God exists, but of whether we are intelligent enough to present adequate reasons for affirming God's existence. Speculative thinking begins with the known and proceeds to the unknown; religious thinking begins with the unknown within the known, with the infinite mystery to which the finite alludes. For Heschel our certainty of the reality of God comes about as a response of the whole person to the mystery and transcendence of living. This response is based on an ontological presupposition, the verification of which is attained in rare moments of insight.[8]

Knowledge does not come into being simply as the fruit of thought. Every genuine encounter with reality is also an encounter with the unknown and involves a "rudimentary, preconceptual knowledge." We do not truly know an object unless we have first experienced it in its "unknown-ness." All creative thinking begins with the awareness that the mystery we face is incomparably deeper than our knowledge of what we face. Our encounter with reality does not take place on the level of concepts, for concepts are like second thoughts; they imply an accommodation of reality to our minds. The living encounter takes place on a level prior to conceptualization. Speculation, theorizing, verbalization—all are efforts to clarify the insights that preconceptual experience provides. In religious and artistic thought, especially, there is a great disparity between what one encounters and what one expresses in words and concepts. Obviously, in the religious situation we do not comprehend the transcendent; we witness it, we are present to it. Our knowledge here is inadequate, and our statements fall far short of reality, because our awareness and our insights cannot be conceptualized or verbalized.

Awareness is prior to knowledge; experience is prior to expression. As we move from awareness to knowledge, we acquire clarity, but we lose immediacy; as we move from experience to expression, we acquire distinctness but lose genuineness. This movement becomes a divergence or a distortion only when our preconceptual insights are lost in our conceptualizing, or when our encounter with the ineffable is cast aside in our acquisition of knowledge, or when the religious situation is made subservient to dogmatic formulation. All religious thought and expression is to some degree a sublimation of that presymbolic knowledge that awareness of the ineffable provides. We must make a constant effort to recall and to keep alive the "meta-symbolic relevance" of our religious concepts. This indeed is the task of Heschel's philosophy of religion. There is a perpetual temptation to give primacy to religious concepts and dogmas because these represent something we can possess and understand; in doing this we forgo the immediacy of insights and forget that the known is but a faint reminder of God. Concepts, symbols, dogmas must not become obstacles to transcendent reality; rather they should be regarded as windows through which the light of eternity may brighten the many facets of our day-to-day living.[9]

RESPONSE TO THE MYSTERY

All our religious insights are rooted ultimately in wonder and amazement, in the depth of our awe, in our awareness of the ineffable. It is precisely from our *inability to experience* that which is given to the mind that certainty of the reality of God is acquired. It is the allusion to transcendence encountered everywhere that challenges our deepest understanding. Our certainty of God's reality comes from the wonder, awe, and amazement before that mystery of life which is beyond all rational discerning. Faith is our response to this mystery that confronts us, our response to the challenge that everyone at some time must acknowledge.[10]

Faith is not a mark of capitulation, but a way of moving on to a higher level of thinking. Faith is not a defiance of human reason but a sharing in divine wisdom. Faith demands that one rise to a higher level of awareness in order to sense "the allusions, the glory, the presence," in order to sense "the urgency of the ultimate question" and the supreme relevance of the eternal. Faith, our believing in God, implies our attachment to the highest realm of mystery. This indeed is its essence: our faith enables us to reach the realm of the mystery. Our experience of awe, wonder, and mystery does not confer any knowledge of God, but it does lead to a level where the question about God becomes an inescapable concern.

In Heschel's mind no one can honestly deny the existence of God. Certainly there are some who are always absent when God is present; such persons may only present their reasons, or "alibis," for not being able to bear witness, an honest confession of their inability to believe. Being able to have faith is a sign of humanity's greatness; it is an act of freedom, asserting independence from our own limited faculties. The ultimate question is an ever-present challenge; we encounter it wherever we turn; there is no way of ignoring it. We cannot remain non-committal about a reality on which the meaning and manner of existence depend. We have to make some type of affirmation; the pressure of existence drives us into a situation where we must decide between "Yes" and "No." Whatever our decision, we implicitly accept either the presence of God or the absurdity of denying His presence. Denial of God's presence is at the same time an assertion that the universe is all alone save for the company of humanity, and that the human mind surpasses everything that lies within and beyond the universe. Unless we forget those moments of insight when we truly glimpse the ineffable, we cannot make such an assertion.[11]

On the other hand, if an individual remains indifferent to the moments of inspiration and insight, no amount of speculation will illumine the darkness. To seek God in order to solve one's doubts or to appease one's skepticism or to satisfy one's curiosity misses the whole point at issue. Certainty of God's existence does not come about as a logical corollary or as a leap from the logical to the ontological realm. Nor is the assertion of God's existence an addition to what is given in our awareness of the ineffable. Rather the statement that "God is" is in itself an understatement, for it means less than what our immediate awareness contains. The certainty of God's existence is a transition from what we immediately apprehend to a thought about what we immediately apprehend; it is a transition from the experience of being overwhelmed by the presence of God to a conscious awareness of His existence. In sensing the sacredness of all reality, we become aware of transcendent reality, of the absolute reality of the divine. In asserting that God exists, we bring this overpowering reality down to the level of conscious thought. Thus our belief in the reality of God's existence does not come from possessing an idea of God and then postulating its ontological counterpart. The ultimate reality, God, comes first in our immediate awareness; our reasoning about Him comes second. Heschel moves from the ontological to the speculative order, reversing the common trend in dealing with the God-question in which the movement is from the speculative to the ontological.[12]

Knowledge, not faith, is the fruit of our curiosity and speculation. Proofs for the existence of God do not generate faith, although at times they may strengthen it; rather it is human existence itself, our being human, that generates faith. Faith is not a convenient shortcut to God, a leap across endless theories of critical speculation; it is not an assent to a proposition, but an attachment to transcendence, to the meaning beyond mystery. As Heschel summarized it so well in the 1962 edition of his classic work *The Prophets*, faith is "trust in Him, in whose presence stillness is a form of understanding."[13]

There is no such thing as faith at first sight. The person who is swift to believe is also going to be swift to forget. Faith does not spring into existence out of nothing, like a treasure found inadvertently, like an unearned and total surprise. We do not stumble into faith. As has already been explained, there are antecedents to faith such as wonder and awe, reverence and radical amazement, at all the things that we apprehend but cannot comprehend, a sense of indebtedness and embarrassment, an awareness of the fallacy of absolute expediency, an awareness of our being exposed to God's presence and of our being called upon and challenged. In other words, what precedes faith is the experience of being human. We must learn to be guided by awe if we are to attain the insights offered by faith. Each day we should strive to deepen our sense of mystery in order to be worthy of attaining and maintaining faith. Callousness to the mystery around us, boredom at the gift of life, apathy toward the people who touch our lives—such are the great obstacles to a life of faith. There is no faith, then, without a strenuous effort, an effort in deed and thought, an effort to live an authentically human life.[14]

Faith is given only to one who lives wholeheartedly in mind and heart and soul, who strives for understanding and not just for knowledge. Faith is rooted in that passionate care for the marvel that is everywhere, a care that extends to all realms of life, holding small things great, taking ordinary matters seriously, perceiving a sacred dimension in one's daily affairs. Far from being an attitude of detachment from reality, faith demands deeper contact with reality, an ability to sense the transcendent within this world's affairs and to entertain a feeling of shame at our unresponsiveness to the holy.

What gives rise to faith is not sentiment or aspiration but a basic fact of the universe, something prior to human knowledge and experience: the holy dimension of all that exists. To have faith is to enter consciously into this dimension where we already abide by our very existence; it is a "blush in the presence of God." But some people wear masks that thwart their spontaneous sensitivity to this holy dimension of reality. At times we wear so many masks that we no longer know our true face. Faith comes only when we stand face to face, allowing ourselves to be seen and to commune, to receive a ray of God's glory and to reflect it.[15]

Faith is not something we acquire once for all; it is an endless pilgrimage, an insight that must be re-acquired at every single moment. Faith does not come to an end with the certainty of God's existence; it is the beginning of an intense desire to reach out to Him who is beyond mystery, a constant effort to listen continually to the eternal Voice that challenges us at each turn and that no one can forever ignore. Faith is the moment in which the soul of an individual "communes with the glory of God." Far from being a type of insurance policy, a source of comfort and security, faith implies a readiness for martyrdom. For faith is an act by which, in transcending the self, one responds to Him who transcends the world. This response is a sign of the essential dignity of the human person, which lies precisely in one's ability to rise above the ego, to ignore one's own needs, and to sacrifice one's own interests for the sake of the holy. This inner urge to look for meaning beyond the tangible and finite, to rise above one's own wisdom, is the root of all religious faith.[16]

We must recognize, too, that faith is the achievement of efforts accumulated over the ages. One does not live alone in faith; individual faith is not of itself sufficient; it must be guided by the unforgettable heritage of the past. There is a collective memory of God in the human spirit, and we partake of this memory through our faith. Remembrance is of great importance in faith; in fact, to have faith is to remember the ancient moments. Recollection is an act of holiness; we sanctify the present by remembering the past. The one who chooses to live by faith finds himself or herself in a community of countless men and women of all ages, races, and nationalities to whom it was manifest that one person with God can withstand all malice, all injustice, all deceitfulness. The community of faith endures forever, in spite of violence, in spite of division, in spite of desertions.

However, to have faith does not mean simply to dwell in the shadow of the past; we pay homage and reverence to those great moments and to the great men and women who responded heroically in such moments. But we cannot merely accept teachings and doctrines of the past and call it faith. In the realm of faith only one who is a pioneer may also be an heir. Spiritual plagiarism leads to loss of integrity as well as loss of identity.

Authentic faith demands more than an echoing of tradition. It is a creative event, an act of the whole person, of mind and will and heart. It involves sensitivity and understanding, engagement and attachment; it is not a permanent possession but an attitude one may gain or lose. There are times when wonder is dead, when ultimate questions have no meaning for us. There are also times when there is nothing but wonder, when mystery is within easy reach. The situation that gives rise to faith may consist in moments of wonder, awe, and radical amazement, or the flash of insight in those isolated instances when we are stirred beyond words by an experience of the momentous reality of God or by the intense darkness of suffering and despair or by a glimpse of the beauty, peace, and strength that radiate from those who are devoted to Him.

Such experiences or inspirations may be rare events. For some people they pass like shooting stars, in a flash with nothing to remember; in others they kindle a light that is never quenched, a certainty that life has meaning and that beyond all mystery and absurdity there is someone who cares. The remembrance of such experiences and loyalty to our response in such moments are the key forces that sustain our faith. In this sense we may say that faith is fidelity, loyalty to an event and loyalty to our response. The response lasts a moment, but the commitment continues. Faith does not remain stationary; we must continue to pray and continue to respond to the challenge in order to remain attached to His presence.[17]

Thus faith comes only after constant and diligent care, with the insistence on remaining true to a vision; it is the fruit of a seed "planted in the depth of a lifetime." Faith is by no means a passive state; it is an active desire to keep alive our responsiveness to God, a responsiveness that cannot be imitated but remains unique with each person. We are incapable of grasping the divine unless we are at the same time sensitive to its supreme relevance. As Heschel writes so often: "God is of no importance unless He is of supreme importance." The ways by which we are aware of God's presence in our lives must be studied carefully. So often the most precious gifts come to us unnoticed; we remain unaware. God's grace resounds like a "staccato" in our lives, and only when we retain the seemingly disconnected fragments are we able to grasp the theme. It is a discovery of a new sensibility, a sensibility to the present moment; this is a key achievement, for the present is the presence of God. "Things have a past and a future, but only God is pure presence."[18]

FAITH AND BELIEF

When Heschel uses the term "faith," he normally means the act of faith, that moment of communing with the glory of God, which should be clearly distinguished from "belief" and "creed," which are indicative of the way one expresses faith. Belief is the acceptance of a proposition as true on the ground of either internal evidence or authority. To believe something is to be convinced of its truth, to affirm a judgment so that it may become part of my approach to life; belief or creed represents something that I may possess. Faith, on the other hand, is an act of the whole person, of mind and will and heart; it implies sensitivity, understanding, engagement, attachment, not an easy, secure achievement. It never is an arrival, but implies being on the way, a constant effort to shed our callousness. Belief is an assent to an idea, while faith is consent to God; belief is a relation to a proposition or dogma, while faith is a relation to God. Belief refers to what we know, while faith surges beyond knowledge and apprehension; it refers, not to the knowable, but to that which transcends knowledge. Faith implies involvement in the mystery of God, while belief implies acceptance of dogma and creed. Faith comes with the discovery of our being needed and commanded; it comes with the realization of our importance in God's design. Furthermore, belief is a self-conscious act, a personal conviction; in belief I am aware that I, myself, am accepting something as true. In the utter awe and amazement in which faith is born there is no place for such self-awareness. How monstrous it would be, writes Heschel, to consider faith an act by which we give our expert opinion and personally grant recognition to God, as though to extend to God a certificate that He exists!

Belief is allegiance to a verbal formulation, while faith implies a profound awareness of the inadequacy of words, concepts, and formulas. Belief without faith would be an empty act, with as much spiritual significance as a computer printout proving the existence of God. Faith is the staking of one's whole life on the truth of transcendent mystery. It begins with embarrassment, with being overwhelmed, with being silenced; its only adequate expression is an exclamation, not a sober assertion. Faith is the joy of living a life in which God has a stake, the joy of being involved with God. Faith is expressed through dogma and creed, but it must never be confused with dogma and creed. Dogmas are tentative not final, intimations not descriptions. They are a translation of the unutterable into a verbal expression, but "the original is known to God alone." If we lose sight of this, then dogma and creed become forms of verbal idolatry. What is needed is the effort to share the moment and insight to which they are trying to testify.[19]

This is not to say that dogma and creed are unnecessary appendages to faith. The moments of insight and of rapport with divine reality are rare and fleeting. How can these moments be conveyed to the long hours of day-to-day living? How are our faith-insights to be communicated to others so that we may unite with them in a fellowship of faith? Dogma and creed are attempts to respond to these problems.

The adequacy of dogma depends on whether it claims to embody the truth or to allude to the truth. If it attempts the former, dogma is an arrogant failure; if it attempts the latter, then dogma may be illuminative of faith. Dogma must point to the mystery of God; it does not unveil the mystery. Dogma should serve as a way of thinking about the divine, not mark an end to that thinking. Dogma should augment the role of faith in confronting humankind with a sublime challenge, and not merely satisfy human curiosity or fulfill a human need. Dogma should serve as a pointer to ultimate truth, and not become a substitute for that truth. The divine can be so easily obscured in dogma and creed. Once dogma ceases to be allusive, it becomes an obstacle, hindering us from discovering in our own lives those moments of encounter with the divine that are the basis of real faith. The truth, meaning, and joy of faith are found beyond dogma in that which can be neither conceptualized nor verbalized. A living faith involves the recognition of the inadequacy of dogma and creed.

By means of a creed faith is transformed into conventional terms of reason. Such terms come and go; what is meaningful at one time may be scandalous at another; what is clear today may be a travesty tomorrow. Faith and reason complement one another; neither is all-inclusive or self-sufficient. Without reason we would not know how to integrate the insights of faith into the concrete issues of everyday living. While the worship of reason would be arrogance and would betray a lack of intelligence, the rejection of reason is cowardice and betrays a lack of faith. An undiscerning faith, a faith that rejects the use of reason, is akin to superstition. If we confuse ignorance with faith, we are inclined to regard as exalted whatever we fail to understand, as though faith begins where reason and understanding end. It is not necessarily a virtue to be convinced without proofs, to be overly ready to believe. Faith is not an easy road to security. We must not cease to question our faith and to ask what God means to us. Does God represent an alibi for ignorance? or the white flag of surrender to the unknown? or an excuse for unwarranted comfort and cheer? or a way of cheating fear or loneliness or despair? An unreasoned faith, a blind faith, is a denial of our humanity rather than the flowering of our efforts to be authentically human. Although many look on faith as an answer to all human problems, Heschel views faith as a challenge to all human answers. Faith is a consuming fire, burning away all pretensions. To have faith is to be in labor, to be in labor for the cause of God.[20]

What is the cause of God? Is it always veiled in mystery? Is the demand that faith makes upon our lives also immersed in the ineffable? The God whose presence in the world we perceive remains anonymous and mysterious. The experience of awe and amazement is necessary, but of itself it is not sufficient to find the way from awe to action. The mystery toward which faith directs us can be approached, but it cannot be entered; intellectually we abide outside the mystery, even though spiritually we may abide within it. True, it is more important to believe than to understand; in faith one can disregard the deficiency of reason, but one cannot live on mystery alone. To be aware of the ineffable is to be aware that something is asked of us. We are driven by faith both to know God and to conform to His ways. But this leads us to the brink of contradiction: in order to know God and His ways we would have to give expression to that which cannot be expressed.

When I seek to understand another person, the success of my efforts depends not only on me but on the willingness of the other to be open and to be understood. Our understanding of God cannot proceed regardless of His agreement. We must assume He plays a role in our efforts for understanding. In other words, our understanding of God depends not only on our efforts to approach Him but also on His willingness to be approached. No matter how lofty our aspirations, unless we are assisted, we will remain spiritually blind. Human initiative is certainly necessary, but the achievement depends on God. Only one who endeavors to seek receives divine assistance to find.

We may assume also that God is not at our disposal always and everywhere. There are moments when He chooses to meet us, and there are moments when He chooses to hide His face. All ages are not the same. There are ages when men and women are chosen to be prophets, and there are ages when the voice of prophecy is muted. We may pray equally to God at all times, but this does not necessarily mean that He speaks equally to us at all times. Throughout human history God has communicated Himself in many ways and on many different levels. [21]

FAITH AND REVELATION

Religious insights often perish or become terribly distorted as they travel from the heart to the lips. They often become "casualties of the soul's congested traffic"; we are aware of so much more than mind and heart can bear. Thus, although the intuition of the divine is universal, there is hardly any universal form to express it. Human expressions of the divine often differ widely and even contradict one another.

Furthermore, not everyone experiences these moments of insight with the same degree of intensity. The sparks may be powerful enough to light up a single life, but not strong enough to illumine the whole world. Has God ever said: let there be light for *all* the world to see? The moments of insight are directed toward a single soul. Has God ever addressed Himself toward a community, a people, a world? Has He left no trace of Himself in history for the sake of those who have not the strength always to be in search of Him?

Those who share in the heritage of Israel, Jew, Christian, and Muslim, believe that the mystery is not always evasive; they believe that the mystery confided itself at rare moments to certain chosen ones. Even though we are unable to express God, God is able to express His will toward us. It is above all through His word that we know that God is with us. We would be in a state of bewilderment if it were not for the guidance we received. But how do we know when this guidance is truly divine guidance? If one should appear in our midst claiming to bear a divine communication, would we necessarily accept the communication as such? Do we accept a message as divine because of an inner compulsion? We may have inner obsessions that are scarcely of divine origin. If a message is to be stamped as authentically divine, it must stand on its own and be saturated with a unique meaningfulness that would clearly identify it as being of divine origin.[22] Where do we find such a message?

In his 1955 treatise on the philosophy of Judaism, *God in Search of Man*, Heschel treats of three aspects of revelation: the idea, the claim, and the result. It is easy to talk about prophecy and revelation, but what do we mean by such terms? Are we speaking of fact or fancy, myth or mystery? Has God disclosed His will to certain chosen ones for the benefit of the whole of mankind? This is not just a personal issue; it is one that concerns the entire history of humanity. For biblical revelation professes to respond to the supreme question: What is it that God demands of us? Unfortunately we no longer hear the question; it is one with which the world is no longer concerned. Unless the question again becomes one of paramount concern, there is little hope of understanding what biblical revelation is trying to convey.

Heschel believes that resistance to revelation in our age is based on an understanding of humanity as either too intelligent and powerful to be in need of divine guidance or too small and inconsequential to be worthy of divine guidance. The notion of humanity's self-sufficiency is an old one and has gained increasing momentum in the last several centuries. Its adherents argue that the fate of humanity depends on our social awareness and our use of power. The capacity of our technology to solve so many problems is considered to be a foreshadowing of our ability to solve all problems. At the same time many are coming to recognize the fallacy of such reasoning and are coming to an acceptance of truths that prophets and saints have always known: that bread and power alone cannot save humanity, that there is a passion for arrogance and cruelty that only the awe and fear and love of God can soothe, that there is a suffocating greed in humanity that only holiness can suffuse, that liberty without righteousness and compassion is terrifying, that humanity without God is meaningless. The assertion that humanity has no need of divine guidance is itself a measure of humanity's arrogance and shortsightedness.

On the other hand, our advanced technology reveals more and more how insignificantly small the human race is in relation to the whole of the universe; in addition we have used this technology at times to accomplish monstrously evil designs. How can any member of the human race be worthy of being approached and guided by infinite holiness?

Yet the more we realize how dangerously powerful we have become, the more we realize the need of the human race for divine guidance. We possess the power and the ability to obliterate life on our planet. If God has any concern at all for this world, if it is not simply a trifle in His eyes, then humanity must be important enough to have received some type of spiritual guidance at rare moments of its history. There must be some counterweight to this immense power of destruction, some voice that has spoken clearly and forcefully, with a spiritual power equal or greater than our capacity to destroy.

Biblical revelation, speaking to us in the name of God who is at once all-powerful and all-just, represents an eternal "No" to this destructive power of humankind. As we applaud the feats of civilization, biblical revelation undercuts our complacency and reminds us that God, too, has a voice in human affairs. Only those who are numb to the true state of affairs, or those who shun society rather than stay within it and fight the seemingly hopeless battle for a more human and compassionate civilization, would resent its restraints on human liberty.[23]

If there are moments when a genius may speak for the whole of humanity, may there not also be moments when a prophet may speak for God? If the energy of the sun and of the soil can be channeled into a blade of grass, may it not be possible for the spirit of God to touch the minds of certain chosen persons? While it may seem incredible that we look upon words containing a "breath of God," we are forgetting, perhaps, that all around us we are looking upon works that reflect His infinite goodness and wisdom.

There are some who want to impose a dogma of total silence upon God. They act as if God had never spoken, or as if humankind were too deaf to hear. Yet why should we assume that the divine is forever imprisoned in silence? If this world is the creation of God, why should there not be within His work some signs of His expression? While the claim of the prophets may seem overwhelming to the point of incredibility, the complete silence of God would be incomparably more staggering and totally incredible.

Thus we may say, at the very least, that the idea of revelation is not an absurdity and that no one can validate a claim for the impossibility of revelation. Yet even when an idea is plausible, it need not necessarily be factual. Perhaps one's belief in revelation is simply wishful thinking; perhaps God does not meet human expectations. The Bible, however, does more than posit the idea of revelation; it makes a claim to convey the will of God. What support does this claim deserve from us?

For Heschel, the surest way to misunderstand revelation is to take it literally, as though God dictated to the prophet as one would dictate to a secretary. This basic error of literal-mindedness assumes that words have only one meaning. But words and things stand for different meanings in different situations; biblical revelation can be understood in many ways and on many different levels. We should not restrict ourselves to one single meaning. The mystery of God's omnipotence hovers over the whole of revelation. From God came the mystery of a divine utterance, and a word, a sound, reached the ear of a prophet. Just as the spirit of His creative power brought the world into being, so the spirit of His revealing power brought the Bible into being.[24]

We cannot grasp the nature of revelation itself because it pertains to the realm of the ineffable. As with all other terms expressing the ultimate, we can only point to its meaning without fully portraying it. Revelation itself conveys a mystery. Just as our concepts are completely inadequate in trying to describe God, so is it with revelation; the mystery ever eludes us. We may say that God speaks, that His spirit bursts forth from its hiddenness, but what actually took place is as unimaginable to us as it was unbelievable to those who were witnesses to it. We cannot grasp the mystery; we can only answer, or refuse to answer, its claim upon us. To ignore the mysterious nature of revelation would be a serious oversight. The issue is indeed a baffling one. Out of the darkness came the voice to Moses, and out of the darkness again comes God's word to us.

Revelation should not be rejected on the grounds that it cannot be explained. Many of our own experiences, expecially those that are most unique and precious, cannot be communicated to another. It is precisely that which is most personal and most real that is at the same time most difficult, if not impossible, to share with another. To communicate is to make something understandable; a deeply personal experience must be removed from the singular and the unique and expressed in general and universal terms. The spark of uniqueness is extinguished in this "atmosphere of generalities." What is true of our own experiences must be especially evident when we consider the impact of the transcendent upon the human mind. Such an experience is incomparable. The authenticity of revelation lies in its uniqueness, in its being different from all other events in which people are involved.[25]

Revelation means that somehow a person was able to endure the shattering presence of God; in revealing His will, God concealed His power and glory. The constant biblical references to the cloud that surrounded each theophany to Moses is indicative of the basic truth that in all revelation there is concealment. God's voice is manifest, but His essence remains hidden. Mystery stands between God and the people, but revelation implies that the divine will stands above the mystery, that there is meaning beyond the mystery.

Revelation means also that the endless distance between the divine and the human has been bridged, that the darkness is pierced, that the heavy silence is overcome. Israel was told that God is concerned with human affairs, that not only is humankind in need of God, but God is in need of humankind. It is such knowledge that makes the person formed by biblical faith immune to despair. Truth is not something timeless and detached from human affairs, but a way of living involved in all our actions. The source of truth is found at particular moments in particular events. There are no substitutes for revelation or for prophetic events. The word of God is not an object to be contemplated; rather it is to be accomplished in our lives. It enters the world as a demand, so that religious and spiritual values are not only aspirations within us, but responses to a transcendent command.

Revelation should be seen above all as an act in the drama of God's search for a people; again and again the people falter and flee from His word, but the quest continues. It is not the people's quest for God, but God's search for a people that forms the central theme of biblical revelation. God is not a power aloof from creation, but a reality that seeks and pursues and calls upon humanity. Biblical religion originated through divine initiative and not through human efforts; it is not a human invention but a divine creation. The people would not have known God if God had not approached the people; His relation to the people precedes the people's relation to Him.

Revelation is contingent on the concern and initiative of God. Ordinarily He is silent and His will remains hidden. Revelation implies a departure from this state of silence. God turns from conditions that conceal to conditions that reveal; eternity enters a moment. From the human perspective, receiving a revelation is witnessing how God turns toward His people. It is not an introduction into the divine reality as such; rather, the prophet is caught up in this divine event of God's turning, of His coming out of His hiddenness to become audible to His people. This turning is the beginning of communion.[26]

The God of Israel spoke through events in history, revealing Himself through these events rather than in things or places. Each of these events is unique; thus revelation is an event that is happening not always, but only at unique moments of time. In Hellenic thought, as well as in some Eastern religions, time is considered to be empty, irrelevant, almost unreal, especially when compared to eternity. History was considered to move in changeless cycles. It was the achievement of Israel to have experienced the importance of history and of time. Biblical faith claims that time is exceedingly relevant for it is pregnant with the seeds of eternity. Certain events that have taken place in time are of decisive importance for human destiny; we find here the triumph of time over space as history becomes a unique witness to God.

This is indeed a new insight. Non-biblical religions found divine mystery in the processes of nature, seeing in these processes reason for reverence and adoration; history did not convey any lasting religious significance or involve anything like a spiritual commitment. Time and history for non-biblical religions are basically monotonous and meaningless.

Biblical faith professes that history as a whole has a meaning that transcends any of its parts. It holds that God is involved in our actions, that meaning is given primarily in the temporal, in the tasks before us here and now. Great are our human possibilities, for time is only a bit lower than eternity, and history is a drama in which both we and God have a stake. In this drama we are confronted not only with the silence of God but also with His voice, which communicates to us what to yearn after, what to pursue, what to expect.[27]

Thus belief in revelation claims that God's word enters our world through unique historical events, pleading with His people to accomplish His will. Some events, like some works of art, are of great significance in themselves; our interest in them endures even after they are gone. There are also events which never become past, which faith continues to make present. The great events of biblical revelation overcome the dividing line of past and present; in them one with faith sees the past as happening now in the present.

Is there any evidence to support this claim of biblical revelation to be the bearer of God's word and God's will? Heschel suggests that we look at the recipients of this revelation (who for him consist primarily of Moses and the prophets) and at their message.

It would be difficult to press the charge that the prophets were victims of an illusion, of some type of mental derangement. The prophets dealt directly with issues and problems of their own times, yet the solutions they propounded appear to be relevant for all times. This has led peoples of every generation to place the prophets among the wisest of all persons. Their message, ringing with universal truths, was ages ahead of human thought at that time. If this is the product of mental derangement, then perhaps we should all be ashamed of our sanity. And to assume that the subconscious was the source of the prophetic experience, that revelation was the expression of a drive hidden in the heart of the prophet of which he was unaware, would presuppose as the source of that subconscious drive a spiritual power so wise and so holy that one would have to identify it with the divine.

One cannot propose solid arguments for asserting that the prophets simply invented a tale. They had no vested interests to protect; they had no desire for power or prestige; they took no pride in their accomplishments. God's revealing word inflicted a bitter taste on the prophets; their reward was loneliness, misery, mockery. They considered themselves servants of God's word. The act of receiving revelation was not a significant fact for them; the significance of prophecy lay with those to whom God's word was to be conveyed, in bringing God's word to bear upon the reality of the people's life. Revelation, for the prophets, was but a prelude to action.

Moreover, it is inconceivable that the prophets fabricated the claim of revelation. They condemned the lie as a fundamental evil; they placed God's demand for righteousness above the demands of country and of sanctuary. Generation after generation they exhibited the highest passion for truth and the deepest contempt for sham and hypocrisy. We cannot believe that these same persons schemed and conspired to deceive the people of Israel.

What, then, gave the prophets the certainty that they were experiencing a divine event and not simply some figment of the imagination? There were no outward signs to support the authenticity of their claim that theirs was indeed a divine revelation. It was easier for them to convey in words the will of God than to convey in words what they experienced in the act of revelation. The only sign we have lies in the claim that the prophetic experience was one of being exposed to, overwhelmed and taken over by, God in the act of His seeking those whom He desires to send to His people. In revelation it is not so much a case of God's being an experience of the prophet as of the prophet's being an experience of God.

To one who is spiritually insensitive and closed to faith there are no proofs to demonstrate the truth of this prophetic claim. Proofs may support a certainty one already possesses; they may make evident what is already intuitively clear to a person, but they are of little help in initiating certainty. Proofs cannot unveil the mystery for all people to behold. Perhaps the only things we can do is to open our minds and hearts to the prophetic word and respond to its demand. For in the final analysis it is the word the prophets convey to us that supports their claim, just as it is history itself that gives support to their word.[28]

The message of the prophets, and of the Bible as a whole, stands as its own witness. If there is anything that ever deserved to be called a divine revelation, it is the Bible. The Bible shatters once for all any illusions we have of being alone. God does not stand aloof from our anxiety and suffering; our struggle to be human is a response to the demands of revelation. The Bible contains the threat and complaint of God against the wicked, as well as the cries of the oppressed who demand justice of God. It records not only the insensitivity and stubbornness of the people, but also the promise that above all evil and all punishment stands the compassion of God.

Anyone who seeks an answer to the ultimate question "What is demanded of me?" will find that answer in the Bible. Our human destiny is to be a partner rather than a master. We have a task, a law, and a way. The task is that of redemption; the law is to do justice and to love mercy; the way assigned to us is, in Heschel's words, the secret of being *"human and holy."* When we are overcome with fear and surrounded by despair and futility, biblical revelation offers its central hope: namely, that history is gradually paving the way for the coming of the Messiah. The Bible truly represents our "greatest privilege."

Biblical revelation is categorical in its demands, yet full of compassion in its understanding of our human situation. Nowhere else do we find such love and respect for all that is truly human. No greater insights concerning the frailty and the glory, the agony and the joy, the misery and the hope, of humanity have ever been expressed. Whoever seeks words to express that deepest longing of the human spirit, the longing for prayer, will find them in the Bible. Its concern for particular historical situations has in no way deterred it from imparting an everlasting message. It bespeaks the hope of a united humankind and provides guidance toward the creation of such a unity. It addresses itself to nations as well as to individuals. It continues to evoke justice and compassion and to echo God's demand as well as His concern and love. It is the source of the finest yearnings of Western civilization. It has provoked more goodness and holiness than we shall ever know. So much of what we call noble and just is derived from its spirit. It continues to open to us an understanding of what God means, and of the need to achieve holiness through justice. And with unceasing vigor it loudly proclaims that worship of God without justice is an abomination and a blasphemy.

Biblical revelation discloses God's love for His people; it helps us recognize that all that is genuinely meaningful to us is also sacred to God. It explains how to make holy not only the life of an individual, but also the life of a people. Those who strive to embody its ideal and fail are offered new promise; those who turn their back on it court disaster.

If we should deny that the Bible is the bearer of divine revelation, then we would be proclaiming that all the spiritual achievements of Judaism, Christianity, and Islam are built on a colossal lie; we would be saying that some of the finest exemplars of the human spirit have succumbed to deception, not truth. The Bible has as its foundation either a deception or an act of God. If the Bible is rooted in deception, then there is no hope of achieving truth; there is no hope of relying on the human spirit; there is no hope of being human. There would be nothing left for humanity except despair.[29]

This summary should indicate the manner in which Heschel argues for the idea, the claim, and the result of revelation. He is speaking primarily to those who are driven by their experience of the world to a recognition of a transcendent demand and challenge upon their lives, and who thus understand that something is required of them. Such men and women are not left alone in their quest; they are assisted in moving from awe to action by the divine revelation given to the people of Israel through the prophets and to all of us through the Bible.

Let us consider now another aspect of Heschel's spirituality to which both faith and revelation direct us: his understanding of God.

NOTES

1. Cf. *God in Search of Man*, pp. 6–7; and especially "Depth-Theology," *Cross Currents*, 10, No. 4 (Fall 1960), 317–25 (repr. as "Depth Theology," in *Insecurity of Freedom*, pp. 115–26).
2. *Man Is Not Alone*, pp. 5–8.
3. *God in Search of Man*, p. 39; *Man Is Not Alone*, p. 19.
4. *God in Search of Man*, pp. 45–47, 74; *Man Is Not Alone*, pp. 25–30.

5. *Man Is Not Alone*, pp. 33–34.

6. Ibid., pp. 54–58; *God in Search of Man*, pp. 102–104. This does not imply, of course, that dogma and doctrine are everywhere a hindrance to one's encounter with God through the world; Heschel points out how they may be an asset to such an encounter. But for one whose life is blindly ruled by dogma and creed, there is a narrowing of vision and a consequent eclipse of God.

7. *Man Is Not Alone*, pp. 59–65; *God in Search of Man*, pp. 105–11.

8. *Man Is Not Alone*, pp. 68, 71–77; *God in Search of Man*, pp. 111–14.

9. *God in Search of Man*, pp. 115–16.

10. Ibid., p. 117.

11. *Man Is Not Alone*, pp. 81–82; *God in Search of Man*, pp. 118–20.

12. *Man Is Not Alone*, pp. 83–85; *God in Search of Man*, pp. 119–21.

13. *The Prophets*, i 143.

14. *God in Search of Man*, pp. 152–53; *Insecurity of Freedom*, pp. 199–201.

15. *Man Is Not Alone*, pp. 88–91, 237–38.

16. Ibid., pp. 87, 174–75; *God in Search of Man*, p. 117.

17. *Man Is Not Alone*, pp. 160–65; *God in Search of Man*, pp. 130–32, 137.

18. *Man Is Not Alone*, pp. 88, 92; *God in Search of Man*, pp. 143, 153.

19. *Man Is Not Alone*, pp. 165–67; *Insecurity of Freedom*, p. 177.

20. *Man Is Not Alone*, pp. 159–60; *Israel: An Echo of Eternity* (New York: Farrar, Straus & Giroux, 1969; repr. 1977), p. 224.

21. *Man Is Not Alone*, p. 94; *God in Search of Man*, pp. 128–29.

22. *Man Is Not Alone*, pp. 98–101; *God in Search of Man*, p. 163.

23. *God in Search of Man*, pp. 168–71.

24. Ibid., pp. 172–74, 178–81.

25. Ibid., pp. 184–89, 221.

26. Ibid., pp. 196–99; *The Prophets*, ii 216.

27. *God in Search of Man*, pp. 205–208.

28. Ibid., pp. 211–34, passim.

29. Ibid., pp. 238–47, passim.

3

The God of Care
and Concern

ABRAHAM HESCHEL'S APPROACH TO GOD is at once wholly biblical
and deeply personal. To the Jewish mind, he once wrote, the understanding of God is achieved "by sensing the living acts of His concern." God takes interest in the fate of the individual person; the
moral and spiritual state of humanity engages His attention. Thus,
if one were to choose the most dominant characteristic in Heschel's
understanding of God, there is no doubt that the choice must be
God's concern or pathos; the divine pathos is at the heart of biblical
revelation.

Heschel's elaboration of pathos, found primarily in the 1962 edition of his great classic *The Prophets*, represents one of his major
contributions to the field of biblical literature. He has also supplied
us, indirectly perhaps, with the personal motive why pathos is so key
to his approach to God, when he wrote that, although it may be one
of the most baffling of mysteries, nevertheless, for the one whose life
is open to God "His care and concern are a constant experience."[1]
Pathos is so crucial to Heschel's understanding of God because
God's love and concern were for him such a constant experience.
For the person of biblical faith any understanding of God must begin with this experience of an ever-faithful love and concern; it must
begin with some sense of the divine pathos.

PATHOS AS FUNDAMENTAL

Divine pathos is the foundation for the relationship between God
and humanity; it implies the constant concern and involvement of
God in human affairs; it is crucial to any understanding of prophetic
inspiration. The prophets of Israel are those who have been granted
a vision of the world *sub specie Dei*; they have glimpsed reality as

reflected in God's mind; they have somehow experienced the pathos of God. The divine pathos is the key to inspired prophecy. God is involved in the life of His people; a personal relationship binds Him to Israel. The prophet is an associate or partner of God, not just His mouthpiece. Heschel's analysis of the prophetic writings reveals that the fundamental experience of the prophet is a fellowship with the feelings of God; it is a *"sympathy with the divine pathos,"* a oneness with the divine consciousness which comes about through the prophet's participation in the divine pathos. In a sense the prophet lives the life of God: he hears God's voice and he feels God's heart.[2]

This is the basis for the fierce anger and intense indignation that so often flow through the prophetic writings. What to some might appear to be literary hyperbole—namely, the prophets' raging against mistreatment of the widow, against manipulation of the worker, against callousness toward the poor—is in reality an attempt to express a profound sensitivity to the pathos of God. This profound sensitivity is the direct antithesis of the apathetic indifference so commonplace in the prophetic era, as well as in our own. We look upon single acts of cheating in business or lying to our neighbor as slight, something that can easily be overlooked; to the prophets such acts are a disaster. We look upon simple injustices as passing episodes, scarcely noticeable; to the prophets they are catastrophic deathblows to existence. This "immoderate excitement" of the prophets, their excessive language, their violent outbursts are all traced by Heschel to their confrontation with the divine pathos which made them acutely aware of the "abysmal indifference to evil" which surrounds humanity in every age. It was not a question of magnifying guilt but of clarifying the greed and selfishness and exploitation that was (and is) so prevalent. What often appears to the casual reader as the gross exaggeration of the prophets is in reality a glimpse of God's concern for the plight of humanity. Humankind writhes in agony; no human voice can adequately convey its suffering. Yet the prophet has become for Heschel the voice that God bestows to the pain of the plundered poor, to the silent agony of a creation profaned by the powerful and the wealthy. God has thrust a burden upon the soul of the prophet, the burden of His concern, of His vision, and the prophet is bowed and stunned at the fierce greed he perceives. Behind the condemnation of the prophet lies the rage of God.[3]

Heschel sees an enormous gulf between the prophets and us. The moral status of our society, for all its weakness and ambiguity, seems nonetheless fair and decent; to the prophet it is dreadful. Our goals and standards are rather modest, our sense of injustice rather tolerant, our moral indignation rather timid. Yet human violence and oppression are unending, unbearable, and too often unopposed. While we are content with business as usual, in the prophet's eyes the world reels in confusion. The basis for this gulf between the prophets and us lies in the prophet's ability to grasp the concern of God, to disclose the divine pathos.

The prophet's reflection on the pathos of God brings about a communion with the consciousness of God, that is, a oneness with the concern of God for the plight of humanity. If the prophet pictures the wrath of God as harsh and dreadful, it is because he knows how profound and extensive God's love is. If God's threatened punishment seems to be so overwhelmingly destructive, it is because of His concern for righteousness and His intolerance of injustice. The human mind seems incapable of grasping the true dimension of human cruelty and exploitation. If God's anger is fierce, it is because humanity's cruelty is enormous. If the God of Israel demands justice from His people, it is because of His great love for His people. But this love is not exclusive; nor does it turn aside from the wrongdoing of the beloved, blindly forgiving every fault. Although God loves Israel, He also possesses a passionate love for what is right and a burning hatred for what is wrong.[4]

Thus in the writings of the prophets justice is not important simply for its own sake. God's demand for justice is rooted in His compassion for humanity. Injustice is condemned, not because a law has been broken, but because a human being is being harmed. The preoccupation of the prophets with justice and their passionate condemnation of injustice grow out of their sympathy with the divine pathos. They are intoxicated with the awareness of God's concern for His people and for all humanity. What is at stake here is the primacy of God's involvement in history. As Heschel points out, it is more accurate to look upon the prophets as proclaimers of God's pathos, as speaking not so much for the idea of justice as for the God of justice, or, better, for God's concern for justice. What the prophets are proclaiming is God's "intimate relatedness" to humankind. It is this fact that places all of life in a divine perspective. Each person is a concern of God. Pathos, this divine concern for creation, and especially for the human person, is "the very ethos of God."[5]

The fact that the Lord of the universe should care how an obscure individual treats widows and orphans is staggering to the imagination; it is incompatible with a mere rational approach to an understanding of God. The prophetic understanding of God was achieved, not by analysis or induction, but by fellowship with Him, by a type of "living together." What is revealed to the prophet is not the abstract divine essence but rather the personal and intimate relation of God with the world. The prophets do not seek to disclose or impart new truths about the divine Being. What they know about God is His pathos, His relatedness to Israel and to humankind. Revelation means, not that God makes Himself known, but that He makes His will known; it is a disclosure not of God's being, but of His will and pathos, of the way in which He relates Himself to His people. The prophets experience no revelation of God's essence but only of His relatedness. Thus their writings deal not so much with humanity's vision of God as with God's vision of humanity. The Bible is not an expression of humankind's theology but of God's anthropology. It tells us nothing about God in Himself, but only of His relatedness to humankind. What was revealed to Israel was not the mystery of eternity but the knowledge and love of God for humanity. The only events in the life of God the Bible speaks about are acts done for the sake of His people: acts of creation, of redemption, of revelation. Thus it was never the goal of Israel to know absolute transcendence, but rather to ascertain what God asks of His people. It was an aspiration to commune with His will rather than with His essence.[6]

Quite obviously, human actions affect God, bringing Him joy or sorrow, pleasure or pain; they may grieve Him or they may please Him. God is never detached from His creation; He is intimately affected by it. Thus the God conveyed to us by the prophets possesses not only intelligence and will, but above all pathos; this basically is the prophetic consciousness of God. The God of Israel does not judge the deeds of His people with apathetic aloofness; these deeds are of intimate and profound concern to Him. God is not outside the range of human sorrow and suffering. Rather, He is personally involved in and aroused by the fate and conduct of His people.

Pathos, then, denotes not simply an idea of goodness, but a dynamic, caring relationship between God and His people. The unfolding of biblical history is the unfolding of the fullness of God's love and care. The very call of Abraham is experienced as care. Abraham's unquestioning response to the sacrifice of Isaac is rooted in the experience of God's response to his plea for Sodom. It was the certainty of God's love and mercy toward Israel that empowered the prophets to accept His anger.

Pathos implies that the human predicament is also a divine predicament, for God has a stake in the human situation. Sin is more than a failure for the individual; it is a frustration for God, because the human person is not only the image of God but also the perpetual concern of God. The idea of pathos brings a new dimension to human existence. Never has humanity been taken so seriously as in the prophetic writings. Whatever one does affects not only one's own life, but also the life of God insofar as the divine life is directed toward humanity. The human person is raised beyond the level of mere creature by the pathos of God and becomes "a consort, a partner, a factor in the life of God."[7]

The divine pathos bridges the abyss between humanity and God. There exists a reciprocal relationship between God and humanity, consisting not only in humanity's commitment to God, but especially in God's engagement with His people. The disparity between God and the world is overcome in God, not in humankind. Pathos is the focal point of eternity and of history; it is the "epitome of all relationships" between God and Israel. What the prophets confront is a God of compassion, of concern, of involvement. Pathos makes the living encounter between God and His people possible; in pathos the divine and the human meet.

Heschel's theology of pathos expresses the uniqueness and richness of the concept, as well as its essential contribution for our understanding of the religious situation. It is indeed, in his words, "a theological category *sui generis*." It is a term that means God is never neutral; He is always partial to the poor, the oppressed, the exploited. Pathos denotes, not a human experience as such, but the object of a human experience. It is something which the prophets confront as current and present in history, and which forms the real basis for dialogue between God and His chosen people. What characterizes the prophetic writings is not foreknowledge of the future but "insight into the present pathos of God."[8]

Apathy vs. Sympathy

This emphasis on the divine pathos places Heschel in sharp contrast to a long tradition of both Jewish and Christian theologians.[9] The approach of traditional theology is often imbued with philosophical presuppositions that have their origin in Hellenic thought. The classical philosophical concepts of perfection, impassibility, self-sufficiency, and infinity clash sharply with Heschel's portrayal of divine pathos. Divine perfection was seen as incompatible with change, for change connotes imperfection. Divine self-sufficiency placed God beyond the range of human suffering and concern. Spiritual perfection consisted in rising above all affections, becoming entirely free from all passion in order to be like God who is impassible. This was especially true in Christian spirituality, which often demanded that one extirpate all feelings and all passion.

Yet what biblical revelation presents to us is not a God who is self-sufficient and apathetic, but a God who is intimately concerned and involved in creation, and who is aroused by the conduct of humanity. Divine pathos makes every decision of God provisional, dependent upon humanity's response. The biblical Lord is a God of justice and mercy who calls upon an individual to return, to repent, and by repenting thus to effect a change in what had been decreed.

Does our conception of the greatness of God demand that He be emotionally insensitive to human agony rather than profoundly moved? Must divine judgment be a generalized abstraction rather than a concern for this particular human person, a feeling for the person, an emotional awareness of the person? If we are to conceive of God not as a passive outsider but as an active participant, then the category of divine pathos is indispensable. To conceive of God as detached and unemotional would be totally alien to the biblical mentality. The Hellenic ideal of apathy is in sharp contrast to the biblical ideal of sympathy. The ideal state of the Greek gods is one of happiness and serenity, while the prophets picture for us a God of concern and compassion.

Heschel thus opposes traditional theology's "God of abstraction," a self-subsisting First Cause that dwells in the lonely splendor of eternity, unaffected by anything outside of itself. This is not the God who hears the cry of the orphan, who listens to the prayer of the widow, who gathers in the tears of the sorrowing. For the person of biblical faith the denial of humankind's relevance to God is as inconceivable as the denial of God's relevance to humankind.

There is no doubt that this theology of pathos denotes a change in the inner life of the divinity, and as such it is much more in keeping with the thought of process theology than with that of traditional theology. A theology rooted in Hellenic thought considers God as impassible in His essence, remaining absolutely and forever without change. In such a theology pathos would contradict the absolute transcendence and independence of the divinity. To attribute pathos to God would be a denial of God as the Absolute. Pathos implies a change from one state to another, and as such it is incompatible with the idea of a First Cause that is both unmoved and unchangeable. Pathos is likewise incompatible with the Scholastic notion of God as *actus purus*, which is another way of expressing the essential immutability of God by denying any admixture of potency in the divine being. Passion, implying change, would not be compatible with the true being of God as *actus purus*. The notion of God as perfect being is not biblical in origin; it is a product of Hellenic thought, not of biblical writings; it is a postulate of reason, not of biblical theology.

It should also be noted again that the *way* one thinks about God is as important for Heschel as *what* one thinks about God. The reflective or philosophic way commences in ignorance and rises from concept to concept to the idea of the perfect Supreme Being. The religious or situational way begins with embarrassment, moves from insight to insight, and arrives at the vision of a transcendent Reality whom one acknowledges as the source of embarrassment. Thus one cannot describe God; one can only praise Him. This is why Heschel stresses that in asking about God we are really examining ourselves. Are we truly sensitive to the grandeur and supremacy of what we ask about? Are we wholeheartedly concerned with what we ask about? Unless we are involved, unless we approach the question situationally, we fail to sense the issue.

The philosophical inquiry into being as being becomes in Heschel's theology the inquiry into being *as creation*, that is, being as a divine act. Theologically there is no being as being; there is only a continuous coming-into-being. Thus, philosophically the supreme concept is being; theologically and biblically the supreme concept is God, and the biblical God is a God of mighty deeds. The

Bible says not how God is but how God acts. It relates nothing about God in Himself, nothing about His essence. It speaks about God in His relation to the world; it portrays His acts of pathos, His acts in history.

This theological approach with its emphasis on pathos is quite open to the charge of being anthropomorphic. Yet in one sense all "God-talk" is open to this charge. Is it any less anthropomorphic to speak of God's love and justice and mercy than it is to speak of God's compassion or anger or sorrow? Furthermore, as Heschel argues, absolute selflessness combined with supreme concern for the poor and the exploited could hardly be regarded as basically a human characteristic. No human personality in the Bible is characterized as merciful, gracious, slow to anger, abundant in love and truth, faithful in love to the thousandth generation. As a theological category pathos is much more a genuine insight into God's relationship with humankind than a projection of human qualities upon God. Absolute selflessness, total giving, mysteriously undeserved love are characteristics far more of the divine sphere than of the human. Insofar as these characteristics are found in human nature, to that extent is a person indeed the image of God, endowed with attributes of the divine. It would be more proper to consider prophetic passion as theomorphic than to consider divine pathos as anthropomorphic. So also rather than label God's unconditional concern for justice as anthropomorphic, it would be better to regard humanity's concern for justice as theomorphic. The idea of the divine pathos, then, is not so much a personification of God as it is an illustration of God's concern, an illumination of His relatedness to His people.

Philosophy conceives of God in the image of an idea. The word "God" may denote a supreme form working within the universe, or the wisdom and intelligence reflected in nature, or an omnipotent ruler, or the First Cause. But none of these ideas conveys the reality of God. How, asks Heschel, does one move from saying the word "God" to sensing the reality of God? Here again the prophetic writings help us, for the prophets portray God "*in the image of personal presence.*" For the prophets God is not an idea of whose truth we are convinced; rather God is a Being who is "supremely real and staggeringly present." They never use the language of *essence* but rather the language of *presence.* They do not try to describe God; they try to make Him present, and in doing so only words of grandeur and intensity are of any help.[10]

Heschel warns of two errors to avoid in our attempts to understand God. One he calls the "humanization" of God; this leads to the conception of God as so allied to His people that, whether they do right or wrong, He would not fail them. In other words, He becomes so much *our* God that He ceases to be truly *God*. The second error is the "anesthetization" of God which so emphasizes the mystery and otherness of God that He becomes completely divorced from creation, an indifferent supreme Power who has nothing to say to humankind; in this case there is so much emphasis on the notion of *God* that He ceases to be *our* God.

One of the great challenges, then, for biblical faith is the reconciliation of this awareness of God's transcendence with the experience of His overwhelming presence and concern. Any pretense that this challenge is adequately met would be specious and misleading; it is precisely the challenge involved in using inadequate words that drives the mind beyond all words. All biblical expressions about God are woefully inadequate, but when taken to be *allusions* rather than descriptions, understatements rather than comprehensive concepts, they are helpful in bringing us to a sense of the reality of God. Indeed, all expressions of divine pathos are efforts to set forth the reality and aliveness of the God of Israel.

THE WRATH OF GOD

Many ancient peoples worshipped gods that were merciful or wrathful; what was new with the revelation to Israel was the recognition that God's mercy and wrath were expressions of a *"constant care and concern."* The divine pathos embraces the whole of reality; all beings and events have a reference to God. One of the basic premises of biblical faith is not simply that there is an ultimate origin, but that there is also an ultimate concern. All of human life is both a concern of God and concerned with God.[11]

This is especially important when considering the biblical expressions of divine wrath. There is a certain ambiguity when speaking about the pathos of anger. Although anger may often become a vice, it would be wrong to identify all anger as evil. It may touch off deadly explosive forces and in this sense be a curse, but anger may also be a blessing. Its contrary, patience, while commonly held to be a virtue, may be a slothful quality when it is indicative of a lack of righteous indignation. The writer of Ecclesiastes (3:8) reminds us that there is a season for everything, "a time to love and a time to hate."

From a psychological viewpoint anger is seen as intense displeasure leading to temporary loss of self-control, to compulsive reactions, and to a desire to avenge or punish. In this sense anger is a passion that one should attempt to curb or eliminate. However, the anger of God as conveyed by the prophets should be viewed in the light of a theology of pathos, not of a psychology of passion. The prophets never considered the anger of God simply as a spontaneous outburst; it was always a response to the conduct of the people. The prophets take pains to account for these outpourings of divine wrath in order to demonstrate that the anger of God is not a random, blind, explosive force; rather, it is willful and purposeful, motivated by a concern for what is right and wrong. It should not be considered apart from the divine pathos, of which it is an aspect. As a mode of God's responsiveness to His people, it is conditioned by His will and aroused by the people's sinfulness. The wrath of God clearly indicates that God's relationship with the people is never an indiscriminate outpouring of good, regardless of the people's response. There are a demand and an expectation that come with this relationship. Heschel calls God's anger "righteous indignation" brought about by the mean, shameful, and sinful conduct of His people; it is ultimately God's impatience with evil.

The prophetic writings are a reminder that, unlike most of us, God is never indifferent to evil. It is precisely His care and concern for humankind that permit the kindling of such intense wrath. All too often we remain neutral or unmoved when wrong is done to others. This massive indifference to evil is often more insidious and more dangerous than evil itself. It bespeaks a silent justification, making possible the easy acceptance of attitudes and actions which otherwise would have been clearly recognized as wrong and sinful. The exploitation of the poor may be to us a slight wrongdoing; to God it is a disaster. Our reaction is often a tolerant disapproval; God's reaction is such that no prophet can adequately convey the divine wrath that is enkindled.[12]

There is a limit beyond which patience and forbearance cease to be a blessing. God's forgiveness must never be mistaken for indulgence or complacency; never is forgiveness absolute or unconditional. If it were, it would easily be mistaken as a license for vice.

Anger is a reminder that one may need forgiveness, a forgiveness that cannot be presumed. God may be long-suffering and compassionate, but He is also demanding and insistent that His people be faithful in their response. It is because of the people's infidelity that God is led to the pathos of anger. The people whom He had chosen and redeemed from slavery, whom He had destined to bear witness to His redemptive love and to be a light to the nations, had betrayed the covenant, worshipped idols, and abandoned Him. They remained deaf to the pleas of the prophets, and eventually God's patience turned to anger. But the pathos of anger is transient; it is not a fundamental attitude. God's anger passes, but His love and concern go on forever.

In other words, the pathos of anger is contingent on the actions of the people. It is the people who provoke it, and it is the people who may bring about its revoking. The people clearly have the power to modify God's designs, for His wrath is instrumental and provisional; if the people should modify their conduct, then the divine anger would fade. For beyond God's anger and demand for justice lies the mystery of His compassion. Heschel puts it quite simply: "The secret of anger is God's care." There is perhaps no clearer truth conveyed in the prophetic writings than the certainty of His care, the fidelity of His concern. Biblical consciousness begins, not with humankind's concern for God, but with God's concern for humankind. The most glaring truth for the prophets is the presence of God's concern for His people and the people's lack of concern for God. God's wrath is never looked upon as an emotional outburst, but rather as an essential aspect of His constant concern. His heart is not made of stone; as a loving Father He is intimately affected not only by what His people do to one another, but also by what He Himself must do to them. God's wrath is indeed a "tragic necessity," both a calamity for humankind and an affliction for God. God does not delight in His anger; He deplores its tragic necessity. Yet, even though He must punish, He will not destroy. God remains ever the master of His anger.[13]

The terrible threats of divine punishment often ring harshly in our ears today; they seem to token a lack of moderation. We would prefer a God who is soft, tender, familiar, a source of comfort and security. Moreover, we are scarcely aware of the sufferings inflicted on the poor and oppressed by those who would make a mockery of

God's demand for justice. It is precisely God's involvement in these sufferings which explains His particular concern for the downtrodden and contrite. A faith that is ensconced in sentimentality will succeed only in weakening the pursuit of justice and truth. It is the pathos of anger that strengthens God's demands for righteousness. Only when mildness and kindness have failed to conquer evil is anger proclaimed. God's anger, then, should be seen as a counterpart to His love, a help to achieve that justice which is demanded by His love and concern for His people.

THE DIVINE INITIATIVE

Heschel never tires of repeating that Israel's faith did not come as a result of its quest for God. The people did not discover God; God discovered His people. The Bible is a record of God's approach to His people, His drawing ever nearer to them. The whole biblical conception of the relation between God and His people begins with God's call and is followed by the response of the people. All the key religious events in the Bible belong to what Heschel calls "anthropotropism," that is, they are experienced as the turning of God toward humankind. It is the consciousness of living under a God who calls upon us, turns to us, is in need of us. In anthropotropic experience one is affected by the impact of events which one does not initiate but in which one feels a transcendent attentiveness focused upon oneself. The unique quality of biblical faith is this awareness of a God who helps, who demands, and who calls upon His people. It is a sense of being reached for, being sought after, being found; always the initiative comes from God.

Without a God who cares, our universe would become an inferno. No human ear could capture the agonized cry of humanity. There is such a dreadful disproportion between human misery and human compassion. Callousness is, perhaps, our outstanding failure; we have such a minuscule grasp of the suffering that surrounds us. One could not endure so much misery, so much callousness, were it not for the certainty that God listens to our cry. This basic insight of biblical faith, the mystery and grandeur of the infinite concern of God for His people, is essential to our sanity and our survival. God is immediately and personally concerned. We are not alone.[14]

Pathos, then, is fundamentally this *"divine attentiveness and concern."* The whole of the biblical message reflects this awareness. The prophets share in and convey this divine attentiveness to humanity, this involvement by God in history, this divine vision of the world. There is a hidden pathos that hovers over the history of humankind. There is a divine attachment concealed from the eye, a divine concern unnoticed or forgotten, which permeates the whole of creation. Humanity lives not only in time and space, but also in the dimension of God's attentiveness. It is this divine concern which is at the root of the prophets' mission to Israel and which is basic to all biblical theology. What makes the difference between pagan and prophetic religious experience is this consciousness of the divine pathos. This is the most precious of insights: to become aware of God's participation in existence, to experience this divine attentiveness. For Heschel the theme and claim of biblical theology is God's concern for the people and the people's relevance for God. It is this care of God that constitutes humanity's greatness. Each person stands for the great mystery of being God's partner. God is indeed in need of us.[15]

PARTNERSHIP WITH GOD

Perhaps the richest and most comprehensive theme used to describe the relationship between the divine and the human in Heschel's writings is that of partnership. Clearly, the God of Israel is not detached from, or indifferent to, the joys and griefs of His people. Rather, life is a partnership of God with His people. God is a partner and a partisan in our struggle for justice, peace, truth, community. Authentic, vital needs of a person's body and soul are a divine concern. That is why human life is holy. Because of His need for a people, God entered into a covenant with humankind through Israel for all time, a mutual bond embracing God and the people, a relationship to which not only the people but also God are committed. God takes humanity seriously. The person of biblical faith knows not only God's mercy and justice, but, even more important, God's commitment to humankind. In this awesome truth are rooted the meaning of history and the grandeur of our human destiny.

Biblical consciousness is characterized by two aspects: it is a consciousness of an ultimate commitment as well as a consciousness of

an ultimate reciprocity. Essential to biblical religion is this awareness of God's interest in humanity, the awareness of a covenant, the
awareness of a responsibility that lies on God as well as on us. Our
task is to concur with His interest; we are to carry out His vision of
our destiny. God needs a people for the accomplishment of His
goals. Religion, in the light of biblical tradition, is a way of serving
these goals or ends of which we are in need, even though we may
not be aware of them. Biblical religion should help us to feel the
need of these goals.

Jewish life, indeed all life rooted in biblical faith, is life shared
with God. God has not thrown us into the world and abandoned us.
He shares in our labors; He is partner to our anxieties; He partakes of
our sorrows. A person in need is not the exclusive and ultimate subject of need, for God is in need with the person. To have God as a
partner is to remember that our problems are not exclusively our
own. When beset by difficulties, one ought to remind oneself that
God is in need just as we are in need, that He is in need with us.
Human living is partnership with God. For Heschel the very essence of Judaism consists in this awareness of the reciprocity of God
and humanity, of humanity's togetherness with Him who abides in
eternal otherness. The task of living, as well as the responsibility for
living, is both His and ours. We have rights as well as obligations.
Our ultimate commitment is also our ultimate privilege. God is
now in need of us because He freely chose to make us partners in
His enterprise, partners in the work of creation.[16]

There is in each person an unquenchable need for what is lasting, a need to worship and to revere. This unquenchable need is
often erroneously transformed into self-aggrandizement or into a
search for a guarantee of personal immortality. Biblical faith indicates that this need is the need to be needed by God, to fulfill the
need of God. It teaches that each person is in need of God because
God is in need of each person. Our need of Him is but an echo of
His need for us. God has, as it were, a vested interest in the life of
each person. But this is a truth that must be discovered from within;
it cannot be imposed from without. It cannot be preached; it must
be experienced.[17]

Biblical faith, then, concerns not only our search for God, but,
more important, God's search for humankind. God is unwilling to
be alone; a personal relationship, an intimate concern, bind Him to

humanity. He has chosen humanity to praise, reverence, and serve Him by the accomplishment of His ends in creation. Our search for God is not only a human concern, but a divine concern. No person is simply a disinterested bystander. Each one is indispensable to God; each is a need of God. Heschel summarizes the whole of the biblical history of salvation with his oft-repeated phrase: "God is in search of man." The human person is both a creature who is constantly in search of self and a creature of whom God is constantly in search. Our faith in God is in response to His call, a call that goes out again and again, a call to accomplish His goals for our world, a call to become a partner with Him in truly humanizing the society in which we live.[18]

All the prophetic writings center in a single revelation. There is a continuity, an all-embracing meaning that flows through every insight of the prophets. Every word they preach reflects the covenant of God with Israel, as well as the demands of that covenant. As a result, the affairs of everyday life are treated not as isolated incidents, but as parts of a great cosmic drama. God has a stake in human history; He has a stake in what takes place between persons. There exists within each of us a far greater kinship with the divine than we are wont to believe. Each of us is a need of God. Behind the various manifestations of His pathos is one motive, one need: the divine need for human righteousness. Righteousness is God's part of human life. Injustice and oppression bring suffering to humanity, and consequently they are a blot upon the conscience of God. Yet people continue to act as they please, doing wrong, capitulating to their greed, abusing the weak, insensitive to the fact that their actions are an affront to God, not realizing that the oppression of the poor is a humiliation of God, a blasphemy against God. What characterizes biblical religion is faith in this profound concern of God for humanity, faith in God's commitment to humanity, in terms of which faith one seeks to shape one's life and attempts to find sense in history.

Although the universe may be considered God's masterpiece, an even greater masterpiece is in the process of being created through history. To complete the grandeur of this work, God needs the help of humankind. Justice and righteousness are the molds in which God wants the living history of humanity to be shaped. However, instead of fashioning the clay according to the mold, we tend to destroy the mold altogether. As a result, the world is full of iniquity and injustice. God needs mercy and righteousness, goals that can be satisfied only in living history, in time, not in the temples and churches of religion. Humanity is charged with God's mission, chosen as God's partner in the realm of history. Justice is not merely a human convention or value; it is a transcendent demand, reflecting a divine concern. It is not merely a relationship between persons; it is a divine need, an act involving God. To do justice is, indeed, to be the partner of God.[19]

Yet beyond justice, in Heschel's thinking, lies righteousness. While justice is strict and exact, giving each person his or her due, righteousness implies benevolence, kindness, generosity. Justice may involve strict legality, while righteousness implies a burning compassion for the oppressed. Justice without righteousness is in danger of being dehumanized or deified, that is, pursued with such legal exactitude that it becomes destructive of persons. One must always remember that beyond all justice lies God's compassion. Concern for justice is ultimately an act of love.

This demand for justice and righteousness is indicative again that the God of Israel is personally concerned for His people, stirred by their conduct and their fate. The Lord of creation, who is transcendent and beyond human understanding is full of love and compassion, of grief and anger. He stands in a passionate relationship to humankind. His love or anger, His mercy or disappointment, are aspects of His profound participation in the history of His people, and of all peoples. The various manifestations of His pathos are rooted in one primary motive, namely, the divine need for human righteousness. We are neither lords of the universe nor masters of our own destiny. Our life is not our own property, but a possession of God's. It is this divine ownership and partnership that makes human life so sacred.

For Heschel there exists an eternal appeal in the world: God is beseeching humankind. Some are startled by the appeal; others remain deaf. It is a cry addressed to us all. An air of expectancy hovers over human life. Something is being asked of us, of all of us. What is it that God most desires of us? It is not primarily prayer or sacrifice. "What then, O Israel, does the Lord your God ask of you? Only to stand in awe of the Lord your God, to walk in His ways, to love Him and to serve Him with all your heart and soul" (Dt 10:12). God is all too often a stranger in our world. Our task is to bring Him back into the world and into our lives. [20]

GOD AS CHALLENGE AND DEMAND

This God whom we have made a stranger is not an explanation for the enigmas of the world, not a solver for the problems of our world, not a guarantor for our personal salvation. He is an eternal challenge, an urgent demand. He is not a mystery to be revealed or a concept to be pondered, but a question addressed to us as individuals, as nations, as the whole of humanity. He is an outcry wrung from the hearts and minds of the human family, and it is urgent that we somehow sense this religious concern.

Writing a few years before his death, Heschel stated that the major religious problem we face is the "systematic liquidation" of our sensitivity to this challenge from God. The human person is to be understood in terms of transcendence, but this transcendence is not passive; it is a challenging transcendence. Each of us is continually being challenged; a question is being asked of us. The moment we disavow this living transcendence we are truncated, reduced to a level on which our distinctiveness as human beings gradually disappears. What makes one human is one's openness to transcendence that lifts one to a higher level than oneself. Unfortunately, we have become overwhelmed by the power we have achieved and have succumbed to the illusion of sovereignty. Blinded to the truth of the human situation, we are deaf to the question that is asked of us. [21]

God reaches us as a claim. Religious responsibility is responsiveness to that claim. It is by our response to that claim, our becoming partners of God, that we achieve the fullness of our humanity. The essence of living a human life lies in being challenged, being called. We must pray for the wisdom of how to respond to that challenge. Living of itself is not enough. Certainly, just to be is a blessing, and to live is holy. But being alive is not the answer to the problem of living. As Heschel repeats many times, to be or not to be is *not* the question; rather the vital question is *how* to be and how not to be. This is the question that helps us to recall the meaning of being human and the deep responsibility involved in just being alive. In one sense the meaning of God is precisely the challenge of "how to be." The tragic disease that afflicts contemporary society is the tendency to forget the "vital question"; this is a disease that could prove fatal and end in disaster. One of the primary purposes of prayer in a life of biblical faith is to help one recall *passionately* the perpetual urgency of this vital question. In fact, there is no real faith without confrontation with Him who demands of us justice and righteousness. In our struggle to achieve humanity not only must we renounce the ugliness of avarice, envy, hatred, arrogance; we must face a claim, an expectation. We are called to partnership. There is a pressing urgency to become engaged in the work of justice and righteousness. To be moderate in the face of this demand would be offensive. Our goal cannot be merely an accommodation; it must be a transformation. A mediocre response to God would be a profanation.[22]

The task set forth by the Bible, then, is to live in a way that is compatible with God's presence. Humanity's response to this task determines the course of history. The prophets have nothing but disdain for those for whom God's presence represents primarily comfort and security; for the presence of God ought to represent a challenge, an incessant demand. God is compassion but not compromise; He is justice, but not a solution to the problems of justice. The Lord who created the world manifests His presence within the world, as well as in the Bible and in the sacred deed. The world, the word, and the deed are full of God's challenge, as well as His glory, but we must learn to be present to His presence. Too often, however, our greed, our self-righteousness, our callousness dull our sensitivity and profane His silent, patient presence. "For God is everywhere," writes Heschel, "save in arrogance."[23]

THE PRESENCE AND GLORY OF GOD

Even though we do not know what God is, we do know where He is. We cannot describe His essence, but we are able to share His presence and to feel the anguish of His dreadful absence. We are so often immersed in our own selfishness that we forget where He is. We forget that even our self-concern is a reflection of a divine concern. Yet there is a way of keeping ourselves open to the caring presence of God. There are moments when we feel challenged by a power that is beyond our own will, that gnaws at our heart and robs us of independence by its judgment of our actions. It is as though we had no privacy, no retreat, no escape. There is a voice that knows no mercy and reaches everywhere with its challenge and demand.

More and more we are beginning to realize that a sense of the sacred is as vital to us as the light from the sun. A true sense of joy and beauty and security lies in our recognition of the sacredness of life. If we allow the light of this sacredness to be quenched, the darkness will fall upon us like thunder. All life hangs by a thread—the thread of our fidelity in responding to the concern of God.

Yet our fidelity is so feeble and confused. The world that has been given to us in trust has exploded in our hands. A stream of misery, grief, and oppression has been unloosed which leaves no one's integrity intact. We have become callous to catastrophe. What hope is left when this callousness stands like a wall between our consciences and God? We have trifled with the concern of God, and now we reap the fruits of our thoughtlessness. The taste for goodness has all but vanished from the earth.

For Heschel and for the Hasidic tradition in which he was reared, the actual eating of the forbidden fruit by Adam was less serious than his hiding from God after he had eaten it. Adam represents each one of us; his hiding from God is thus our hiding from God. The will of God is to be present in our midst and to be manifest to the world, but by betraying His trust and defying His will we have turned our back on Him and walked away. Yet in His compassion God continues to ask "Where art thou?" When we hear that question, when we shed our alibis and try to respond, then the wall built by our callousness begins to crumble away. God is never distant from the honest and repentant heart, for the biblical God is not essentially a hidden God. His hiding, like His wrath, is a passing phenomenon brought about to a great extent by the infidelity of His people. It is not that God is absent or obscure; it is we who have concealed Him. He is waiting to be disclosed, to be admitted into our lives and into our world. Like the child in the game of hide-and-seek who hid himself and then became dismayed because his friend had ceased to look for him and had instead gone away, so also God may say: "I hide, but there is no one to look for me." If God is in hiding, He is waiting for us to disclose His presence.[24]

This should not be a difficult task for us. The whole earth is full of God's glory; this for Heschel is an affirmation that the whole world is full of His presence. Just as some people are able to make their presence felt here and now without saying or doing anything, just as some are able to communicate silently something of their interior power and strength, so also the outwardness of the world communicates something of the indwelling greatness of God. There is a divine radiance that conveys itself without words. It is sensed in grandeur, and yet it is more than grandeur; it is a living presence. This glory or presence is not an exception, but an aura that surrounds all things; it is the spiritual setting for all reality. If the perception of this glory is a rare occurrence in our lives, it is because we have deadened our sense of wonder and thus fail to respond to the presence. This is a failure due above all to our callousness, which for Heschel is the root of all sin. It is akin to the biblical "stubbornness of heart" or "hardness of heart." The prophets had to reproach Israel continually for this lack of sensitivity. In their darker moments the prophets would complain that this callousness was the permanent condition of the people, yet it was a condition that could be overcome.

The glory of God enhances not only the grandeur of the world, but the grandeur of time. Each moment is precious, for time bears a treasure open to everyone. Each moment is a majestic expectation, for each moment announces God's subtle arrival. Time is the presence of God in our world. On the human side, awareness and response are needed, for the divine presence is retained only in those moments in which we try to be present and in which we try to let God enter our daily deeds. Thus we are called upon to make the moment sacred, to unfold this divine presence, to sanctify time. Only three elements are required to sanctify time, says Heschel: "God, a soul and a moment." These three are always found wherever we take our stand. To turn away from this task of the moment, this task to sanctify time, is to introduce a boredom into life that could well end in despair.[25]

The presence of God is also discovered in His word, in the Bible. Here again, if we are to discover the biblical presence of God, we too must be present. Presence is not so much a concept as a situation. One must be involved with the prophets if one is to understand them. Presence is not disclosed to those who remain uninvolved, or to those who are merely intellectually curious, or to those who are concerned solely with their own narrow points of view. Presence is not perceived by those who understand only the story, but who miss the pathos, who possess an idea of God but who have no sense of the reality of God. One must live with God's word intimately and be ready to give oneself wholly to its demands. We can discover the presence only by allowing ourselves to be addressed by the Bible and by being responsive to it. Unless we are truly confronted by the word, unless we are in genuine dialogue with the prophets and respond to them, the Bible ceases to be Holy Scripture; it ceases to be God's word.

If we are genuinely to understand the Bible, we must accept it for what it is. If we are to discover its unique quality, we must recognize its unique authority. This is the paradox of biblical faith. In the Bible words are more than instruments of expression; they are vessels of divine power, conveying the mystery of creation and disclosing the source of all meaning. The Bible is a never-ending expression of an eternal concern: God's concern for humanity. It is not so much a book to be read as a drama in which we are called to participate; our participation is our response. When God confronted the prophets, He confronted the whole of humanity; when He addressed the prophets, He addressed each one of us. If there is a passionate commitment to the Bible, it is not rooted in any test of its truthfulness. Such commitment rather comes from that prophetic awareness that enables one to acknowledge "Here is the presence of God."[26]

For the biblical mind ultimate reality is not mystery. Beyond mystery is the God of righteousness who rules the world and who has chosen to enter a covenant with humanity so that God has need of each person. Ultimate meaning and ultimate wisdom, then, are found not in the world but in God. The only way to share in wisdom is through a relationship with God, a relationship that begins, paradoxically, in ignorance. Heschel distinguishes two types of ignorance. There is an ignorance that is dull and barren, the result of indolence, and that leads one to complacency and conceit. But there is another ignorance that is keen and penetrating, the result of one's perception of the ineffable, and this ignorance leads to humility. The beginning of wisdom is found in this latter ignorance, in the awareness of the ineffable and of the grandeur and mystery of living. To know reality in its true significance is to know the world in its relationship to God, that is, to understand that all things are His servants. We are not alone in celebrating God. We join all creation in its song of praise to Him. Our kinship with nature is above all a kinship of praise, for all things praise God. "We live," writes Heschel, "in a community of praise." While the technological mind dwells primarily on what is manageable and controllable in nature, the biblical mind emphasizes the marvel and mystery of nature, that nature which is not a part of God but an allusion to Him. These two outlooks are not mutually exclusive; on the contrary, they ought to be complementary. The biblical mind, however, never perceives nature in isolation from God, and this is the basis for genuine wisdom. For the world is both an act of God and a gateway to God.[27]

This brief analysis of Abraham Heschel's approach to God provides strong evidence that God's care and concern were indeed for him a constant experience. He was a man with an intense awareness of God's presence and with a prophetic insight into the pathos of God. This God-centeredness of Heschel's led him to a deeper appreciation of the strengths and weakness of religion, of its need and value, and of the consequent responsibilities for men and women of faith. Let us turn our focus to this very important aspect of Heschel's spirituality.

NOTES

1. *God in Search of Man*, p. 21; *Man Is Not Alone*, p. 144.
2. *The Prophets*, i 14, 24–26.
3. Ibid., 4–5.
4. Ibid., pp. 50, 80.
5. Ibid., pp. 216–18.
6. *Man Is Not Alone*, pp. 129, 143–44; *The Prophets*, ii 264–65.
7. *The Prophets*, ii 3–7.
8. Ibid., 9–11.
9. Ibid., 27–52.
10. Ibid., 54–55.
11. Ibid., 57–58.

12. Ibid., 61–65.

13. Ibid., 65–74; *God in Search of Man*, pp. 127–28.

14. *The Prophets*, II 219–20; *Insecurity of Freedom*, p. 254.

15. *The Prophets*, II 263–64; *God in Search of Man*, p. 158.

16. These themes are repeated often in Heschel's writings. Cf., for example, *Man Is Not Alone*, pp. 241–43, 269; *Insecurity of Freedom*, p. 194; *Who Is Man?* pp. 74–75.

17. *Man Is Not Alone*, pp. 247–48; *Insecurity of Freedom*, p. 13.

18. *Man Is Not Alone*, p. 215; *God in Search of Man*, p. 136.

19. *The Prophets*, I 198–201, II 146.

20. *Man Is Not Alone*, pp. 244–47.

21. "Choose Life!" *Jubilee*, 13, No. 9 (January 1966), 37.

22. "On Prayer," *Conservative Judaism*, 25, No. 1 (Fall 1970), 8.

23. *Man Is Not Alone*, p. 145.

24. Ibid., pp. 145–54; *The Prophets*, I 16.

25. *God in Search of Man*, pp. 82–85; *Insecurity of Freedom*, p. 32.

26. *God in Search of Man*, pp. 253–55.

27. Ibid., pp. 56, 94–98.

4

Religion and
Human Existence

"It is hard to define religion," Heschel wrote in the mid-1950s; "it is hard to place its wealth of meaning into the frame of a single sentence." We cannot expect, then, to find a concise definition of religion in any of his writings, but we do find that he has much to say about it. Earlier I discussed faith as the full flowering of the human; here I am concerned with showing the essential relationship between religion and human experience which is so important for Heschel's concept of religion. Neither faith nor religion can be understood apart from an understanding of the human.

Religion possesses vitality only when it is deeply rooted in human existence. The institutions, rituals, symbols, and creeds of religion must spring from human experience. If religion is vapid or unappealing, it is often due to our having forfeited the antecedents of religious faith: namely, the insight and commitment springing from human experience which are essential to religion's meaning. We must cultivate, rather than suppress, those human moments that precede a religious response to ultimate demand.

Without continuously nourishing a sense of the ineffable we cannot grasp the meaning of the holy. Our minds are so often imprisoned by platitudes and labels that the notion of God is robbed of all reality. We must try honestly to sense once again the sheer mystery of being alive, the mystery we experience when truly confronting the world around us.[1]

Origin of Religion

One of the ideas most frequently stressed in Heschel's writings points to the sense of the ineffable as the cradle of genuine religion. It is not precisely the sense of the ineffable itself, or the experience of wonder and amazement, but rather one's attempt to respond to this experience which gives rise to religion. As Heschel wrote in his classic work *God in Search of Man*:

> Religion is the result of what man does with his ultimate wonder, with the moments of awe, with the sense of mystery. . . . Thus it is not a feeling for the mystery of living, or a sense of awe, wonder, or fear which is the root of religion, but rather the question *what to do* with the feeling for the mystery of living, what to do with awe, wonder, or fear.

He goes on to say that what gives birth to religion is not intellectual curiosity but "the fact and experience of our being asked." In spite of all the obstacles that come from within and without we are driven by an awareness that something is asked of us, that we are being asked to live and act in a way that is truly compatible with the grandeur and mystery of living. Heschel comes back to this notion later in the same work: "The root of religion is the question what to do with the feeling for the mystery of living, what to do with awe, wonder and amazement. Religion begins with a consciousness that something is asked of us." What is decisive here is the realization of our own great spiritual power, the power to answer the question of God. Each one of us is caught up in an eternal request seeking to elicit an answer from us. This is the origin of religion.[2]

The experience of wonder and awe, the sense of the ineffable, become the cradle of religion when they give rise to a sense of personal indebtedness. This sense of personal indebtedness, rather than an experience of absolute dependence, provides for Heschel a more accurate understanding of the central basis for religion. God is not only a power we depend on; He is also a God who makes demands. This certainty that "something is asked of us" means primarily that there are ends toward which we are to strive, divine goals in need of us for their accomplishment. Religious living consists in striving for those goals that are in need of us. Unlike other values, religious values and goals evoke in us a sense of obligation. They present themselves as tasks to be accomplished rather than simply as objects of perception.

Religious persons then are driven by an awareness that something is being asked of them, that they must live responsibly, that is, that they must be responsive to the challenges and demands that accompany the experience of awe, wonder, and mystery. Hence the emphasis by Heschel that the religious question is *what to do* with awe, wonder, and mystery. Thinking *about* God, rather than responding *to* God, begins when we are no longer caught up in awe and wonder; in other words, thinking *about* God occurs when we move from a situational to a conceptual approach to reality. Obviously, our being asked implies that we may either answer or refuse to answer. But the more deeply we listen, the more we nourish the experience of awe and mystery, the more we are enabled to overcome the callousness and arrogance that alone would form the basis of a refusal.[3]

Thus in Heschel's thought the very characteristics that are so essential to human living and that give meaning to a person's life—namely, the experience of wonder and of the ineffable, as well as a sense of indebtedness and of being challenged—are also essential to his understanding of religion. Authentic human living and authentic religion, the human and the holy, are essentially interrelated.

Heschel rejects forthrightly any psychological theory that would place the origin of religion in a human feeling or need. Such theories may help to explain a person's receptivity of religion, but human feelings or needs are incapable of creating religion. The essence of religion has nothing to do with the satisfaction of human needs. Certainly, as men and women seek to control and exploit the forces of nature, they often seek the use of divine power to come to their aid. Such intentions and practices, however, smack not so much of religion as of magic, which is the deadly enemy of religion and its very opposite. Though one cannot prove that magic has preceded religion everywhere, the confusion of magic with religion cannot be denied. This was a danger against which Israel had to battle again and again. It is a struggle that has continued through the ages. A central focus of the prophets was their firm opposition to such opportunism under the guise of religion.

Even to root religion in the quest for personal salvation is to reduce it to a sophisticated magic. As long as one sees in religion the satisfaction of one's own needs or a guarantee of immortal life or a device to bring about personal security, one is serving not God but oneself. Heschel is quite emphatic on this point: "*religion is not expediency.*" We miss God completely when we think of Him as an answer to a human need, as though not only the wealth and goods of nature, but even the Author of nature, too, had to cater to the human ego.

Thus religious thinking and acting are often very deceptive. There is a constant danger of believing what we desire rather than of desiring what we believe; the temptation is ever before us to transform our need into God rather than to adopt God as our need. We may assume it is God we believe in, but in reality "God" may often be simply a symbol of our own personal interests or a symbol of the values espoused by society or government. One's concern for God may thus be a concern for one's own ego. Hence the role of religion in our lives must be constantly re-examined. The point here is that transcendence is the test of genuine religion and of religious truth. For Heschel the unique and essential meaning of a human being lies in the ability to satisfy ends that go beyond one's ego. Though our natural concern may be "What are others doing for us?" religion teaches us to ponder what we may do for others and to realize that no person's ego is worthy of being the ultimate end. Religion begins, not as a feeling or emotion within us, but as our response to goals and situations outside of ourselves. Religion recognizes that God is *the* human need, and thus the goals of God must become the goal and interest and concern of humanity. This also demands that we oppose whatever is contrary to these goals within ourselves, including our own interests and needs, whenever they collide with God's will.[4]

Religion means, then, that we strive to say "No" to ourselves in the name of a higher "Yes." One of the primary purposes of religious tradition is to keep this higher "Yes" alive and to teach men and women the true demands that are being made upon them. That is why Heschel writes that "*religion consists of God's question and man's answer.*" Religion is our response to the expectations of God. Far from being the *satisfaction* of a need, religion ought to be the *creator* of needs. Its task is to convert divine ends into human needs, "to convert the divine commandment into a human concern." Heschel sees this as one of the purposes of religious education. If we fail in this, if we fail to convert the divine command into a *human* concern, then it remains merely an obligation, uncongenial to the human heart, a duty but not a joy, creating a state of constant irritation between the religious person and the task to be accomplished. Religion provides an answer for what ought to be the ultimate questions of every human being: Who needs me? What am I here for? Once one becomes oblivious to ultimate questions, then religion itself becomes irrelevant for there is no longer an awareness of our being needed, of our being a need of God's.

In Heschel's thought, then, both faith and religion must be rooted in human experience if they are to be properly understood. Just as faith ought not to be studied in total separation from moments of faith, so also we ought not to study religion in complete detachment from the acts, events, and experiences that give rise to it. Religion comes to light in moments when one's whole being is shaken with unabated concern about the meaning of all meaning, when one's ultimate commitments are suddenly questioned, when all foregone conclusions are abruptly shattered. When reduced to dogmas and definitions, to codes and catechisms, religion becomes little more than a "desiccated remnant of a once living reality."[5]

Religion, with its demands and visions, is not a personal luxury but a matter of life and of death. Its message is often diluted by routine and superstition. The task that confronts us is to recall the urgencies and emergencies of human existence, those deep cravings of the spirit, the many ways in which the voice of God comes to us and to which the demands of religion are an answer. Religion tries to counteract the boredom and apathy of human existence by pointing to every moment as an extraordinary occasion and to every action as a precious opportunity. For the spirit of God is present wherever and whenever we are willing to accept it, and religion is what one does with this presence.

Closely allied with this notion is Heschel's association of religion with "ultimate embarrassment," another essential component of our being human. Ultimate embarrassment is the awareness of the world's being too great for us, of the grandeur and mystery of reality, of our being present at the unfolding of an incomprehensible eternal saga. Ultimate embarrassment underscores the absurdity of one's sense of sovereignty and the fallacy of absolute expediency. Not only does it precede religious commitment; it is the touchstone of religious existence. The self-assured person is convinced that he or she does not need God in order to know how to live: "I am a good person without going to the synagogue or church." The religious person, imbued with a sense of embarrassment, would never say "I am a good person" but rather prays daily "Forgive us, Father, for we have sinned."[6] That is why Heschel may also say that religion is what one does with one's ultimate embarrassment.

Heschel at times does speak of religion with a certain vagueness—as the answer to our ultimate questions, as what one does with presence or wonder or ultimate embarrassment—but when he speaks in this way, he is dealing primarily with the prolegomena of religion, with those human experiences that give birth to religion. He becomes much more specific when speaking of religion from the vantage point of Judaism. Here generalities become specifics. The essence of religion is not found in any inward state of the soul or absolute feeling, as though a religious person possesses sentiments too deep to manifest themselves in ordinary deeds, or religion were a plant that could thrive only "at the bottom of the ocean." Rather, for the faithful Jew "religion is not a feeling for something that is, but *an answer* to Him who is asking us to live in a certain way. *It is in its very origin a consciousness of total commitment*, a realization that life is not only man's but God's sphere of interest."[7] For Judaism it is not enough to say "God asks for the heart." Heschel would not be comfortable with St. Augustine's formula "Love God and do what you will." God is asking the Jew to live in a particular way; the life of the faithful Jew is the response to this quest of God. Judaism lived in the concrete makes very little sense unless it is seen as the answer to a most important question: "What is God asking of me?" This should lead to a discussion of such matters as the role of law, deeds, and the like, but we will deal directly with these points in the following chapter. For our purposes now it is enough to emphasize the importance of the above question not only for Judaism, but for all religions. One of the great contributions of religious education would be to bring about the genesis of this question in each one's mind and heart: What is God asking of me? For Heschel genuine religion must be imbued with the realization that something indeed is being asked of us.

The response to this question by the religious person must be one of total commitment. Heschel elaborates on this point in many of his writings, but especially in his last complete work, A *Passion for Truth,* in which he draws comparisons between two dominant religious figures of the mid-nineteenth century, the Hasidic *tzaddik* Reb Menahem Mendl of Kotzk (the "Kotzker"), and the Christian existentialist Søren Kierkegaard. Heschel contends that both these men saw the essence of religion as warfare; to live one's religious commitment means to defy, to proclaim, to oppose. Religion implies a commitment to do battle against spiritual inertia, indolence, and callousness. Without such commitment one would merely drift with the changing tide and evade the challenge; such evasion and routine destroy the fabric of religious life. Kierkegaard's "leap of faith" is not a once for all venture but must be renewed continually lest it succumb to inertia. Religious faith presumes a resolution of the will. For the Kotzker, too, there are no easy ways; what one achieves without effort "is not worth a candle." To be a Jew means to struggle uphill where no steps can be taken lightly, yet the task urges us on. For both Kierkegaard and the Kotzker the voice of faith is resonant with power, but faith is not easily won; it is gained only at the cost of great spiritual anguish. Religious faith is not the facile acceptance of a tradition or creed; nor can it be inherited from one's parents or ancestors; each person must earn it. One can never be at ease in the life of faith, but to one who is truly committed, fidelity in the pursuit of one's religious duty implies a demand that also brings solace.[8]

In concluding this section it should be evident that it is indeed difficult to compress the breadth and depth of Heschel's thoughts on the meaning of religion into a single sentence. Nevertheless, if we should attempt what Heschel did not, we would do well to summarize the preceding pages by defining religion in Heschel's writings as *the committed response to the demands of God.*

Dangers and Weaknesses of Religion

Religion exists not for its own sake but for God's sake. Institutional religion, what Heschel calls the "human side" of religion, with its creeds and rituals and laws is a way to the goal, not the goal itself. The goal is "to do justice, to love mercy and to walk humbly with thy God." When religion attempts to segregate God, it falls into error; it forgets that the true sanctuary has no walls. When the human side of religion becomes the goal, when religion exists for its own sake, when the temple becomes the ultimate end, then religion becomes a façade for idolatry. Unfortunately, religion has often succumbed to this tendency to become parochial and self-seeking, as if the task were to increase the might and beauty of its institutions or to enhance its body of doctrine rather than to ennoble human nature. When this occurs, religion becomes more a sower of prejudice than a beacon of truth, abrogating the sacred rather than sanctifying the secular.

The achievements of religion in this world must not be idolized. We must not regard any institution as an end in itself; a temple that has come to mean more than a reminder of the living God is an abomination. To equate religion and God is idolatry. God alone is supreme. Anything else regarded as supreme is an idol. Even the laws of the Torah are not held to be absolute. Nothing may be deified, whether book or hero or institution. To ascribe divine qualities to anything, no matter how sublime it may be, is to distort both the thing itself and our concept of the divine. Biblical religion must be a voice raised against this human tendency to convert means into ends; it should be a challenge to the sovereignty of any created value, whether it be the ego, the state, or the cosmos. Nothing exists for its own sake; all is set in the dimension of the holy, endowed with the imprint of God.[9]

Another facet of this danger of religion is the tendency to make a god out of dogma, or to allow dogma to become, as it were, a vicarious faith. Judaism does not deny a role to dogma, but it refuses to give exclusive primacy to dogma because it realizes that what we believe in goes far beyond the range and power of human expression. Underlying the pre-eminence of dogma is an intellectualism that claims that right thinking correctly expressed is the most important aspect of religion. But for biblical religion *right living* is what counts most. A dogma represents only a partial grasp of the religious situation. The adequacy of dogma depends on whether it claims to express the mystery of God or to allude to the mystery of God. If the former, it is doomed to failure; if the latter, it is a help and an illumination. To be adequate, dogma must point to the divine mysteries, but not picture them; it serves as an allusion, but not as a description. It is difficult to restrain dogma to the role of a humble signpost, and so it frequently becomes an obstacle to faith. It is easier to believe in dogma than to believe in God. The inner craving to possess an authoritative fixed set of principles replaces the necessity of constantly searching for the way of faith. Dogmatic stability often takes precedence over personal initiative and spontaneity. If it is to fulfill its purpose, dogma must be recognized for what it is, a summary or epitome of faith, not a substitute for faith.[10]

The decline of religion's influence in Western society is due for the most part to religion itself and not to the physical or social sciences or to a so-called secularism. Religion is to blame for its own defeats. It is not so much that religion was proved to be wrong in this or that instance as that it simply became "irrelevant, dull, oppressive, insipid." Religion today makes few demands upon us. It is prepared to offer comfort and edification, but it lacks the courage to challenge our idols or shatter our callousness. The problem, in Heschel's eyes, is that religion has become "religion," that is, it has become identified with institution, dogma, law, ritual. It is no longer an event; its acceptance no longer involves risk or responsibility. Life calls for dramatic exaltation, and religion offers routine and repetition. It has achieved respectability by muting its demands and surrendering its values. When faith and worship and love are no longer the hallmarks of religion, when religion itself is no longer a living fountain, when it places more emphasis on authority than on compassion, then the voice of religion becomes meaningless, a noisy gong or a clanging symbol.[11]

Heschel applies this critique in an explicit way to Judaism, but the Christian reader will easily grasp the parallel weaknesses present within the Church. In a 1953 address to the Rabbinical Assembly of America, later expanded for his *Man's Quest for God*, Heschel speaks of the dignity and precision of those Jewish services in which all the right things are done. The ceremonies are carried on with great decorum. However, one key element is missing: *life*. Everyone knows in advance what will take place. There are no surprises, no spiritual adventures, no sudden outbursts of devotion. Nothing unpredictable is going to happen to the one who prays; one attains no new insights into the words one reads or into the life one lives. Monotony is the motto; the fire once present in worship has been extinguished. The temple has become the burial place of prayer. People continue to attend services, but one could scarcely call it a service *of God*, or *divine* worship. They repeat the words "Forgive us for we have sinned" or "Thou shalt love the Lord thy God with all thy heart" with no thought of the meaning of what they say; the words are spoken in lofty detachment "as if giving an impartial opinion about an irrelevant question." Complacency prevails in our houses of worship. The temple may be clean and tidy, but prayer has become an empty gesture, because people either lack faith or are too bashful to admit that they would like to take prayer seriously.

And so they develop the habit of praying by proxy, letting the rabbi or the cantor do the praying for them. Thus prayer becomes an impersonal exercise. People who are otherwise sensitive, vibrant, alert suddenly become in the synagogue listless, lazy, aloof. Many suggestions can be proffered for improving temple attendance, yet they all miss the core of the problem; as Heschel warns, spiritual problems are not going to be solved by administrative techniques.

Religion today has lost sight of the person; it has become an impersonal affair involving mere institutional loyalty. Its emphasis is on external activities rather than on the stillness of commitment. It is concerned more with what is done publicly than with what takes place in the privacy of one's heart. Inwardness is ignored, and so we treat ourselves as though we were made in the image of a machine and not in the image of God. No longer mindful of this sacred image, we become deaf to the command to live in a way that is compatible with this image. Religion must return to what is personal and intimate.[12]

In A Passion for Truth Heschel cites the critiques of both Kierkegaard and the Kotzker against institutionalized religion. Much of their critique he would make his own, although he would not follow them in their almost total rejection of "the world." Kierkegaard claimed that religion as it was taught and lived was counterfeit; he resented not so much the failure of the Church to approach the Christian ideal as its refusal to admit its failure. He condemned what he saw of worship in the established Church as a mockery and a forgery. True worship of God consists above all in accomplishing God's will, but this type of worship is distasteful to most Christians. Christianity aims at the total transformation of a person through renunciation and self-denial, but the Church again and again suppresses or slurs over whatever in the Christian message would make life difficult or would hinder one from enjoying life. Kierkegaard felt strongly that anyone who wished to be a disciple of the truth must live a life that would be totally free of anything that might be called enjoyment! The Christian must be prepared to renounce everything, any attachment to temporal affairs or to human relationships for the sake of relating absolutely to God, while the Church must stop trying to bring almost everyone and anyone into its fold. And so Kierkegaard considered it his mission to liberate people from the conceited notion that they were Christian. Too many who may never enter a church and never think about God arrogantly call themselves Christian as a matter of course. In place of Luther's ninety-five theses Kierkegaard would have but one: Christianity does not exist.

The Kotzker, in a similar stand, saw Judaism as basically a self-satisfying routine of obedience to law and tradition. Most people thought that being a Jew required little or no effort; one need only follow the well-worn path of facile adherence. One was simply born a Jew and had merely to conform to one's Jewish environment. The Kotzker was distressed at the shallow religious commitment of the masses; he denounced the complacent scholarship, the desire for respectability and material acquisitions, the unquestioning obedience. Too many rabbis were canonizing spiritual mediocrity. Like Kierkegaard, the Kotzker railed against those who would suppress or omit what he regarded as decisively Jewish: namely, voluntary renunciation. In order to struggle for the truth one must first divorce oneself from the world, for God demands our direct and undivided commitment; anything that would lessen this commitment must be avoided. The Kotzker did not demand a total sacrifice of life's comforts or an ascetic self-denial, but he sought a depreciation of mundane pleasures so that one might live one's life with greater independence from the world. Only then would one truly be able to serve God. The point here is that the Jew, too, must be prepared to renounce everything, all attachments and relationships, in order to relate absolutely to God. In the eyes of both Kierkegaard and the Kotzker, religion had made the life of faith too easy, removing from it all sense of the heroic, encouraging its followers to be satisfied with a job half done and to accept compromise as a norm. They both were acutely aware that religion must constitute a demand, not a consolation or comfort; complacency must be fought on every level. Religion must exact a radical transformation in its adherents and tolerate no pretense, no masks, no compromise.

Critics of Kierkegaard and the Kotzker might well complain that their religious ideals were meant for spiritual giants and not for ordinary men and women, that a moderate piety is better than no piety in our day-to-day living, and that a life of accommodation and compromise might in some way be justified. But the crucial question to ponder, as raised by Heschel, concerns the goal and expectation of religion and of religious faith: "Should its requirements be adapted to the weaknesses of human nature or should human nature be raised to the level of greatness?" In an ambivalent world where so many are afflicted with spiritual tepidity and uncertainty is such "pure religion," as espoused by Kierkegaard and the Kotzker, possible in any way? Men and women for the most part find distasteful the search for a rigorously honest interiority. Life lived on the exterior is more familiar and secure, and so our inner selves generally remain vague and obscure unless some type of personal or social catastrophe forces us to look inward. In today's disintegrating world the critique of Kierkegaard and the Kotzker takes on a new relevance. Only integrity can save us and restore religion to its proper role.[13]

Religion then must be the subject of constant criticism to determine what is authentic in its claims and teachings and what is not. Religion is subject to distortion from without or corruption from within. It may become a yoke that tends to subdue rather than nurture the human spirit, or it may become an altar on which the power of the soul may be kindled in holiness. Frequently religion absorbs ideas that are not indigenous to its spirit; even its finest traditions may be defiled through pride, arrogance, or superstition. And it is such an easy step from zeal to bigotry and prejudice.[14]

In a 1960 conference on "Depth-Theology"[15] Heschel explores another aspect of religion which he calls the heart of religious existence. From without, religion appears to consist in ritual and myth, in sacrament and dogma, in deed and scripture. But there is another element which takes place within the person, the innerness or interiorization of religion; through this vital ingredient ritual and myth, dogma and deed are internalized. At times this dimension of depth is missing in our religious experience: "the word is proclaimed, the deed is done, but the soul is silent." There are other moments when the whole soul is aflame. For some the objective deed is so sacred and effective that the interior element is of little importance. For others the inner moment is the vital principle, the "culmination of existence." This is the moment that Heschel considers to be so crucial to religion. Theology strives for communication and universality; depth theology strives for insight and uniqueness. Religious tradition is perpetuated by theology, but without the moments of interiorization this tradition is in danger of becoming irrelevant and ineffectual. Depth theology combats the smugness and arrogance and intellectual self-righteousness that at times threaten religion. It centers on what happens to a person in moments of confrontation with ultimate reality, moments in which the whole person is involved with all that one feels and acts and thinks. These are the moments, so essential to religion and to faith, in which decisive insights are born.[16]

We return, then, to the experience of that mystery before which one is reduced to reverence and silence. Reverence, prayer, and faith go beyond acts of reason, just as religion itself is beyond the limits of reason. Religion exists only where there is a sense of wonder; its real meaning can be understood only in terms compatible with a sense of the ineffable.

THE ROLE OF PRAYER

In a talk at Union Theological Seminary in 1958 Heschel admitted that it is indeed "presumptuous" to speak about prayer. We are fortunate, however, that Rabbi Heschel proved to be a presumptuous person, for he wrote and spoke often on this topic, and we are the richer for it. Prayer is central to any full understanding of religion, and it is clearly essential for Heschel's thoughts on religion. There is no religious act in which prayer is not present. Heschel insisted frequently in his writings, as noted earlier, on the need to divorce religion from any notion of expediency or self-interest. Religion is not expediency, and of all the things that one does, the least expedient is prayer; it is the least worldly and the least practical and hence an act of "self-purification." Prayer as a way of insight is the acceptance of the spirit, which is another way of saying that prayer is the acceptance of the presence of God; it is the first and most basic of the sacred acts of humankind.

Heschel provides us with no devices, no techniques, no specialized form of prayer. Rather, the whole of one's life is a training to pray. "We pray the way we live." It is not surprising, then, that above all it is a sense of wonder, of mystery, of the ineffable which enables us to pray. If we close ourselves to what is beyond sight and reason, if we close ourselves to the mystery of being, then we also close ourselves to prayer. If the rising of the sun and the changing of the seasons is nothing for us but the cyclic rule of nature, there is no reason to praise the Lord for the sun and for life. If we live in the illusion of total intelligibility and of complete and ultimate self-reliance, then there is no room for prayer in our lives. To pray is to take notice of the wonder and to regain a sense of the mystery that touches all things; it is simply our humble response to the surprise of being. When we are confronted with the mystery of living and dying, of knowing and not knowing, of loving and of being unable to love, it is then that we pray and address ourselves to the One who is beyond mystery. Life can be so embarrassing when we compare our smallness and pettiness to the tacit glory in nature. Only one response is adequate: gratitude for witnessing the wonder and for being gifted to serve and to praise.

Prayer may also be rooted in a sense of compassion, a sensitivity to evil and suffering and to one's countless infidelities to God and neighbor and self, a sensitivity that leads to the experience of not being at home in the world. This experience is intensified with the awareness that God Himself is not at home in this universe in which His will is defied and His kingship denied. From this point of view, the world is corrupt and God is in exile, and to pray means to bring God back into the world and to establish His kingship at least in this place at this moment. To pray means to expand the presence of God, just as in a similar way to worship means to make God present, to make Him immanent. To this extent God's presence in the world depends on us. What underlies much of Heschel's approach to prayer is the certainty of God's being close to us and the necessity of His coming ever closer.[17]

Prayer is our attachment to the divine, it is "the essence of spiritual living." There is at times a deep yearning to escape from what is mean and sordid, from the discord and ambiguity that surround us, and yet we may feel so weak and powerless to achieve the peace of prayer. In such a case, prayer is arrival at the border across which is the dominion of God. All our forces are placed before Him with the wish that all be taken away which cannot enter the realm of God. It is not the case that we step out of the world when we pray; rather, we see the world in a different light. Nor is the focus of prayer upon the self. The self is no longer the hub or center of living; what takes place at the moment of prayer is a movement from self-consciousness to self-surrender. One may spend hours meditating about oneself or stirred by the deepest sympathy for another, but this is not prayer. Prayer comes about in the complete turning of the heart toward

God, toward His goodness and power. It is the momentary absence or disregard of personal concerns and of self-centered thought which constitutes the act of prayer. Feeling becomes prayer when we forget ourselves and become aware of God. All thought of personal need is absent, and only the thought of divine grace is present. Even in prayer of supplication the hope for help or protection may be the motivating force leading us to prayer, but the hoped-for results are not what fill our consciousness at the decisive moment of prayer. We may, for example, be begging God for bread, but there is one moment at least, the moment of true prayer, when the mind is directed neither to our hunger nor to food, but simply to His mercy.

In prayer God becomes the center toward which all our forces tend. We lose our narrow self-interest and grasp the situation from God's point of view. In the light of prayer we are able to discern what is true and what is false, what is important and what is trivial; by growing in communion with the will of God we see our present situation in its relation to God and we behold the worth of our efforts and the meaning of our deeds. Prayer helps us to discover and clarify our true aspirations. It leads us to those ideals which we ought to cherish and strive for. It gives us the opportunity to say what we believe and to stand for what we say. Prayer has the power to revive and to keep alive "the rare greatness of some past experience in which things glowed with meaning and blessing. . . . Night will come, and we shall again gather around its tiny flame."[18]

AN INVITATION TO GOD

Thus the issue of prayer is not prayer itself but God. When anointed by prayer, one's thoughts and deeds are caught up into the endless knowledge of an all-embracing God. Prayer is like a crucible in which time is molded into the likeness of eternity. Its essence lies in the transcending of self, in surpassing the limits of what is human and in relating to the divine. One cannot pray unless one has faith in one's ability to "accost" the infinite and merciful Lord. But relation with God is not my achievement; it is a gift from on high. Before I pray, I must believe in God's willingness to draw near and in my ability to clear the path for His approach. Far more important than my desire to pray is God's desire that I pray; far greater than my will to believe is God's will that I believe. My praying would be an absurdity if it were not God's will that I pray or if He should not desire my prayer. The fact that God waits for my prayer is what gives meaning to prayer.

In praying we invite God to intervene in our lives, to become the Lord of our lives, to allow His will to prevail. So often we have allowed His gentle whispers to be drowned by our desires and whims, but now we disentangle ourselves from this stupid conceit and respond to His request for our service. In prayer we submit our interests to His concern, seeking an alliance with what is ultimate truth. Prayer involves, then, a self-examination of the heart in order to realize what it means to live as a child of God. The goal of prayer is to let God participate in our lives and to make His concern our own. Through prayer a living contact is established with God, between our concern and His will. That is why Heschel refers to prayer as spiritual ecstasy. We try to see our hopes in God's light, and our life as truly His affair. We begin by letting the thought of God permeate our minds, by realizing before whom we stand and entering into a state that leads through beauty and stillness to understanding and devotion.

From the perspective of Judaism prayer is not a substitute for sacrifice; prayer *is* sacrifice. It is no longer the sacrifice of a lamb or some other object; it is now the sacrifice of the self. In moments of genuine prayer, the faithful Jew surrenders vanity and insolence and abandons bias and envy. One places all one's forces before God; the word becomes an altar. One no longer sacrifices, for one is the sacrifice. Prayer is a risk for God's holy ones; it is a gamble full of peril. Each one who prays is a priest in the temple of God's universe. Each person may thus purify the world and build it up, just as each may contaminate the world and bring it to destruction.

All who pray share a common certainty that prayer is an act that "makes the heart audible to God." It is not a thought or word rambling alone in the world, but an event that has its beginning in us and its ending in God. In prayer we pull ourselves together, gathering our will and our memory, our thoughts and our dreams into a single direction.[19]

Even though prayer is an outgrowth of one's whole way of life, the thought processes of one engaged in prayer are radically different from those of one who is not engaged in prayer. The course of consciousness which one pursues, the way of thinking by which one regularly lives, are remote from the consciousness and thinking necessary for prayer. To be able to pray one must disengage oneself and adjust to another type of consciousness and thinking. For one who is praying a fixed formula, one must confront the word since, in Heschel's view, one becomes a praying person by means of the word. Words may appear to be familiar and trite, but each word of prayer is a repository of the spirit; each is a commitment. There is no pretentiousness in prayer. We stand for each word we pray. Outside of prayer we speak words, but the words are silent. In prayer the words speak. What is needed for prayer then is "to confront the word, to face its dignity . . . and to sense its potential might."

It is in this context that Heschel distinguishes between prayer of expression and prayer of empathy. The latter is the more common; it begins with our reading the words of the prayer and leads to an empathy for "the ideas with which the words are pregnant." The word comes first, and the empathy or feeling follows. In the prayer of expression, we experience the urge to set forth some personal concern before God. Here the concern and desire to pray come first; the word or expression follows. In this prayer we may often arrive at thoughts that lie beyond our power of expression. In actuality the two types of prayer are intimately connected. Genuine expression involves empathy, while profound empathy generates expression. There is no empathy without expression. Any genuine response to the liturgical word involves the whole person and calls up so much that is ordinarily hidden. We all bear within ourselves a vast accumulation of unuttered sorrow and guilt, of hope and joy. In prayer these feelings strive for an outlet and begin to move our minds toward expression. It is not that the goal of prayer is self-expression, but rather that the supreme goal of prayer is to express God and to discover the self in relation to God.[20]

BECOMING KNOWN BY GOD

This emphasis on the discovery of self in relation to God leads Heschel in several of his writings to stress that in prayer one endeavors to become "a thought of God," "the object of His thought," not to know God but "to be known to Him." When we pray we seek not to possess God as an object of knowledge but to be wholly possessed by Him, to be an object of God's knowledge and to sense this. In the moment of prayer, God is not object but the subject; we strive in prayer to deepen a mutual allegiance. We pray in order that we ourselves may be brought to God's attention. To pray is to endeavor "to make our life a divine concern." We approach God by discovering ourselves as the object of His thought. The ultimate human aspiration is to be an object of His knowledge. We live in God's mind when God abides in our life. In turning toward God we experience God's turning toward us. Our awareness of God is a reflection of God's awareness of us; our knowledge of God is transcended in God's knowledge of us. We ourselves become object, and God becomes the subject. We cannot aspire toward God without His first choosing us; we can think of God only insofar as God thinks of us. The essential element is "our being seen and known by Him." This is the basic content of our understanding of God. Thus the ultimate object of theological reflection, as well as the ultimate basis for prayer, is this transcendent divine attention to humankind, the fact that each one is apprehended by God. "There is no self-understanding without God-understanding."

While prayer, for Heschel, is an outpouring of the heart before God, an emanation toward Him of all that is precious in us, he does not consider prayer to be a dialogue with God; we do not carry on a conversation with God or communicate with Him. Rather we make ourselves communicable to God, we expose ourselves to Him, we want to listen and to be judged. Instead of dialogue Heschel prefers the metaphor of prayer as immersion, similar to the ancient Hebrew custom of repeatedly immersing oneself in the waters as a way toward self-purification. Thus in prayer the "I" becomes an "It." The discovery of prayer is that what is "I" to me is basically an "It" to God. Prayer begins as an experiencing of myself as an "It" in the presence of God. The closer one draws to the presence of God in prayer, the more one realizes that the "I" is but dust and ashes. One becomes an "I," a person, by becoming a thought of God.

For the person of faith no human misery could be greater than being forsaken by God, no human life could be so empty as one deserted by God. The fear of being forgotten is thus a powerful motive spurring one to bring oneself to the attention of God, to live one's life so that it is worth being known to God. How may we ever become worthy of being known to God, of being a matter of concern to Him? Heschel finds the answer in prayer, for it is prayer that affirms the preciousness of the human person. "Prayer may not save us, but it makes us worthy of being saved." All prayer either implicitly or explicitly contains the plea: "Do not forsake us, O Lord."[21]

Prayer is thus an *"ontological necessity"* if one is to become an "I." It is an act that constitutes "the very essence" of the human person. "He who has never prayed is not fully human." Prayer is indeed the "quintessence of life." Again, it is clear that Heschel's thought does not permit a divorce of the human and the holy. If one is not a person of prayer, then one is not fully a person, and such a one tends to look upon prayer as a hobby to be indulged in periodically. The person of prayer, however, knows that prayer is a privilege to be earned through existence by the life one lives. This endowment with the gift and capacity to address God is at the heart of human dignity; it must be considered part of the very definition of a human person for it is our "greatest distinction." The reverence that is owed to every single human being is based upon this ability and right "to pray, . . . to worship, to utter the cry that can reach God." But if in our vanity and conceit we betray God day after day, we doom ourselves to a superficial, shadowy existence, and we live in a "ghostly mist of misgivings." Our human potential remains unfulfilled. If we forfeit our ties with God, we walk the earth as mere skeletons of humanity, craving what is missing in our lives. Vicious deeds, felt or committed today, destroy the roots of tomorrow's prayer. Vulgarity deadens that sensitivity that is so crucial to prayer in our lives. And when we discard God from our lives, God is not alone, but we are alone no matter how much we attempt to deny or cover up the truth. To live without prayer is to live without God. The constant avoidance of prayer creates a gap between ourselves and God, a gap that is in danger of becoming an abyss. Yet perhaps we may recover to weep on the edge of the abyss, and a yearning may softly move in to help us pass over the gap with "the lightness of a dream."[22]

Prayer is much more than a cry for mercy or some sort of spiritual improvisation. Prayer is the summation of what a person is; it is the whole of that person expressed in a single moment. If prayer is to live in us, we must live in prayer. Prayer depends upon the total moral and spiritual situation of a person; it depends upon a soul within which God is at home. To pray is to sense the presence of God, and the presence of God means the absence of despair. In the stillness of sensing His presence one also senses His mercy. Anguish and despair turn to joy as one directs one's entire person upon God and knows only His presence and His mercy. Prayer may last but a moment, but it is the essence of a lifetime.[23]

PRAYER AND WORSHIP

Prayer is closely associated with worship and is, obviously, one form of worship. For Heschel prayer and worship have a similar meaning: to expand God's presence in the world, to make God immanent to our world. God is transcendent, but our worship and prayer make Him immanent. This is one aspect of the idea that God is in need of us: His being immanent to the world depends upon us.

Moreover, the ideal for the Jew is neither to pray alone nor to worship alone. Jewish tradition insists that one pray with, and as part of, a community. So also public worship is to be preferred over private worship. Yet there is an essential connection between private prayer and worship and public prayer and worship. Each depends upon the other for its existence. Ignoring this interconnection would be fatal to both. Much of our ability to pray comes from the community and from tradition. We have learned to pray by listening to the voice of prayer, by being part of a community that stands before the face of God. Some who desire authentic prayer feel that this can be accomplished only in private prayer. They are driven away from the community because of the sterility of public worship. Yet Heschel insists that private prayer cannot survive unless it is inspired by public prayer and worship. The way of the loner, an exclusive concern about one's personal stand before God, cannot long endure. Piety in isolation from the community is ultimately impiety.

From the biblical perspective one stands before God not alone but always as a member of the community. Our relationship to God is not as an "I" to a "Thou" but rather as a "we" to a "Thou." Thus we do not pray as individuals set apart from the rest of the world. Each act of worship is caught up in the eternal service given by the whole of mankind. Each act of adoration is carried out in union with all history. Yet Heschel reminds us that prayer is primarily an event that takes place within individual souls. The integrity of public worship depends upon the depth of the private worship of all those gathered in community to worship together.[24]

Worship, like prayer, is linked to our capacity for wonder and amazement. Yet as there is need for daily wonder in every human life, so also is there need for daily worship. The surest way to suppress our ability to grasp the importance of worship is to become mired in boredom and indifference. There can be no worship in our lives if we take for granted each of the joys or defeats of living. No matter how much routine there is in daily life, it must not dull our sense of surprise that there *is* a daily life. Indifference is the death of any kind of spiritual living. Thus worship without wonder is an illusion; it is meaningless. And if worship is meaningless, human living becomes an absurdity. [25]

To worship is to move to a higher level of existence and to see the world as God sees the world. True worship should lead to moral living. That is why the prophets stressed that the worth of worship is dependent on the moral life one lives. Where immorality prevails, worship is detestable for there is no effort being made to see the world from God's perspective. Deeds of injustice vitiate both worship and prayer. We cannot drown the voices of the poor and the exploited with the noise of our hymns, or appease God simply with increased offerings. Worship cannot be a substitute for righteousness. It is precisely because the prophets recognized the value of cultic worship that they insisted that there is something far more precious than sacrifice. Cultic worship possessed a sacred authenticity, a role and procedure of its own, a mysterious glory. It differed from all other human pursuits; it conferred special blessings. Through the sacrificial acts a person was transformed, entering into a relationship that was precious to God and vital to the person. Through the sacrificial offering one offered oneself to God. This was undoubtedly a holy sphere, and because of its holiness it was closely criticized by the prophets. The people were making a mockery out of cultic worship because their deeds proved their sacrifice to be a lie.

This immediate devotion to God, which is worship, is the essence of religion. Yet religion in turn places such a stress on justice and compassion and kindness in our dealings with one another. Prophetic religion is claiming that righteousness is God's stake in human history. Those who ignore or exploit the poor have simply not grasped the world from God's point of view. God's need for mercy and righteousness cannot be fulfilled merely in worship; it is a work that must be carried out in history. It is within this realm of history that we are charged with God's mission, a mission that is made known through prayer and worship.[26]

THE PROPHETIC RELIGION OF SYMPATHY

Those who have *par excellence* grasped the world from God's point of view are, of course, the prophets. It was their task and their grace to convey a divine understanding of the human situation. Heschel defines biblical prophecy as the *"exegesis of existence from a divine perspective."* Prophecy involves both a way of thinking and a way of living. More often than not, because of the divine perspective that they brought to the human situation, the prophets were at odds with society, condemning its habits, its assumptions, its complacency, its idolatry. Their basic goal was to reconcile humanity with God, a reconciliation that required confrontation with human ignorance and pride, with abuse of freedom and resentment of God's involvement in human affairs. The prophets force us to question whether freedom implies self-assertion or response to a demand, whether the relationship between the divine and the human is one of conflict or of concern.

The prophets, swept up into God's vision and God's pathos, as mentioned in the previous chapter, were men who were bowed and stunned by humanity's enormous capacity for evil. They were men of intense indignation who felt so fiercely about what are perhaps even more in this age daily occurrences throughout the world: depriving the laborer of his recompense, trampling upon the needy, taking advantage of the poor and the powerless. They felt so fiercely because they heard so deeply. The prophets were concerned with the plight of humanity because God Himself is so caught up with the plight of humanity. Their intense sensitivity to what is right and wrong is but the expression of their intense sensitivity to God's concern for right and wrong. For the prophets God is a challenge and an incessant demand. To the prophets God is seen as preoccupied with human concerns and with the concrete realities of history rather than with the timeless issues of eternity. Whatever has bearing upon good or evil in human affairs is of utmost importance in the eyes of God.[27]

One's response to the divine depends to a great extent on how one apprehends the divine. If one looks upon the divine as absolute perfection, one responds with fear and trembling; if one considers the divine to be omnipotent will, one responds with unconditional obedience; if the divine is sensed as pathos, one responds through sympathy. Thus it is with the prophets who are stirred by the deepest sympathy for God's concern. Sympathy is the prophets' way of responding to the divine situation, of meeting the demands addressed to them in moments of revelation.

When the prophets, then, describe the wrath of God enkindled because the rights of the poor are violated, or because widows and orphans are oppressed, it is not the cruelty of God but the concern of God they are conveying. Indirectly they are also highlighting the evil of that indifference that so often grips the so-called decent or respectable or pious members of society. What is fundamental to the prophetic consciousness is this awareness of the divine pathos. The prophet does not simply hear a divine message and then convey it. Rather he is swept up into the divine pathos and is convulsed by it to the very depths of his being. That is why prophetic religion is called by Heschel a "religion of sympathy" and the prophet himself a *"homo sympathetikos."* An unemotional intellectual analysis is not compatible with the religious understanding and consciousness of the prophets. The prophetic mentality is more at home with an emotional religion of sympathy than with a rote religion of unquestioning obedience. The pathos of God overwhelms the prophet, taking possession of his heart and mind so that he will speak and act courageously against the abuses prevalent in his society. The prophet must try to convey in human language the infinite emotion of God. What seems to us to be hysterical exaggeration must appear as constraint to the prophet, given the enormity of his task. Prophetic sympathy comes about as a result of the powerful emotion with which the prophet responds to what he has sensed in the divine.

Religious sympathy is concerned not so much with self-conquest as with self-dedication; it is aimed not at the suppression of emotion but at its redirection, actively cooperating with God and identifying, insofar as one can, with the concern of God. Sympathy implies an openness to the presence of another and a feeling "which feels the feeling to which it reacts." Prophetic sympathy, then, is an openness to the presence of God and a bearing within oneself of an awareness of what is happening in God; in other words, the prophet and God share a common feeling.[28]

Feeling, however, is not enough. Prophetic religion is *not* a religion of sentimentality. Feeling must give way to actions, actions that will help to overcome the misery and injustice that are so widespread. Without action the tension and anguish remain. Pathos and sympathy are demands, not goals. Prophetic sympathy provides a sense of challenge and commitment which demands concrete action. It enables us to understand the inner accord of the prophet with God, his zeal, which flows from this emotional harmony, and his anger, which motivates him at times to turn away even from his own people. Sympathy does not lead the prophet to a knowledge of the divine pathos; it presupposes such knowledge. Through this shared common feeling the prophet becomes sensitive to the divine insight into human actions and into the events of history.

For Heschel this deep awareness by the prophet of God's concern for the world, this communion of the prophet with God's love and suffering, is of such authority that it may provide a basis for understanding religious commitment; it helps to clarify for us the "ultimate meaning, worth and dignity of religion." The unique aspect of prophetic existence lies in being attuned to God. No one outside of the prophets can know the degree and intensity of such accord. It is not just a feeling; it is an entire way of living and of being that is an essential characteristic of prophetic existence.[29]

Prophetic religion, then, can never be identified with temple worship and sacrifice. Worship that comes from an avaricious and oppressive people is fraud and illusion. When the temple cult is preceded or followed by evil deeds, it becomes an absurdity. The primary way of serving God is not through offerings and songs, but through love and justice and righteousness. Our works of justice are not a favor we confer on society; they are as much a necessity for human life as breathing. They must be a constant preoccupation if we are to live humanly, if we are to live in God's image. The prophets portray justice and righteousness as inherent in the very essence of God and as identified with the ways of God; they are an *a priori* of biblical faith.

Doing justice is thus a requisite for every person. It is the supreme commandment of God, one that cannot be fulfilled vicariously by society or government or church or any other social body. In almost all cases the exploiters are the powerful who can skillfully justify their actions; the exploited are the powerless who are unable to plead their cause. Those whose personal interests are not affected either way do not become involved; if they happen to witness the callousness and cruelty of others, they tend to obliterate the memory and to silence their conscience. Who then is left to plead for the powerless? The prophetic vocation may be described as a call to defend those who are unable to plead their own cause. The prophets may be characterized as "outside agitators" who protest when wrongs are inflicted on others and who meddle in affairs that on the surface appear to be neither their concern nor their responsibility. And so the prophet may be described as a person "who is not tolerant of wrongs done to others."

The prophetic demand for justice is not satisfied simply by our actions in the political and social sphere; it involves also our relationship with God. Justice is not just a matter of deeds; it is also a matter of the heart. Injustice flows from a heart that is false, a heart that is far from God; it flourishes wherever there is insensitivity to the afflictions of the poor. The biblical term for justice, *mishpat*, refers to all actions that contribute to fulfillment of the covenant, to the authentic relationship that should flourish between the people and God and between persons. The prophets equate knowledge of God with knowledge of all that God does, such as His kindness, His justice, His righteousness. Yet knowledge of God is also equated with what persons do, such as justice, righteousness, concern for the poor and needy. Those who do justice are those who know God. Knowledge of God, then, is manifested through our actions toward others, sharing in our hearts God's concern for justice. Knowledge of God is prophetic sympathy in action.[30]

UNIQUENESS OF PROPHETIC RELIGION

The prophets remind us that the relationship that exists between God and Israel is not a legal contract but a personal covenant. The covenant is an extraordinary agreement, establishing a reciprocal relationship, a juridical commitment. Yet prior to the covenant stands God's love, the basis for divine pathos. This implies that the relationship of God and Israel is an emotional engagement, one of con-

stant concern, involvement, tension. The life of God interacts with
the life of the people. To live in the covenant is to partake of the
fellowship of God and Israel. Prophetic religion is what one does
with God's concern for the whole of humanity.

Prophetic religion, rooted in pathos, is in sharp contrast with
those religions that picture the divine sphere as one of tranquillity
and peace, an existence without cares, and hence a sphere that
would be remote from, and indifferent to, worldly affairs and politics. Such religions consider divine transcendence as total detachment and aloofness from the world; it would be absurd for the divine
to be concerned with the affairs of this world. The divine is immu-
table, imperturbable, impersonal, self-sufficient. For the prophets,
however, it is not immutability or self-sufficiency that characterizes
the divine but concern and involvement. Pathos means that every
divine decree is provisional and contingent upon the response of the
people. The ultimate is not a blind or inscrutable or hostile power
that would force humankind to submit in resignation, but a God of
justice and mercy. The order He has established is not a rigid, unchangeable structure, but a dynamic drama that unfolds in history.
Behind the stern and stinging words of the prophets stand a love and
compassion for humanity. "Have I any pleasure in the death of the
wicked, says the Lord God, and not rather that he should turn from
his way and live" (Ezk 18:23)? Every time the prophets predict disaster, they are in reality exhorting to repentance. Along with cen-
sure and castigation the prophets also bring consolation, promise,
and the hope of reconciliation. Beginning with a message of doom,
the prophets conclude with a message of hope.[31]

The prophetic sympathy with the pathos of God also differen-
tiates the prophets from the mystic and the ecstatic. The ecstatic
seeks to experience illumination from God and strives ever anew to
achieve this goal even by use of various stimulants. Ecstasy is characterized by detachment and separation from society, by a rejection
of civilization; there is a depreciation of consciousness and of the
human coupled with the belief that the less there is of consciousness
and the human, the more there is of the divine, of God. All this is
comparatively unknown to the prophets. The prophet does not seek
inspiration; it comes against his will as he is seized by God. Without
preparation or inducement the prophet is called to hear God's voice.

The prophet's intense concern with humanity and with society is incompatible with the ecstatic mentality. Prophecy is meaningless without a message to be conveyed to the people.

Ecstasy is often based on a theology of radical transcendence; it comes about as the result of an effort to force one's way to Him who is considered to be wholly above the world. In the biblical tradition, however, God is not isolated in absolute transcendence; the Creator manifests His presence within the world in concern for His people. He is accessible to our prayer, and His fidelity testifies to an absolute reliability.

The mystic tends to conceal; mysticism is a private affair for the individual, centering on personal salvation and personal illumination. The mission of the prophet is to reveal; the prophetic experience is for the sake of the people to lead them to a greater service of God; it is essentially intertwined with the people. Mysticism, rooted in a longing for a world beyond this world, strives for a perception of timeless reality, for the mysteries of heaven and the glories of eternity. The prophets, on the other hand, are concerned with the affairs of the marketplace, with the life of the people. The prophets hear the word of God as expressive of His concern for the world here and now. Thus the attention of the prophet is directed toward the social and political issues of the day. While the mystic is absorbed with the infinite, the prophet is concerned with the finite, with the arrogance and hypocrisy, with the cruelty and idolatry of God's people. The prophets display no hostility to civilization but only to the abuses contained therein; the world and its fate are of crucial significance to them.[32]

Even when the prophets called for justice and kindness toward the weaker members of society, they never considered themselves to be spokespersons for the people. They spoke at all times in the name of God. Their concern for the people could never be separated from their concern for God. Their whole personality exhibited a sympathy with God. This touches on what Heschel considers to be the basic characteristics of the biblical prophets: namely, the certainty of being inspired by God, the certainty of speaking in His name, and the certainty of having been sent by God to the people. This is the staggering claim to which the prophets attested again and again.

Prophecy comes into existence through God's grace. The prophet encounters a word spoken from a Presence. It is as though God stepped forth from the mystery and incomprehensibility of His being to reveal His will to humanity. A decisive mark of prophecy is this transcendent aspect. The prophetic experience is one of being overwhelmed or overpowered by God's word addressed exclusively to oneself for the people. The biblical Lord is a God who demands and judges, and the prophet is sent to bring the demand and judgment to the people.

Finally, biblical prophecy serves as an illumination for the people and their history. Each prophet regards his message as a continuation of what was spoken by earlier prophets, for ultimately the God who speaks to the prophets is the God who spoke to Abraham. Prophetic experience may well have occurred to many people in many parts of the world, but a series of prophets, stretching over many centuries from Abraham to Malachi and forming the basis of a prophetic religion is a phenomenon, as Heschel points out, which has no parallel. These prophets are among the wisest of persons: through their message we are ushered into the central drama of humanity. So many of the ideas that are of ultimate importance, so many of the values we cherish dearly, we owe to them. Clearly it is through his scholarly and meditative approach to the prophets that Heschel derived many of his insights into the meaning of religion.

Religion must center on God's care for His creation. The prophet is one who responds with sympathy to this care for creation, a care for God's care. Sympathy opens us to the living God; if we do not share in this divine concern, we cannot know the living God of the prophets. To share this divine concern is to recognize that God is indeed a challenge and that religion is thus a demand.[33] God speaks to us in the dimension of history and in the language of human situations. His need is for mercy and righteousness, a need that can be satisfied only in the realm of time and of history, and not simply by visiting temples or kneeling in pews. Religious living has nothing to do with trivialities; it is arduous and demanding. We must not sell salvation cheaply. And religious commitment is not just an appendage to human existence, a convenience, as it were, or an afterthought. As Heschel never tires of emphasizing, religious commitment is "the heart and core of being human."[34] One cannot be genuinely human without also being genuinely religious. Again, the human and the holy cannot be sundered.

From this overview of religion in the writings of Heschel, we turn

now to his understanding of Judaism, the religious commitment
that was central to his life and the subject that occupied so much of
his research, his prayer, his writings.

NOTES

1. *Man's Quest for God*, p. xiii; *Insecurity of Freedom*, p. 176.
2. *God in Search of Man*, pp. 111–12, 162.
3. *Who Is Man?* pp. 109–10; *Man Is Not Alone*, p. 215.
4. *Man Is Not Alone*, pp. 232–34, 248–49; *Man's Quest for God*, p. xiii.
5. *Insecurity of Freedom*, pp. 7–8, 199; *God in Search of Man*, pp. 7–8; *Man Is Not Alone*, p. 249.
6. *God in Search of Man*, pp. 373, 384; *Who Is Man?* pp. 112–14.
7. *Man's Quest for God*, pp. 107–108; *Man Is Not Alone*, p. 175; *God in Search of Man*, p. 293.
8. *Passion for Truth*, pp. 183–88.
9. *God in Search of Man*, pp. 414–15; *Man Is Not Alone*, pp. 236–37; *Insecurity of Freedom*, pp. 8–9.
10. *God in Search of Man*, pp. 330–31; *Man Is Not Alone*, pp. 168–69.
11. *Insecurity of Freedom*, pp. 3–4; *God in Search of Man*, p. 3.
12. *Man's Quest for God*, pp. 49–52; *Insecurity of Freedom*, pp. 12–13, 206.
13. *Passion for Truth*, pp. 110–12, 123–26, 150–52, 315–18.
14. *God in Search of Man*, pp. 10, 317.
15. "Depth Theology," in *Insecurity of Freedom*, pp. 115–26.
16. Ibid., pp. 116–19.
17. *Man's Quest for God*, pp. xiii–xiv, 5; *Insecurity of Freedom*, pp. 258–60.
18. *Man's Quest for God*, pp. 6–8; *The Prophets*, ii 221.
19. *Man's Quest for God*, pp. 9–19, 58–59, 71.
20. Ibid., pp. 24–32.
21. *Man Is Not Alone*, pp. 128–29; *Man's Quest for God*, pp. 10–11; *Insecurity of Freedom*, pp. 255–57; *The Prophets*, ii 267–68.
22. *Man's Quest for God*, pp. 11–12, 18, 69, 78, 94.
23. *Insecurity of Freedom*, pp. 254–57.
24. Ibid., p. 258; *God in Search of Man*, p. 156; *Man's Quest for God*, pp. 45–46.
25. *God in Search of Man*, pp. 43, 49, 119.
26. *Man's Quest for God*, p. xii; *The Prophets*, i 196–98.
27. *The Prophets*, i xiv–xv, 3–5; *Insecurity of Freedom*, p. 11.
28. *The Prophets*, ii 64–65, 87–89.

29. Ibid., 89–91.

30. Ibid., I 199–211.

31. Ibid., 12, II 10–20.

32. Ibid., II 138–45.

33. Ibid., 189, 212–13, 264.

34. "What We Might Do Together," *Religious Education*, 52, No. 2 (March–April 1967), 136.

5

The Demand
To Be Human

MUCH HAS ALREADY BEEN INTIMATED of Heschel's understanding of Judaism, yet before I attempt to delve more deeply into this area of his thought, the limits, if not the arrogance, of such an undertaking should be clearly acknowledged at the outset. There is an understanding of faith and an insight from faith which will be locked forever in the heart of each one who professes "I believe." There is an area of intimacy between each believer and God that no one else may enter. When I speak of Judaism, I am speaking of that which was perhaps closest to the heart of Abraham Heschel, but I address myself primarily to that understanding of Judaism which Heschel shared with his readers. Furthermore, this attempt comes from one who, though a spiritual Semite and sympathetic to Judaism, does not share that faith-perspective, and yet who finds in the writings of Heschel one of the most comprehensive, clear, and meaningful explanations of one person's understanding of his Jewish faith.

Judaism had many different connotations for Heschel. It meant being chosen, belonging to a people; it implied a relationship to the land of Israel, as well as a demand of cosmic significance. Judaism is more than creed and doctrine; it is living in covenant with God and in observance of the law; it is a remembrance of sacred happenings. Judaism is a religion of history; it demands both the acceptance of certain basic teachings as well as an attachment to certain decisive events. Doctrine and event are inseparable. Judaism is a quest for right living, a quest for what is to be done here and now; it serves as a reminder that there is something of divine significance reflected in the life of each person.

Toward the conclusion of his epic *God in Search of Man* Heschel summed up his thoughts on this topic: "To be a Jew is to renounce allegiance to false gods; to be sensitive to God's infinite stake in every finite situation, to bear witness to His presence in the hours of His concealment; to remember that the world is unredeemed. We are born to be an answer to His question." The ultimate price that Jews have had to pay throughout history for their way of life attests to the "absolute significance" of Judaism. The universal relevance of Judaism consists, at least partially, in the role it plays in humanity's struggle to maintain its humanness by conveying the taste of eternity in its daily living. The survival of the human family depends on the conviction that "there is something that is worth the price of life." Heschel sees this something in the recognition that Israel did not discover God, but was discovered by God; the Bible records above all else God's approach to His people and His love for His people. Judaism stands forth as "God's quest for man." [1]

Heschel returns to this theme in many different ways in a number of his works. Speaking in Jerusalem in 1957, he reminded his listeners: "Judaism is not a matter of blood or race but a spiritual dimension of existence, a dimension of holiness. This dimension comes to expression in events and in teachings, in thoughts and deeds. . . . Judaism is an *anchor of ultimate significance* to a tottering world." A year later in a talk to American rabbis he pointed out that Judaism should stand for *"education for reverence,"* endowing its people with a spirit of prayer and sensitivity. The emptiness, the injustice, and the arrogance of our civilization cry out to heaven; Judaism must wage war against the vulgar, against the idolizing of power, a war that is "incessant, universal." In 1967 he wrote that Judaism can never be reduced simply to faith in a supreme being called God; rather, it is trust in Him "who is in need of man, involved with all of us, remembering and waiting for His promise to come to pass." Judaism is convinced that history is the realm of divine meaning, and consequently Jews have the responsibility to trace God's itinerary through the maze of seeming contradictions in history; thus Heschel writes: "We are God's stake in human history. We are the dawn and the dusk, the challenge and the test." [2]

COVENANT AND ELECTION

To speak of Israel as "God's stake in human history" or as "God's quest for man" is to underscore the vital role of election and cove-

nant for Judaism. There is probably no other notion so basic to biblical faith and to Judaism, and yet so commonly misunderstood, as
that of the divine election of Israel. Heschel refers to the belief that
God had chosen Israel to carry out His mission to the world as both
a "cornerstone" of Hebrew faith and a "refuge" in times of peril and
distress. Yet from the biblical age to the present this cornerstone has
become for so many a stumbling block, and the refuge has become
simply an escape. The prophets had to remind the people again and
again that chosenness must not be confused with divine favoritism
and in no way implied immunity from punishment. On the contrary, as God's chosen people Israel would all the more be severely
judged and chastised for its failings.

The idea of a chosen people never connotes in the Bible the idea
of a superior people. Israel did not first choose God; God chose
Israel, but this in no way suggests that Israel was preferred over other
nations because it was somehow better than the other nations. A
chosen people means simply "a people approached and chosen by
God." It does not infer that there is any special quality inherent in
the people; rather it points to "a relationship between the people and
God." Nor does chosenness in any way imply that God was exclusively involved in the history of Israel and oblivious to the history of
other nations. Isaiah reminded the people that the God of Israel was
also the God of Syria and the God of Egypt. Amos put it in very
blunt terms: "Are you not like Ethiopians to Me, O people of
Israel? . . . Did I not bring up Israel from the land of Egypt and the
Philistines from Caphtor and the Syrians from Kir" (Am 9:7)? It
would be difficult to put it in clearer terms: the God who has chosen
Israel is the God of all nations; the history of all humankind is His
concern.[3]

Divine election was in no way meant to be a basis of self-
aggrandizement for Israel; election was for service. Israel was indeed
precious in God's eyes, a preciousness that comes from God's choice,
and God's choice is rooted ultimately in the mystery of His love (Dt
7:8); it is a love for Israel that will never vanish but perdure for all
eternity. God chose Israel for the accomplishment of His grand design in history, to be His witness to the peoples of the world, a light
to all the nations. Israel becomes servant so that God's salvation may
reach the ends of the earth. As servant, it is true, Israel may often
fail to grasp the significance of its mission: instead of opening eyes

that are blind, it may itself succumb to blindness; instead of being
the bearer and witness of God's message, it may at times be deaf to
that message. Yet Israel's failings and transgressions are always trivial
when compared to the immensity of God's love. The experience of
the prophet Hosea, ordered by God to take back his adulterous wife,
Gomer, and to renew his love for her, will forever serve as a model
of God's love for Israel. Despite Israel's many affairs with other gods,
God cannot abandon Israel; He will not forsake her despite her infidelity. The iniquity and the transgressions will pass, but God's love
for Israel, expressed in election, will never pass. Israel's infidelities
may affect God's attitude temporarily, but it cannot bring about a
basic change in God's relationship. God and Israel are bound forever in covenant.[4]

Sinai marked the decisive moment in Israel's history, for it brought
with it a new relationship between God and His people: God became "engaged" to Israel, and Israel accepted the new relationship,
becoming "engaged" to God; God and Israel have become partners.
"God gave His word to Israel, and Israel gave its word of honor to
God."[5] What is so essential to Judaism, in Heschel's view, is this
awareness of God's interest in humankind, this awareness of a reciprocal relationship which exists between God and humanity, this
awareness of covenant. It is a covenant to which both God and
Israel are committed. The holiness of human living is rooted in this
partnership, in the fact that all authentic human needs are a divine
concern and that divine concerns *ought* to become human needs.
God's concern for justice, peace, fidelity, mercy, compassion, community does indeed comprise our basic human needs. The human
and the holy are united in the covenant. What exists, then, between
God and Israel is not only a covenant of mutual obligations, but
also a relationship of mutual concern.[6]

The political ambiguity and practical tensions that come with
this partnership were well portrayed by the prophet Isaiah in his
warnings against foreign alliances. Israel's security was based on its
covenant with God, not on covenants or political alliances with
other nations. Such alliances too often involved preparations for
war, and Isaiah revolted against such steps, looking forward to that
day when all nations would "beat their swords into ploughshares
and their spears into pruning hooks," and war would be a horror of
the past, for no nation would "learn war any more" (Is 2:4). Israel's

covenant with God demanded that the people manifest their belief that the power of God, not the power of politicians, determined the destiny of the nations, and that reliance on God, not reliance on weapons, was the ultimate source of security. God alone is true protection for the people. The people must not yield to the constant temptation of haughtiness and pride, bowing down to the work of their own hands; rather, they should remember to whom they belong.[7]

Loyalty to the covenant would be measured both by the deeds of Israel and by its inner attitude. The prophet Amos condemned the injustice of the people, their evil deeds; God despises the sacrifices of an unjust Israel, so "let justice roll down like waters, and righteousness like a mighty stream" (Am 4:24). Israel's fidelity to the covenant is to be measured by its deeds, by its actions in history. The prophet Hosea, on the other hand, attacked Israel for its idolatry, for its lack of inward devotion, for the emptiness of its deeds. "For I desire love and not sacrifice, attachment to God rather than burnt offerings" (Ho 6:6). Israel's fidelity to the covenant is to be measured by its inwardness, by the motivation or attitude that accompanies the deed.[8] Amos and Hosea are not necessarily in opposition to one another. Each is stressing an important aspect of covenant fidelity. The relation and the tension between external deed and internal attitude, between halacha and agada, have been present throughout the history of Judaism and are discussed frequently in Heschel's writings. More on this will be said below.

In accepting the covenant at Sinai and in giving its word of honor, Israel invested the whole of its future. That moment of acceptance has determined all other moments for Judaism because it committed all future generations to this covenant with God. For Heschel, the very dignity of being a Jew lies in this sense of commitment, just as the very meaning of Jewish history centers on the fidelity of Israel to its covenant with God. For the believing Jew this commitment is what gives life dignity and meaning. Sinai was only a beginning. The acceptance of the covenant is an ongoing event; its fulfillment lies always in the future. The deeds and the lives of God's people help bring about this fulfillment. What was anticipated at Sinai comes about for Judaism in the moment of a good deed. The covenant depends for its fulfillment on this moment and on every moment, on what we do with each moment in relation to

God's will. Heschel speaks of the very rare and very precious consciousness that belongs to Israel; Jews do not live in a void fretting
over the emptiness of time. "We remember where we came from.
We were summoned and cannot forget it." The summons was given
in the covenant at Sinai; it is remembered in each holy deed of the
present moment as Israel and all peoples of the earth move toward
the fulfillment of the covenant in the Kingdom of God.[9]

CENTRALITY OF THE DEED

Judaism is not a religion of an unknown God; it is rooted in the
certainty that God has revealed His will to Israel, and Israel is bound
by the covenant to accomplish that will in its life. So Judaism is
pre-eminently a practical, specific, real affair. The Jew worships
God not so much by symbolic gestures and actions as by the shaping
of life according to the pattern of God's will; worship is found primarily in deeds. Judaism is a religion that deals with the common
deed and with the trivialities of human living and not so much with
the extraordinary and exceptional moments of life. For the Jew religious existence is not confined to prayer, dogma, and ritual. Hewing
stones and building homes, paving roads and planting gardens, are
some of the many ways one praises God. Efforts to reach out to the
helpless and infirm, to console the desperate or the despondent,
serve as reminders that there are deeds in which God is at home in
our world. The spiritual and the material are not antithetical but
interrelated. Judaism seeks to endow the material elements of life
with the radiance of the spirit, to sanctify the everyday, to detect the
marvelous in the common. The predominant feature of Jewish
living then is an "unassuming, inconspicuous piety" rather than
any type of extravagant asceticism; its purpose is to ennoble the ordinary and to endow everyday actions with an eternal beauty. One of
the goals of Jewish living in Heschel's view is "to experience commonplace deeds as spiritual adventures." Thus with each glass of
water pious Jews remind themselves of the eternal miracle of creation: "Blest be Thou . . . by Whose word all things come into
being." The eating of bread, the fragrance of a blossom, the tasting
of fruit, the beauty of a rainbow, the reception of good or bad
news—all become the occasion for invoking God's name and for
renewing one's awareness of Him. The holy is not that which is set

apart or isolated from the world but refers primarily to a quality found in our common and everyday efforts, in simple, individual deeds rather than in public ritual.[10]

Judaism stands unalterably opposed to Luther's central thesis that salvation is achieved by faith alone, and to its corollary that no human activity may be called good because of humanity's sinfulness. On the contrary, Judaism is anchored in the recognition of the absolute relevance of human deeds. Deeds are the expression of one's faith and love of God. The deed is the source of holiness and the way the imitation of God is achieved. Holiness may be found wherever we are and in whatever we are doing, as much in an act of friendship as in a prayer of forgiveness on the Day of Atonement.[11]

Heschel's fullest treatment on the centrality of the deed for Judaism is found in *God in Search of Man*. There he points to three inner attitudes at the heart of Israel's religious existence. First and foremost, there is one's relation to the living God, which is expressed in interior acts of the soul; secondly, there is one's relation to the Torah, in which God's voice is audible and which comes about through study and communion with its words; thirdly, there is one's relation to God's concern expressed in mitsvot (commandments) and which comes about through attachment to the essentials of worship. At the basis of Jewish living is commitment. The problem of how one ought to live as a Jew cannot be solved simply through common sense or common experience. It is principally a spiritual problem with a spiritual logic of its own which cannot be grasped unless it is lived, for spiritual meaning is grasped in acts rather than in speculation.

Thus one must first accept Judaism and live Judaism in order to explore it. By living as a Jew one may then attain faith as a Jew. Deeds do not confer faith, yet one may attain the threshhold of faith through sacred deeds, through fidelity to God's concern expressed in mitsvot. Faith for the Jew may thus be called a *"leap of action."* One's way of living must be compatible with the image of God in which one is created. Yet how should a human being created in the image of God actually live? The image of God may be so easily distorted or forfeited. How does one remain faithful to that image? Our deeds may seem slight, but their aftermath can be enormous. A single deed may have immense ramifications. What is one to do? How ought one to conduct one's life? Humanity has so often abused the power and the freedom with which it is endowed, but that must not lead to despair. It is here that we are confronted by the claim of the Bible: we are not alone, the world is not an empty abyss, God is in search of us. We are indeed responsible for all that we do, but God shares our responsibility. Judaism pictures God as "waiting to enter our deeds," as becoming a "partner to our deeds" through our fidelity to His law. God and humanity have a shared task and a shared responsibility. The task involves achieving the meaning of humanity's existence, as well as that of the whole of God's creation. The biblical law, then, is both a plea of God and a claim of humankind. It spells out God's expectations as well as humanity's aspirations. Religion points to a task within this world, but its goals go far beyond it.[12]

A mitsvah, which may be considered to be both a command and the deed fulfilling the command, is an act that God and the faithful Jew "*have in common*"; it is an act of communion with God, an act of worship. Mitsvah has a wide range of meanings, from the most solemn ritual acts to a humble act of good will, from external deeds to inner attitudes. In its broadest sense mitsvah refers to any act performed in agreement with God's will. The word itself connotes goodness, value, piety, holiness. Mitsvah, rather than law, is the basic unit of Jewish life. The law tells us what should be considered as mitsvah and what should not. Mitsvah is the focal point of Jewish religious consciousness.

The spirit of mitsvah is the togetherness of God and His people, for the Jew believes that God is partner to such acts. A mitsvah is a prayer in the form of a deed. In carrying out a mitsvah it is impossible for the Jew to be or to feel alone, for by this deed one enters into union with God's will and with God Himself. This stress on the basic importance of mitsvah assumes that somehow we are able both to know what God's will demands of us and to meet that demand in our lives. For Heschel this would be an article of Jewish faith; it is a belief that is fundamental to Judaism. Human life is precious because at all times and in all places one is able to accomplish the will of God. This is the reason why despair is alien to the believing Jew.

Thus one may speak not only of an analogy of *being* between each person and God, but also of an analogy of *doing* by which each person may act in the likeness of God. It is through this likeness of doing that a person comes close to God; herein lies the essence of the imitation of God. God's plea to Israel is to *do* what He *is*. Israel is to be holy just as the Lord God is holy (Lv 19:2). Israel achieves holiness by doing, by its fidelity to God's mitsvot, God's command-ments. A mitsvah reflects the hidden light of God's holiness; it mir-rors His infinite love. God has delegated to humankind the power to act in His stead. Our deeds of compassion and mercy, our sharing of another's sorrow or joy, our acts of service and sacrifice—all are part of the effort to act in the place of God. For Israel only one image of God can be fashioned, namely, one's own life as an image of the will of God. By fulfilling mitsvot one is expressing in acts that which is God's will. That is why Heschel repeatedly points out that God needs us for the accomplishment of His goals in the world. In the beginning is God's eternal expectation, an eternal cry in the world calling for a response. Something is being asked of each and every person. In every act of our lives "we either answer or defy, we either return or move away, we either fulfill or miss the goal." There are endless opportunities in life to sanctify the profane, to serve God's ends in this world, ends that transcend our own personal interest. These divine ends or goals are in need of us, just as we are in need of God and in need of serving His ends. What this means is that there is a mutual relationship between each human being and these ends or goals of God: we are in need of justice just as justice is in need of us. These divine goals make a claim upon us; they are spe-cific demands, not just abstract notions; they are experienced as ob-jects of commitment; they are the basis for the certainty that some-thing is being asked of us. These divine goals are in need of our deeds. For Judaism they are expressed in the mitsvot addressed to each person, conveying to each one a task to accomplish here and now in this world. It is the task of living with God at all times, the task of responding to Him who is asking His people to live in a cer-tain way.[13]

In stressing the relevance of the deed, Judaism anchors itself in the concrete actions of everyday living. It is averse to seeking a meaning in life apart from doing; it strives instead to convert ideas into deeds, insights into action, ethical principles into patterns of conduct. What is of highest importance is one's day-to-day living, for it is here that one perceives one's kinship with the divine and the presence of the divine. It is not that the right intention or inward devotion is unimportant, but human living needs so much more

than good intentions or inward holiness. The absence of a right motive will not necessarily vilify the goodness of a deed, for the intention does not always determine the deed. The good deeds of every
person, regardless of the religious motivation or lack of it, will be
rewarded by God. This world needs more than our devotion and
holiness and good intentions, important as these might be. The
world is in need of our deeds and our lives. It is our lives lived in
accordance with God's will that bring redemption to the world.
What one does in one's material, physical existence is directly relevant to God. The mitsvot, for Judaism, are the instruments that
carry God's holiness into the world.

Reason and conscience alone are not the only means by which
we come to a knowledge of the rightness of our deeds. Judaism affirms that God has given humanity not only life but a law. The Jew
is committed to a divine law whose essence is derived from the great
events of Israel's history. It is not sufficient to believe in God; one
must accomplish His will. Jewish living, then, involves a specific
discipline, a commitment to specific actions and obligations. It is
not an attitude to be assumed simply at one's convenience. For the
pious Jew life is a complex of obligations, where deed takes precedence over creed and commitment to God's will takes precedence
over commitment to doctrine. Love of God is expressed by reverence for the law.[14]

To Be What One Does

Granted this centrality of the deed, it must be noted that one's service of God would be inadequate if it consisted only in deeds and
rites. Important as positive deeds are, there are also times when the
silence of sacred abstentions is more eloquent than the language of
sacred deeds. More important, it must be recognized that no sacred
deed is properly fulfilled unless it is done with a willingness of heart
and soul. The relationship between one's deeds and one's inner devotion is of crucial importance, and so Heschel takes great care in
his explanation.

To fulfill a mitsvah is to train oneself in the art of love; to forget
this is to emasculate mitsvot of all meaning. Thus observance of the
law can never be reduced to external compliance; there must be
agreement with both the letter and the spirit of the law. The law is
meant to be not a restrictive yoke placed upon a person but rather a

cry for creativity. Jewish observance includes both external actions that are clearly defined and interior acts of the soul that include right intention and putting this right intention into action. Pious thoughts or intentions locked up within a person are clearly deemed to be incomplete, but so also are deeds performed without any motivation or devotion. A sacred deed consists not only in *what* one does but also in *how* one does it. The mind and the heart are never exempt from participation in the service of God. While Judaism exalts the deed, it does not idolize mere external performance. It calls also for insight and devotion and understanding, for God asks for the heart and not merely for the deed. The law does not demand blind, impersonal obedience. One who observes the law should be spiritually perceptive, for, in Heschel's words, "Judaism is not interested in automatons." The faithful observer should thus recognize that the essence of obedience is the imitation of God. In other words, in one's obedience to the law, in fulfilling a mitsvah, one is indeed imitating God. "*That* we observe is obedience, *what* we observe is imitation of God."[15]

A deed that is performed without devotion or proper motivation may well be relevant because of the good it does for others, but it will have no effect on the life of the doer. Thus the goal for the observant Jew is *to be* what one *does*; Jews must learn how to be one with what they do. A mitsvah touches both the doer and the deed; the means are external, but the goal is internal and personal. One is holy to the extent that one's deeds are pure. Clearly, Judaism is not concerned merely with the performance of deeds; it seeks the transformation of the soul. Even before Israel was told what it must do through the Decalogue, it was told what it must be, namely, a holy people. Thus within Judaism halacha, the science of deeds, must be balanced by agada, the art of being. The purpose of a mitsvah is to sanctify the doer. Judaism is not content with *opus operatum*, with mere external rites or performances.

Heschel strongly criticizes what he terms "religious behaviorism," an attitude that would stress external compliance with the law without the need for inner devotion. Religious behaviorists would argue that the outward deed alone fulfills God's will; obedience to the law is what is crucial; inner devotion is not relevant to Judaism. Supporters of religious behaviorism speak of discipline and observance but never of religious experience or devotion, as though God were not concerned with the interior life. Judaism must not be reduced to legalism. The Torah contains both love and law; it is both a vision and a demand; it is both halacha and agada. A scrupulous observance of the law might well lead one to forget that the law is not for its own sake but for God's sake; such scrupulosity might make one oblivious of the living presence of God in the sacred deed. Jewish observance has at times become so encrusted with customs and conventions that its essential meaning has been lost. Concern for the externals has replaced the engagement of one's whole person to the living God. The law was never meant to become an idol. Jews live and die for God, not for the law. They are to be transformed by their sacred deeds. One is more than what one does. Deeds are outpourings and reflections of the inner self; they may refine the self, but they are not the essence of the self. Yet it is the inner self that is the most urgent problem, for the Torah must permeate all that one is and all that one does. The Jew is to be an incarnation of the Torah.

The goal of the believing Jew is to be a partner of God, and this is achieved in a mitsvah where God and the doer meet. One's task in a mitsvah is to be present to God's presence, to let God enter the deed. Judaism's imperishable homeland is in God's time, but one enters God's time by the path of sacred deeds. These deeds are the ground where one meets God again and again. It is in deeds, not in things, where the meeting with God takes place. Sacred deeds are moments which one shares with God, moments in which one identifies oneself with the will of God. A sacred deed is the divine in disguise, a revelation of the divine. Hence the stress on kavanah, on insight or attentiveness to God when performing a mitsvah. Kavanah implies an appreciation of being able to stand in the presence of God, an awareness of the preciousness of being able to perform a mitsvah. Its acquisition is a lifelong process and is essential to Jewish observance. Its purpose is to direct the heart so that one recognize what one is doing, acknowledging the deed as an imperative of God. With this attentiveness one is not merely doing a mitsvah; one is living what one does.[16]

HALACHA AND AGADA

Halacha of necessity deals with the abstract and impersonal; it speaks in terms of quantity, of the frequency and the amount needed to fulfill one's obligation. It places life into an exact system, defining, measuring, specifying, limiting. Agada deals more with the personal, reminding the Jew of the spiritual goal of a mitsvah, that the purpose of the deed is to transform the doer; it speaks in terms of quality and of consciousness, concerned more with the manner of performance than with its content. Agada deals with a person's relationships to God, to others, and to the world. Halacha looks to details, while agada looks to the whole of life. The one looks to the law; the other, to the meaning of the law. For halacha, then, quantity is decisive, while for agada, which stresses insight and motivation, or kavanah, it is quality that is decisive. Agada looks to inwardness, while halacha looks to externals. The interdependence of halacha and agada belongs to the core of Judaism. To place the essence of Judaism exclusively in one or the other is to miss the mark completely. Halacha without agada is lifeless, and agada without halacha is directionless. Frequently in Jewish tradition agada was either overlooked or considered inferior to halacha. Yet if one reduces Judaism simply to law, to halacha, then its light is dimmed, its essence is perverted, and its spirit is destroyed. The goal of religious living ultimately concerns quality rather than quantity, *how* something is done rather than simply *what* is done. The effort to obey the letter of the law must not curb the spontaneity of one's inner life. If the law becomes rigid, and if observance becomes mechanical, then one has already violated its spirit. Observance of the law involves constant decision, not rote performance. Halacha is meant as a response to the question: "What is God asking of me?" Without the question the answer becomes meaningless, and religious practice is reduced to spiritual sterility. To ask the question is to bring devotion, attentiveness, and spontaneity to halacha. The task of religious teaching is to help each generation to ask the question in its own way. To isolate the law from faith, from inwardness, from the personal is to render the law meaningless.[17]

Yet Heschel also sees any attempt to reduce Judaism to inwardness, to agada, as equally destructive of its essence and meaning. To abolish halacha is the surest way to lose agada. Inwardness alone does not bring humanity closer to God. One may have the purest intention, the noblest aspiration, the deepest devotion, yet unless this is somehow expressed in action, it is in danger of being a mere illusion or a grand delusion. Piety cannot endure without a pattern of deeds. The life of the spirit must be actualized through concrete actions; only in this way can the spirit be fulfilled. Just as a creed is necessary to give expression to one's faith, so halacha is needed to give expression to one's piety. Heschel believes it would be a tragic failure not to appreciate what halacha does for agada. Elimination of halacha would be spiritual suicide and would destroy Judaism's richest source of religious experience. Through halacha the Jew belongs to God not occasionally or intermittently, but essentially and continually. In a personal testimony Heschel writes: "How grateful I am to God that there is a duty to worship, a law to remind my distraught mind that it is time to think of God. . . . I am not always in a mood to pray. . . . But when I am weak, it is the law that gives me strength; when my vision is dim, it is duty that gives me insight." [18]

Halacha and agada can survive only in a symbiotic relationship, a relationship of mutual co-dependence. Without halacha agada loses its substance and its character, its tangible and material expression. It is impossible, Heschel concludes, to determine whether Judaism gives supremacy to halacha or to agada, to Amos or to Hosea. Ultimately, one must recognize that there is a dialectic, a polarity, at the very heart of Judaism, whether one expresses the polarity in terms of halacha and agada, of regularity and spontaneity, of uniformity and individuality, of obedience and understanding, or of discipline and joy. In the abstract such terms appear to be mutually exclusive, yet in actual life they demand one another; they cannot exist in separation from one another. There is no halacha without agada; there is no agada without halacha. Inner devotion, spontaneity, freedom cannot exist without discipline, rule, law. A mitsvah is at once a discipline and an inspiration; it is an act of obedience and an experience of joy; it is an obligation and yet a privilege. The task of the Jew is to discover and to maintain a harmony between "the demands of halacha and the spirit of agada." [19]

To achieve and maintain such harmony is no easy task. Heschel was fully aware of this and deals with it not only in *God in Search of Man* but in a number of other works over the last two decades of his life. How does one acquire the proper motivation, the right intention in performing a sacred deed? Heschel's basic response would be: through the deed itself. To take a negative example: one may perform an act of greed without necessarily being interiorly a greedy person; but if one constantly repeats such actions, consistently acts in a greedy way, then one will soon know greed and be motivated by a spirit of greediness. So also one may perform an act of kindness without really possessing the spirit of kindness; but if one repeats such acts day after day, one could not remain forever deaf to the spirit of the acts one is performing. In other words, deeds not only follow intention; they may also instill the intention. Thus devotion or kavanah comes into being through deeds. The deed brings out what may be lying dormant in the mind. That is why Judaism insists upon the deed and hopes that the intention may follow. It teaches that one must continue to observe the law even if one is not yet ready to fulfill it for the proper intention. A repeated good deed will eventually teach the doer how to act for the sake of God. Such purity of intention is the goal, but the way is through the deed itself. One overcomes self-centeredness not by dwelling on the self but by concentrating on the task. It is the act itself that teaches one the meaning of the act, so that performing sacred deeds will eventually change baser motives. Such deeds are exacting, demanding undivided attention; there is a power in them that purifies one's motives. It is the deeds of life that educate the will; good motives come into being through doing the good. As Heschel put it: "The way to pure intention is paved with good deeds." A person may be filled with selfish motives, but the deed and God are stronger and will overcome such motives. Good deeds are wiser than the heart. Even when one is aware how impure and imperfect one's motives are, performing a mitsvah must still be recognized as humankind's greatest privilege and source of joy, endowing life with ultimate preciousness. For regardless of the impurity, acts performed in imitation of God's will and moments lived in fellowship with God never perish. Whatever we do is only partial fulfillment; the remainder is completed by God.[20]

One might tend to believe that repetition of a deed would lead to lack of interest and apathy, that strict observance of the Jewish law at fixed times and in identical ways would become a matter of routine and mere outward compliance. Heschel insists that the opposite is true, that routine breeds attention, calling forth a response where normally the soul would be dormant. Sacred deeds of themselves bring one to the threshhold of the holy, so that eventually one will be affected by the holy. In doing a mitsvah one exposes one's life to God and thus discovers the divine; in entering into a mitsvah with all one's heart and soul, one is drawn close to God. For acts of holiness reveal God's holiness hidden in each moment of time, and God and His holiness are one.

Thus it would be a mistake to wait until moved by the spirit before seeking to worship God. Such movements of the spirit may be brief and sporadic, and for long intervals the mind may be dull and empty. Judaism's emphasis on the deed implies that in performing a mitsvah one meets the spirit. Yet the spirit is not something we acquire once for all; it is something we must try again and again to pray for and to live with. This is the reason why Judaism emphasizes repetition of rituals, in order to meet the spirit again and again, the spirit in oneself and the spirit that hovers over all reality.[21]

To examine mitsvot in terms of common sense or to look here for rational explanations is to rob mitsvot of their intrinsic meaning. Mitsvot allude to that which is beyond reason, expressing in deeds an appreciation of the ineffable. The purpose of sacred deeds is to make life compatible with our sense of the ineffable. It is not utility that one seeks through a mitsvah but eternity. The criterion for Judaism, and for any religion, lies not in its agreement with our common sense, but in its agreement with a sense of the ineffable. Mitsvot, then, should not be judged according to their reasonableness. Religion ultimately lies beyond the limits of reason; it creates in us the need to serve ends of which we would otherwise be oblivious; it can be understood only in terms compatible with a sense of the ineffable. It may happen that only where reasoning ends does the meaning of a mitsvah begin. Mitsvot seek to give expression to God; they attempt to "utter God in acts." Reverence is not an adequate response to the wonder and mystery that surround us. The deeper our reverence the more we recognize the inadequacy of reverence alone. The whole of one's life must be given in response; one must adapt a pattern of life that is compatible with the ineffable. This, for Heschel, is the basic purpose of Jewish observance. It is Israel's response to the ineffable, to the ultimate mystery that has been revealed as the God of mercy and as a loving Father. The question of how to respond has been answered by specific commandments. Each mitsvah is a response, representing a mating of mind and mystery to create an image of a divine attribute. In the sacred deed there is a meeting of heaven and earth. A mitsvah is not an anonymous or impersonal act; it is a deed done in answer to God's will, responding to what He expects of us.

To one who stands outside Judaism, the mitsvot may well appear to be absurd and lifeless legalisms. To the Jew who does not strive to enter fully into the spirit of a mitsvah, observance may well become a dreary and annoying routine. To the pious Jew, however, the mitsvot are a joyful art, expressions of deep significance, not just of a meaning given once for all, but of new meanings evoked again and again by the performance of sacred acts. Mitsvot are deeds of inspiration, not just acts of compliance; they comprise a liturgy of deeds. Judaism is not concerned primarily with the performance of single good deeds, but with the pursuit of a way of life. Each single deed is woven into the complete pattern of a committed life. Jewish living shapes the whole of one's existence, one's attitudes, interests, and dispositions. Faithful Jews discover in the mitsvot God's presence as it is meant for them, a presence that brings with it a fullness of joy. Thus the deed and its reward are one. The reward of a mitsvah is eternity, not an eternity in the life to come, but an eternal Presence discovered in the deed, in the act itself; a mitsvah is its own reward.

Mitsvot, then, are Judaism's response to the question of how one ought to live in a way compatible with God's presence. Human living is not a private affair; it is what a person does with God's time and with God's world. Mitsvot evoke this awareness of living in a holy dimension, of living in the nearness of God. For the pious Jew each mitsvah is "an encounter of the human and the holy"; each sacred deed expresses an accord between our will and God's will; each such deed helps to repair and illumine a world torn by conflict and hatred. The mitsvot are ways of living in fellowship with God, flashes of holiness that enlighten the path of humankind. They are given for the benefit of humankind: to refine, to ennoble, to discipline, to inspire. Performing a mitsvah implies going beyond oneself and illuminating the world, disclosing the light of the divine to a world often steeped in darkness. Holiness is the outcome of those moments in which the human and the divine meet in the light of a good deed.

Judaism must beware lest it consider the performance of mitsvot as mere ceremonial actions, as actions required primarily by custom or convention. In such cases tradition, and not attachment to God's will, becomes the motivating factor. For Heschel, mere ceremony is paramount to disbelief paying homage to faith. Mitsvot must be recognized for what they are: deeds required by the Torah, deeds that are relevant to God and that are Judaism's way to God. Ceremonies have been created for the purpose of signifying, while mitsvot are given for the purpose of sanctifying, i.e., they confer holiness whether or not one knows precisely what they signify. In performing a mitsvah one recognizes that God is indeed concerned with our fulfillment of His will.[22]

THE DANGER OF SYMBOLISM

The intrusion of this ceremonial mentality into religious ritual and worship is part of a much larger question with which Heschel was concerned, especially in the early and mid-1950s, namely, the question of symbolism, which he interpreted as a threat to Jewish observance. Heschel saw Judaism's growing concern with symbols as a confession that it no longer knows how to encounter reality face to face.

Judaism clearly eschews images of God. "You shall not have strange gods before me" has been understood to mean that this God of Israel could not be captured or localized in any way. At the inauguration of the Temple Solomon confesses: "Behold, heaven and the heaven of heavens cannot contain Thee; how much less this house that I have built" (1 K 8:27). The God of Israel manifests Himself to His people in events, not in things or places. Although Mount Sinai designates the place of Israel's highest revelation, it never became a place of pilgrimage.

In the Bible there is only one symbol or image of God. God created man in His image and likeness, and so whatever is human is also holy. The holiness of the human comes as a gift of God; it is not an achievement of humanity. So much of biblical piety is rooted in this truth. Our reverence for God is shown in our reverence for a human person, just as an act of violence against another human being is a desecration, a blasphemy against God. The basic imperative of biblical piety thus becomes: one is to treat oneself as a symbol of God. Since each of us is a reflection of God, we must keep that reflection pure, guarding God's likeness on earth. The divine symbolism of human persons points to our capacity to be holy as God is holy; it points to our capacity to act as He acts in mercy and in love. This divine likeness may so easily be distorted or forfeited. It is in this context that Heschel deals with symbolism in Judaism. Each person is called upon to preserve this likeness or at least to prevent its distortion. Yet is it possible to prevent this distortion if we have only symbolic knowledge of God and no objective knowledge of God or at least of His will? Heschel saw religion becoming largely a matter of symbols, and he interpreted this as looking upon religion *as a fiction*, useful simply to society at large or to one's personal well-being; there is, however, in this understanding no relation of a person to God but only to the symbol of one's highest ideals. Religion is treated here simply as a form of symbolic thinking.

The premiss of religious symbolism rests on a twofold assumption: (*a*) the infinity of God lies beyond the grasp of our finite minds; (*b*) God can thus be apprehended or expressed only through symbols. Heschel does not accept this conclusion. He argues that if there is no direct knowledge of God, or at least of God's will, we are unable to ascertain the legitimacy of our symbols of God, and hence we cannot take our religious symbols seriously. If we are to judge the adequacy of any symbol, we must possess a knowledge of the reality symbolized that is independent of all symbols. We must have some type of non-symbolic knowledge of God if we are to determine which symbols represent God and which misrepresent God. Symbols are substitutes for direct knowledge of God, and such substitutes distort one's vision as well as one's interior life. In Heschel's view symbolism degenerates into a vicarious religion by giving to symbolic objects an honor that is due to God alone.

Those for whom God is eternally absent or forever silent are the only ones who are forced to accept the substitute of a symbolic knowledge of God. Such is not the case with Israel. The God of the Bible is not an unknown or unknowable God. Israel's faith is rooted in the certainty that God has indeed made His will known to the people. For Judaism the experience of God's will is more powerful and more real than the experience of self. The demand to love and serve God does not refer to symbolic attitudes. The prophets vigorously opposed any notion that God desired simply symbolic deeds. The service of God becomes an extremely concrete affair. Israel worships God not symbolically but by shaping its everyday life according to God's will. The prophets did not speak primarily in symbolic terms but in terms of specific actions. The command to observe the Sabbath or to love one's neighbor as oneself has a clear and literal meaning. Holiness is something that is vital and real. The Torah is not in heaven, nor is the voice of God ambiguous; ambiguity is created by confusion on our part. The Bible tells Israel precisely how it is to act. In performing a mitsvah one is not symbolizing religion; a mitsvah *is* religion, for it is an expression of the will of God. What is most important for Judaism is that God speaks and thus we must try to understand God's speech. The mitsvot are indeed the words of God which Judaism tries to understand and to articulate. [23]

Heschel admits that there is a basic human need for symbolic expression; religion should supply norms for the correct satisfaction of that need. Religious symbolism is a search for God, an expression of what we experience; Jewish observance is a response to God, an expression of what He wills. In performing a mitsvah one's major concern is not the expression of one's feelings but the compliance with God's will. This certainty of being able to accomplish God's will gives a profound meaning to each mitsvah. Judaism has no doubt that there is an ultimate meaning to all ritual acts, but the immediate relevance of these acts lies in their being commandments of God. One may not understand the ultimate meaning of the mitsvot, but Judaism insists on their fulfillment because of its certainty that it understands the will of God. Here again is the role of kavanah in performing a mitsvah. Kavanah is the awareness that what one is doing is indeed God's will; it is *not* an awareness or understanding of the symbolic significance of such deeds. Jewish mysticism does delve into this aspect of the divine mystery whenever it attempts to grasp the ultimate meaning behind Jewish observance. Yet the goal of kavanah is not to understand the symbolic meaning of, or the reason behind, the mitsvot, but to forget all reasons and to try to realize before whom one stands in performing a mitsvah. To achieve such a realization is to forget everything, including the self, and to make room in the mind only for the awareness of God. Such ideal moments may be rare, and they may be attained for only an instant, yet they are the basis for the great joy experienced by the pious Jew in performing a mitsvah. [24]

By definition a symbol is not the ultimate reality; it is always a pointer to a reality beyond itself. For Heschel the ultimate is the very opposite of the symbolic and is not translated into symbols. Symbolic knowledge, which is obtained through analysis and reflection, must be distinguished from immediate understanding, which is derived from an intimate engagement with what is real. Insights into the meaning, for example, of joy or suffering or reality are acquired not through the use of symbols but through direct experience. The religious person lives in the depth of a certainty that comes from immediate understanding: this is what God wants of me. Without that certainty all symbols are useless.

Heschel sees symbols as a snare for anyone who is seeking the truth; they may be appealing because they promise to revitalize beliefs and rituals that have become meaningless, but they succeed only in undermining belief and observance, reducing the Bible to literature and theology to aesthetics. Symbols make no demands on us; they do not involve us in ultimate commitment. They may distort what is literally true or profane what is ineffably real. Authentic faith could easily perish from an overdose of symbolism because symbols weaken the certainty of faith, implying that even God does not succeed in conveying His will to us in unmistakable terms and that thus we have not succeeded in understanding what He demands of us. The uniqueness of the Bible does not lie in its symbolism; nor is symbolism an authentic category of prophetic religion. Other religions might be rich in symbolism, but they lack Israel's knowledge of the living God. The Bible discloses the will of God with utter clarity; it discloses the presence of God in historical events, not in symbolic signs; its uniqueness lies in this.

If God is actual, Heschel argues, then He is able to express His will in unambiguous terms. Symbols are necessary only where ambiguity prevails; they tend to be particularistic, dividing us rather than uniting us. What is needed is immediacy with God, new insight instead of new symbols. The meaning of existence will not be found through a set of symbols. The problems humanity faces are real: oppression, malice, ignorance, deceit; our suffering is deep. Symbols provide no remedy. God's will is either real or a delusion. Our only escape from the quagmire of ambiguity is our certainty that God has spoken to us and has made clear His demands for us and for all humanity.[25]

Heschel's polemic against the role of symbols, rooted in his certainty of our knowledge of God's will, raises many questions, especially for one who does not share the vantage point of his Jewish faith. It must be remembered, however, that his remarks on symbolism are directed primarily to those who share his faith as a Jew and his conviction that the mitsvot are Judaism's response to a God who has made His will clearly known to His people. It is in this context that one must read Heschel's criticism of the dangers of symbol in religion. At this point it might be wiser simply to hear the opinion of another Jew on this matter, Martin Buber, an early colleague of Heschel in Germany prior to the outbreak of World War II. Buber recognizes that the codification of divine revelation into law and statutes demands a deep faith, and he would honor the faith of those who are able to equate Jewish observance of law and statute with the will of God; he would be concerned only if one held to the observance without being concerned about God. At the same time, one's faith might well prevent a person, as it did Buber, from identifying the various legal prescriptions with God's will. "I cannot accept the laws and the statutes blindly," Buber wrote in a letter to Franz Rosenzweig, "but I must ask myself again and again: Is this particular law addressed to me and rightly so?"[26] In other words, Buber is compelled to question how much of what is prescribed by Jewish observance genuinely reflects God's will, and how much of it is our human attempt to interpret God's will. Heschel himself writes in *God in Search of Man* that the full meaning of revelation is not given once for all; the effort to understand God's word must go on continually. Furthermore, biblical laws are grasped through the interpretation and wisdom of the rabbis; without this help the text of the laws would often be unintelligible. Judaism is based upon "a minimum of revelation and a maximum of interpretation"; at the center of Judaism is both God's will and Israel's understanding of that will. Each generation of Jews should bring forth new understanding and new realization. The basic difference between Heschel and Buber on this point seems to lie in the faith-perception of Heschel's which accepts the interpretation and understanding of revelation found in Jewish tradition as a faithful representation of the will of God.[27]

It should not be necessary to add that one should honor and respect the faith-insights and faith-experiences of another, as Buber himself does, without compromising one's own faith-perspective. The ways in which God reveals the mystery of His will are many, and many are the ways in which humankind, led by God's grace, will interpret this revelation.

THE SABBATH: SANCTIFYING TIME

One area of Jewish observance on which Heschel writes with particular eloquence and which would clearly have an appeal to those outside of Judaism, is his view of the Jewish Sabbath. There are few ideas in the history of human civilization that can equal the spiritual power contained in the idea of the Sabbath. Heschel's primary work in this area, mentioned briefly in the first chapter, is *The Sabbath*, published in 1951. In this work Heschel refers to Judaism as a religion whose goal is the sanctification of time; each moment is unique, exclusively and endlessly precious. The Sabbath is the primary means by which the observant Jew becomes sensitive to holiness in time by escaping from the tyranny of the things of space. Space represents that aspect of reality wherein humankind seeks control and dominion over creation. The Sabbath bids one move from the works of creation to the mystery of creation. This implies that one must turn aside from the "profanity of clattering commerce" where so many are yoked to the desire for acquisition in the nervous fury of the marketplace; manual work must be set aside so that one may truly realize that the world has been created and will survive without our help. Let the rest of the week be spent in trying to dominate the world; on the Sabbath we must try to dominate the self, for this is a day set aside for living and not for enhancing the efficiency of our work. The Sabbath marks a respite in the cruel struggle for existence, a truce in all our conflicts whether personal or social; it calls for peace between persons and within persons, peace between oneself and one's environment. The handling of money would be a desecration on the Sabbath, for this day calls on Jews to proclaim their independence of this great idol of the world.

Thus much of the meaning of the Sabbath is expressed by means of abstentions. If God's image should be built exclusively by our rituals and deeds, how obtrusive and awkward it would be. At times silence alone is our only worthy response in the presence of God's glory. The Sabbath bids Jews to abandon their ordinary pursuits in order to reclaim their authentic being, to rejoice simply in the blessedness of what they are as human persons, regardless of their educational achievements, their economic position, their career or work or profession; on the Sabbath one must be free of all social conditions. On other days one may worry about being rich or poor, one may be concerned about success or failure, but on the Sabbath one is lifted to another plane. There is no time here for personal anxiety and care or for anything else that might dampen the joy of this day. This is not the time for confessing or repenting or fasting or mourning. One abstains from toil and strain in order to make this a day of praise. So the Sabbath is more than an interlude; it is the profound consciousness of the harmony between humankind and creation. All that is divine in this world is brought into union with God.[28]

The Sabbath, in Heschel's view, is Judaism's response to the problem of modern civilization. It is not a question of turning one's back on technology or on a computerized society, but of withdrawing a bit in order to achieve some degree of independence from it. This is precisely what is done on the Sabbath, for on this day one lives as though independent of our technological society, refusing to engage in any activity geared toward reshaping the things of space. The privilege and the command given to humankind to conquer the earth are thus suspended for the Sabbath. This also underscores Judaism's attitude toward material possessions, namely, to have them, yet to be able to do without them. It is easy to become a slave to one's own possessions and one's own pettiness. One's inner liberty must be jealously guarded from domination by things as well as by other people. Very few in our society are free from some type of enslavement to things. This is a constant struggle: to live with people and things and yet remain independent. The Sabbath represents a bulwark of strength in this struggle. It proclaims one's ultimate independence of civilization and society, of achievement and anxiety. It does not imply a rejection of the realm of space. Material things are our tools; we work with them; the Sabbath reminds us that in the midst of that work our heart should be set on eternity. Even if Israel is dedicated to temporal pursuits for six days of the week, its soul is claimed by the Sabbath.[29]

Heschel employs an ancient allegory to spell out the relationship of the Sabbath to Israel. In the beginning time was eternal, undivided, and unrelated to the world of space. Then time was divided into seven days, entering into intimate relationship with the world of space. With each day another aspect of the world of space came into being, except on the seventh day. The Sabbath was alone and lonely. This may be compared to a king with seven sons. The six older sons are given his wealth, the youngest is given his nobility with the privilege of royalty. The older six, all commoners, find their mates; the youngest son, the noble one, remained without a mate. The allegory is explained by Rabbi Shimeon ben Yohai: "After the work of creation was completed, the Seventh Day pleaded: Master of the universe, all that Thou hast created is in couples; to every day of the week Thou gavest a mate; only I was left alone. And God answered: The Community of Israel will be your *mate.*" Thus Israel is to be the helpmate of the Sabbath because, for all its spiritual grandeur, the Sabbath is not self-sufficient; it calls for companionship. The Sabbath stands in need of humankind; Israel is destined to meet that need. The Sabbath, noble and holy by the grace of God, still needs all the holiness and nobility that Israel may lend to it. It should be noted that Rabbi Shimeon belonged to that generation which saw Rome crush the revolt of Simon bar Kochba. There was no longer any possibility of rebuilding the Temple in Jerusalem; Israel's sanctuary in space would continue to lie in ruins. This brought about the growing awareness that sanctity is not bound to any particular place. There are fixed times for prayer, but no fixed place of prayer. The Temple lay in ruins in Jerusalem, but synagogues arose in every village. Israel was not alone; Israel was engaged to holiness, to eternity, to the Sabbath. Here was a union that no one could put asunder. The notion of the Sabbath as the bride of Israel serves as an example of God's need for the love of Israel and of all peoples; it illustrates the relationship that exists between God and His very own.[30]

Yet the Sabbath cannot survive in exile, a stranger among six days of profanity; it needs their companionship. All days of the week should be spiritually consistent with the Sabbath; an appreciation of the Sabbath should be ever present in the mind of the pious Jew. The Sabbath is Judaism's awareness of God's presence in the world; it is eternity within time. The Sabbath is but one day, yet its spirit should permeate all days. For Heschel *Shabbesdikeit* (reverence for the Sabbath) represents "the epitome and spirit of Judaism." The whole of life should thus be viewed as a pilgrimage to the Sabbath. The longing for the Sabbath each day of the week parallels that longing for the eternal Sabbath which should mark each day of our lives.[31]

The Sabbath teaches us to look at time in a different manner. We are accustomed to consider time as a measuring device, to distinguish events in the world of space as earlier or later, longer or shorter. Heschel wants to probe beyond this. Does time exist only in a relationship of before or after to the world of space? Is there no meaning to this present moment without a relationship to the things of space? We are so caught up in the world of space that we fail to recognize the ultimate significance of time. We confuse temporality with time. We can never have space without time, but in moments of deep meditation or reflection we are able to have time without space. By temporality Heschel means the relation of space to time. Time appears to be in constant motion, but to the spiritual person it is the spatial objects that are constantly in motion and constantly coming to an end. Time is that which never expires; the world of space is moving through an infinite expanse of time.

Ordinarily time is identified with evanescence or temporality. Yet it is the world of space that conveys the sense of temporality; temporality comes to mind when we are concerned with the things of space. It is the world of space which perishes within time. Time itself does not change; it is everlasting. Instead of the flow or passage of time we should think in terms of the flow or passage of space through time. Time does not die; rather things or persons perish in time. Temporality belongs to the world of space, while time is beyond space and beyond divisions of past, present, and future.

Technology epitomizes humankind's triumph over space, but time remains our greatest challenge; its reality escapes us. We can exert our will on space, shaping and controlling things as we please. Yet time is beyond our reach; it is intrinsic to, and transcendent to, all experience. In this sense time is otherness, akin to the holy, a mystery that hovers over all categories; it belongs exclusively to God. On the other hand, each person occupies a portion of space in an exclusive fashion. Where I am, no one else can be; I am a rival to all others for the possession of this space. But there is no moment of time that I possess exclusively. This present moment belongs as much to others as it belongs to me. As far as time is concerned, we are sharers and contemporaries, not possessors and competitors. In time we are together in fellowship; in space we are isolated in rivalry. It is within time that we are enabled to grasp the unity of all beings, and it is in this dimension of time that we encounter God. Time is God's presence in the world of space; it is God's gift to the world of space.[32]

Time may also be considered as synonymous with continuous creation. God is continually calling the world into being, so that every moment is an act of creation and signals a new beginning. To witness to the marvel of the world's continual coming into being is to recognize that time is rooted in eternity and that God is present in creation through time. If one stands alone, time is elusive; if one stands with God, time is eternity in disguise. The Sabbath and eternity are one.

For six days it is our task to sanctify life by our control of the things of space; on the Sabbath we are asked to share in the holiness that is at the heart of time. One's life may be in tatters, weariness may stifle any hope of prayer, the soul may be parched, yet the silent rest of the Sabbath can still lead one to a realm of endless peace and to an initial glimpse of what eternity really means. In the Sabbath God has given us the beginning of eternity.[33]

REDEMPTION: A DIVINE AND A HUMAN TASK

In one sense one may also look upon the Sabbath as a foretaste of redemption. Heschel considers redemption as basically the disclosure of the divine or of the holy that is hidden and suppressed in our world. This certainly is one purpose of the Sabbath as it is of each mitsvah a Jew performs. Judaism calls upon each person to be a redeemer by recognizing that redemption takes place at every moment of every day. Yet at the same time it would warn us against believing that by our own power alone we are capable of redeeming the world. Good deeds alone will not bring about redemption, but fidelity to God's law will make us worthy of being redeemed. If Judaism had relied exclusively on humanity's power to fulfill God's demands and to achieve redemption, it would never have put such emphasis on the messianic hopes and the promise of messianic redemption. The belief in a coming messianic age implicitly recognizes that even the greatest of human efforts cannot redeem the world. History, for all its relevance, is not sufficient of itself. Nor are we capable by ourselves of overcoming the deep-rooted drive toward evil found in every human being. God asks for the heart, yet the human heart is so deceitful and weak; it represents "our greatest failure." Concern for self permeates all our thinking. The demand to serve God with a pure heart and the recognition of the inability to free ourselves from vested interests represent a tragic tension in the spiritual life. Selfish intent may taint our motivation either prior to or in the midst of performing a good deed, and we face the problem of a self-righteous superiority and vanity following a deed supposedly dedicated to God. The good cannot be free of self-interest.

Here again Judaism's ultimate reliance is upon God. Jeremiah spoke of this in eschatological terms: "Behold, days are coming, says the Lord, when I will make a new covenant with the house of Israel . . . not like the covenant I made with their forefathers. . . . I will set my law within them and write it on their hearts" (Jr 31: 31–34). We await God's redeeming power; all of creation is in need of redemption, but redemption will not come about solely as an act of God. Our human task is to make the world worthy of redemption; our good works prepare the world for ultimate redemption.[34]

Heschel also speaks of the need to separate good from evil if redemption is to come about. The effort to separate the two is what he calls Judaism's greatest redemptive task. Evil thrives so well under the guise of the good, even drawing strength from a parasitical relationship with the holy, for the holy and the unholy, good and evil, exist only in this confused and intermixed state; neither exists in purity. This confusion of good and evil is the central issue of redemption. All history reflects an admixture of good and evil. The redemptive task of separating good and evil implies ultimately that evil will cease to be since it can exist only in this parasitic relationship with the good. Redemption is thus dependent on separating good from evil.

The climax of Jewish hopes lies in the establishment of the kingship of God. A passion for its accomplishment should permeate the life of every faithful Jew. This implies that the ultimate concern of Judaism is not personal salvation but universal redemption. By considering redemption as a continual process rather than as a sudden and dramatic eschatological event, Judaism can emphasize the role each deed plays in the long drama of redemption. We must remember that each sacred deed we perform, each kind word we utter, each ritual prayer we chant represents our own modest contribution to the reduction of distress and to the advancement of redemption. Most important, each one must live as though the redemption of all humanity depended upon the devotion achieved in one's own life. Thus each life becomes an immense opportunity to enhance the good of the whole of creation. The vision of a world free of narrow nationalism and arrogant imperialism, of a world where there will be no more weeping or cries of distress, of a world radiant with the love and joy of God—this "certainty of ultimate redemption" must continue to inspire Jewish thought and action.[35]

This concern for both the human and the divine, for the historical and the eschatological aspects of redemption, is also reflected in the messianic hopes of Israel. From one point of view, the Messiah would be essentially a political figure: foreign rule and oppression would be abolished and the people returned to the land. Yet from a prophetic viewpoint, the messianic age is essentially eschatological; it implies a radical transformation of all creation. History and humanity and all of nature had somehow gone astray, and the only cure is a type of re-creation. The prophets spoke of the Messiah ushering in a new order of things, a reign of everlasting peace that would affect even the wild beasts. Yet there have always been wise Jewish teachers who looked on the messianic hopes of the prophets basically as metaphorical and in a spirit of "realism" interpreted messianic redemption as a type of political renewal and deliverance from foreign powers.

The manner in which the messianic age would come is also viewed in a twofold way. One view sees the Messiah appearing suddenly from heaven in the midst of miracles and wonders to gather together the scattered remnants of Israel to their ancient inheritance. The other view sees the beginning of the messianic age taking place simply by the desire of Jews to live in Palestine and by the willingness of the nations to assist them. Yet here again messianic redemption is not conceived of as an act that takes place without preparation. It is an ongoing process that each person either retards or enhances. The human family needs redemption, but redemption also needs the cooperation of the human family. Our actions affect the course of redemption. We hold the key that can unlock the chains that bind the Messiah. Central to Jewish thought on redemption is its refusal to consider it as either an exclusively divine or an exclusively human achievement. These two views of the messianic age complement each other. The sacred and the secular, the spiritual and the political, the human and the holy are not mutually exclusive. The relationship between God and humankind is reciprocal and interdependent. Our task is "to humanize the sacred and to sanctify the secular." [36]

The ugliness and the violence that mark our world will not last forever. The messianic hope is of a world rid of evil both by God's grace and by our own human efforts, by our dedication to the establishment of God's reign in our lives and in our world. God waits for our cooperation in redeeming this world. He waits for our effort and devotion, and yet we spend so much of our time hunting for trivial satisfactions and for personal gains. The universe was not created for the satisfaction of our greed, our envy, our ambition. Humanity, and Judaism in particular, have not survived the millenia to be dissipated in vulgar vanities. The martyrdom of millions, the suffering and oppression of many millions more, make a demand on our lives. We must consecrate ourselves to God's goal of redemption.[37]

THE ROLE OF THE LAND

Redemption is God's pledge and humanity's hope. For Judaism this is a pledge and a hope that has always been closely associated with the land of Israel. There is a unique association between the people and the land which non-Jews, and especially Christians, must attempt to recognize and understand. Even before Israel became a people, there was the promise of the land. The election of Abraham and of the land came together. The promise made to Abraham was to be a blessing for all the nations of the earth. The gift of the land betokens this greater promise. In Jewish thought the promise of redemption for all the nations is intimately connected with the presence of the people in the land of Israel. Only here may the scattered tribes become a people, God's people, and a light to all the nations. This is the land where the Bible is at home; it is the land where the deepest encounters between God and humankind took place; it is the land where the most precious visions and the most sublime goals were born. Judaism perceives Israel as a land sanctified by the prophets, by the sufferings of a people, and by their tears and prayers over the millenia. It is a sanctity both precious to God and vital to the people. Simply to be in the land is itself a religious experience, a witness to the almost forgotten truth that God is Lord of all lands. For Heschel the rebirth of Israel as a nation is a mystery as well as a clear, unmistakable challenge, a verification of the ancient promise: "I will restore the fortunes of my people Israel. . . . I will plant them once more on their own soil, and they shall never again be uprooted from the soil I have given them, says the Lord your God" (Am 9:14–15).

The redemption for which Israel yearns both for itself and for all peoples is concerned not merely with a life to come. It is concerned with human dignity and justice and compassion here and now. Redemption is to be as concrete as the agony and suffering which the people have endured and which make them worthy of redemption.

Hebrew thought never accepted the Neoplatonic dichotomy between the real, that which is spiritual and eternal, and the apparent, that which is material and temporal. Judaism saw a deeper unity between the two. The promise and the commands of the Bible were never reduced to shadows of heavenly realities; they never became mere allegory. It is the immediate, specific meaning of the words which counts, without denying the intimation of deeper meanings. In Jewish tradition the words of the Bible are relevant both objectively or historically and symbolically or spiritually. Primacy is given to the objective or historical meaning. While searching for deeper meaning, Judaism first considers the words of the Bible in their explicit sense. For the person of biblical faith it is concrete reality, specific human conduct, this material world, which comprises the primary religious challenge. The Bible deals not only with moral and spiritual issues, but also with specific historical events, commands, and promises.[38]

Christianity has tended to move away from the concrete, worldly, historical character of the promises and hopes expressed in the Bible, giving them a completely spiritual or allegorical significance. Christianity thus minimizes what for Judaism is the Bible's plain historical meaning. This tendency, in Heschel's view, has rendered the average Christian incapable of understanding, and often unsympathetic toward, what the Holy Land means to the Jew, or what the people of Israel mean in the concrete historical order and not just as a symbol or a theological construct. Many Christian theologians have been committed to a mode of thought which treats the people of Israel, the city of Jerusalem, the hopes for the restoration of Zion as primarily spiritual entities. The allegorical method, although no longer a force in biblical exegesis, is rooted in the supposition that some meaning, other than what is specifically stated, is the real intention of the biblical author. This approach clearly contributed to Christianity's misreading of Judaism's hopes and goals. The value of the Old Testament, the Hebrew Bible, was seen by many Christian exegetes primarily as a prefiguration or foreshadowing of what would be revealed in the New Testament. Although a wholly different theological understanding has come about through modern biblical scholarship and its search for the literal and historical dimensions of the Bible, much remains to be done to correct the distortions that for so long had dominated the Christian approach to the hopes and promises of Israel.

Perhaps the area of greatest misunderstanding is centered on the place of *Eretz Israel*, the land of Israel, in the faith-perspective of Judaism. Writing in the time of the political upheaval of the late 1960s in the Middle East, Heschel tries to spell out this relationship of Jews to the land of Israel. When the land promised by God was taken away from the Jews by violence through the destruction of the Temple in the year 70 and with the crushing of the Bar Kochba rebellion in 135, the people never ceased to assert their right and title to the land of Israel. This continuous and uninterrupted claim was an essential ingredient of Jewish consciousness and of Jewish faith. It was a claim that was uttered in their homes and sanctuaries, in their books and prayers. The very identity of Jews as a people emphasized this link to the land and the desire to return. Despite all adversity the roots of the people remained in the land; they maintained their passion for Zion; their lives were in constant dialogue with the land.

Jews were not overwhelmed by despair; their hope was rooted in God, in the conviction that He would be faithful to His promises. It was a hope that manifested itself as "yearning and expectation, as waiting and anticipation." It was a hope that evoked scorn and derision from those who despised Jews. To those outside Judaism such hope often seemed to be a senseless dream; for those within, it was an all-absorbing prayer to God. Zionism was born out of this prayer, out of this hope in God's promise, out of faith in the biblical command to the people never to forget their origin, never to abandon hope for Zion and for Jerusalem. Hope and waiting implied, not inaction, but the recognition that the success of any human effort toward redemption remained incomplete, contingent upon the response of God.[39]

Exile from the land was looked upon as an interruption, never as a definitive detachment; it was simply the prelude to return. Zion continued to live on as an inspiration in the hearts and minds of the people. The thought of Jerusalem and the hope for return became an intimate part of Jewish life and prayer; it was the recurring theme of Jewish liturgy. It is found in the words of comfort addressed to those in mourning: "May the Lord comfort you among all those that mourn for Zion and Jerusalem." When a newborn is received into the community, the blessing asks that the child may become worthy "to ascend in the holy pilgrimage of the three festivals." The glass broken at the end of the wedding ritual is a reminder of the destruction of Jerusalem. The dead are laid to rest with earth from the Holy Land placed under their head. In life and in death the Jew is never parted from *Eretz Israel.* Heschel describes the vital importance for Judaism of this relationship to the land: "The Jew in whose heart the love of Zion dies is doomed to lose his faith in the God of Abraham, who gave the land as an earnest of the redemption of all men." Jewish faith is wedded to the land of Israel.[40] And in the face of the political complexities that have engulfed the Middle East over the last four decades, one can only hope with Heschel that the hatred and terrorism that have turned the area into an armed camp may eventually dissolve, and that the healing power of peace and community may replace the insidious destructiveness of suspicion and mistrust. Arab and Jew are kinspeople; they can be a blessing to one another, supplying one another's wants, engaged in research together, sharing knowledge and experience in a dialogue of learning. Arab and Jew must abandon their antagonisms and fears and begin to think in terms of one family. The only alternative to peace in the Middle East is disaster. Arab and Jew must learn to love one another, or else they will destroy one another. Love must have the final word so that both peoples may live in community, sharing their fears and joys and anxieties.

All must be concerned without qualification for the security and well-being of each person everywhere. Harm done to one person is harm done to all. From the biblical perspective that which brings chaos and conflict to the world is fraternal hatred, hatred among kinspeople. Isaiah's reminder to the people that the God of Israel is also the God of Egypt and of Assyria remains no less true today. Judaism's hope and trust in God's promise to plant the people once again on their own soil also includes the further hope that all nations will turn to friendship. Nations will live together when they learn to serve together, responding to the demand of the historical situation.

Heschel views the restoration of Israel to national statehood as a personal challenge to all Jews, demanding creative thought and creative action. It is ultimately a religious challenge that must be seen in terms of the prophetic vision of the redemption of all humankind. It is the obligation of each believing Jew to participate in this continuing process of redemption by helping to bring about the triumph of justice over power, of compassion over callousness, of humility over arrogance so that all of human living may be permeated by a deeper awareness of the divine Presence.[41]

JUDAISM AND CHRISTIANITY

We should not leave Heschel's understanding of Judaism without delving a bit further into his thinking on the relationships and the difficulties between Judaism and Christianity. In an article written for *The Christian Century* in December 1963, Heschel criticizes the many attempts of the early Church to foster in a deliberate manner its contrast with Judaism.[42] Instead of acknowledging its vast indebtedness to Judaism, the Church emphasized its differences. There were many reasons for this, not the least being the expansion of Christianity into the Gentile world of Greece and Rome. The result was a steady process of de-Judaizing the Church. This has affected the inner life of the Church as well as its relationship to Israel past and present. Judaism, the mother of Christianity, was considered to be stubborn and blind; some of the early Christian theologians wrote as if they suffered from a "spiritual Oedipus complex." As a result, the Christian message, originally considered to be an affirmation and culmination of the Jewish message, became instead its repudiation and negation; the new covenant marked the abolition of the old covenant. Instead of acknowledging common roots and common ancestry, the early Church Fathers more often pointed to the contrast and contradiction. Thus we have the erroneous ideas, still prevalent among many Christians, that Judaism upholds a God of wrath and vengeance, while Christianity preaches a God of love; that Judaism is a religion of enslavement to the law, while Christianity is a religion of freedom; that Judaism's outlook is narrow and particularistic, while Christianity's outlook is universal; that Judaism is a religion of fear and punishment, while Christianity is a religion of mercy and forgiveness. Heschel considers this process of de-Judaization as gradually leading the Church to abandon its origins and to alter seriously the core of its message. The Church must decide for itself whether its roots are in Judaism or in pagan Hellenism, and whether it is to be the extension of Judaism or the antithesis of Judaism.[43]

Certainly the Church was clear in its rejection of Marcion, the second-century theologian who denied the relevance of the Hebrew

Bible for Christian revelation. Marcion held that Christianity ought to be free from every vestige of Judaism; the God revealed by Jesus is opposed to the God of the prophets. However, although the Church placed the teaching of Marcion under anathema in the year 144, the spirit of Marcion continues to be alive in Christianity. There is still a strong tendency in some quarters of Christianity, despite the dedicated work of generations of Scripture scholars, to stress the discontinuity between Old and New Testaments, as though the God of Israel was not also the God and Father of Jesus. The opening verse of Matthew's Gospel refers to Jesus as son of David and son of Abraham, yet some scholars are so fascinated by the Hellenistic aspects of Christianity that one would think, in Heschel's view, that Jesus was born in Delphi or Athens instead of in Bethlehem, the city of David. For such scholars God's revelation seems to be everywhere except in the words of the Hebrew Bible.

There is a further problem that comes with modern biblical scholarship: we are sometimes so fascinated about what we can learn *about* the Bible that we tend to pass over what we should learn *from* the Bible. We know so much of the historical, cultural, and literary background of the Bible, yet we often fail to grasp the message of the Bible. We are not open to God's presence in its sacred words. Such openness comes about only through care, involvement, prayer. But the Bible is still with us, and it is always possible to hear and respond to its demands.

Heschel fears that Christianity is sometimes too preoccupied with the heavenly or eschatological aspect of revelation to the consequent neglect of the teaching and of the historical demands of revelation. But it is in the historical sphere that Jesus' teaching on love is to be fulfilled. Yet where there is too much concern with the heavenly realm, with personal salvation, there is a tendency to withdraw from the historical realm and from the concrete demands imposed by Christian teaching, and there is a slackening of concern for the secular and social aspects of human living. The consciousness of the Christian concerned with personal goals is often dulled to the social ills that afflict our society, just as the pious Jew may be too preoccupied with ritual to be sensitive to these same social ills. The world is astir, but Church and Synagogue are often caught up in trivialities. Both Church and Synagogue remain in permanent need of the prophetic call to conversion, in need of those who struggle on the front line to accomplish God's will for our society here and now. The totality of human existence must be exposed to the biblical challenge. There must be an end to cheap grace. Jew and Christian must recognize that religious living is "arduous and full of demands."[44]

In 1965 and 1966 Heschel further developed his thoughts on Jewish–Christian relations in two important addresses, one at Union Theological Seminary where he was the Harry Emerson Fosdick Visiting Professor and the other at the annual convention of the Rabbinical Assembly.[45] This was a period notable for the decree of Vatican II, *Nostra Aetate*, which spoke directly to the relationship of the Catholic Church with Judaism. Rabbi Heschel had earlier accepted an invitation from Pope Paul VI to discuss the problems of Catholic–Jewish relations, especially as they might bear on the deliberations of the Council.

In these addresses Heschel is concerned primarily with what unites Jew and Christian. Jew and Christian have different religious commitments, yet they may meet one another first of all as human beings, with common fears and hopes and longings, with a capacity for compassion and trust and understanding. "My first task in every encounter," says Heschel, "is to comprehend the personhood of the human being I face, to sense the kinship of being human. . . ." Each person is indeed a disclosure of the divine, so that in meeting another human being one encounters God's image, one is caught up in the presence of God. Jew and Christian may differ in matters that are very sacred to each, but each remains in God's image. Their commitments may differ, their conceptions of God may differ, but that does not destroy the kinship of being human. They are united in a common accountability before God, in being precious to God and objects of His concern. The demands placed upon each are different; their proclamations are different; but they confront together the same arrogance, the same iniquity, the same agony. Dogmas and forms of worship may differ, but it is the same God who is worshipped. They share together many of the same sacred writings, many of the same commandments, a common commitment to justice and mercy, and a common sense of helplessness and contrition.[46]

Heschel repeatedly asks how he, as a Jew, can relate spiritually to Christianity, not as a doctrine or an institution, but as a body of human beings throughout the world who worship God as disciples of Jesus. Obviously, in facing the teachings and the claims of the Church, Jews and Christians are strangers standing in disagreement. Yet there are other areas where Jew and Christian meet as sons and daughters, brothers and sisters. We are together in praising God, in obeying Him, in hearkening to His commands. Interfaith, then, demands above all faith. Only out of genuine involvement in the unending drama between God and humankind can Jew and Christian assist each other in coming to an understanding of the historical situation. Interfaith betokens a depth of faith, not an absence of faith; it is not an undertaking for those of shallow learning or immature spirituality. Dialogue between Jew and Christian is not meant to lead to syncretism or to a type of conformity found by depriving Judaism and Christianity of that which is most sacred and unique to each. Nor should dialogue degenerate into debate in an effort to prove the other to be wrong. Any genuine dialogue between Jew and Christian should be aimed at mutual enrichment, with respect for one another's faith-perspective and not with the silent hope that the other will abandon his or her faith-perspective. Thus while fostering cooperation, reverence, and understanding for each other, Jew and Christian must preserve their own individuality. Jew and Christian are committed to contradictory claims, and so there will always be profound disagreements, but such disagreements can be had without bitterness or arrogance or disrespect. Across the chasm Jew and Christian can reach out to embrace one another.

Christians must give serious thought to the need to reverse the de-Judaizing process that began in the early history of the Church; the children must stop calling their mother blind. A world without Israel would be a world without the God of Israel. Jews must ponder the role that Christianity has played and is playing in God's plan for the redemption of all the nations. Judaism is the mother of Christianity and thus has a stake in its history; a mother cannot ignore her child. Jews should acknowledge "with a grateful heart" that it was the Church that made the Hebrew Bible available to all humankind and who brought to the Gentiles the knowledge of the God of Israel. Christians in turn should recognize that Jews in loyalty to their own tradition have a role to play for Christianity by preserving and teaching the riches of the Hebrew scriptures and by aiding in the struggle against the many remnants of the Marcionite heresy still present within the Church. Jews and Christians can help one another in overcoming callousness, in opening hearts to the demands of the Bible, in responding to the challenges of the prophets.[47]

Heschel questions whether religious uniformity is either possible or desirable in our world. The prospect of all humanity embracing one form of religion clearly remains an eschatological hope. The task of preparing for the kingdom of God here and now, however, demands a variety of talents and commitments. It may also require diverse ways of understanding the demands of revelation and different forms of ritual and devotion. The voice of God reaches humankind in a variety of ways; revelation is always adapted to the capacity of the human spirit. And human faith, our response to revelation, is an endless pilgrimage. It is never final; it is always on the way. Holiness is possible wherever the human person stands; it is not the monopoly of any single religious tradition.

Many Jewish teachers have acknowledged Christianity to be a preparation for the coming of the Messiah. This enables Judaism to consider Christianity as continuing to be a viable entity and to acknowledge more easily that Christianity fits into the divine plan of redemption. Christianity, however, often looks upon Judaism simply as a preparation for the Gospel, with the consequence that Judaism is seen as no longer viable; it has outlived its usefulness. Jews are thus ripe candidates for conversion. Heschel sees this so-called "mission to the Jews" as an attempt to have Jews betray the fellowship and dignity and sacred history of their people; it represents an effort to bring Judaism to self-extinction. Such an attitude destroys any hope for dialogue between Jew and Christian. Dialogue demands a mutual esteem for the other's faith and integrity; it is not a confrontation for the sake of conversion. One of Heschel's best responses to such a demeaning outlook is contained in an account of his last meeting with the renowned Jesuit theologian and ecumenist Rev. Gustave Weigel on the evening of January 2, 1964. The two men were together in Rabbi Heschel's study; the next morning Father Weigel would die of a heart attack. Both men were genuinely open to one another in prayer and contrition, acknowledging their deficiencies, their failures, their hopes. Then Rabbi Heschel spoke:

Is it really the will of God that there be no more Judaism in the world? Would it really be the triumph of God if the scrolls of the

Torah would no more be taken out of the Ark and the Torah no more read in the synagogue, our ancient Hebrew prayers in which Jesus himself worshipped no more recited, the Passover Seder no more celebrated in our lives, the law of Moses no more observed in our homes? Would it really be *ad majorem Dei gloriam* to have a world without Jews?[48]

This question, posed by Heschel to Father Weigel, is addressed to all who stand outside the pale of Judaism and especially to Christians whose faith is rooted so deeply in the Hebrew Bible. The fullness of God's design for humankind remains a mystery before which we can only stand in awe. It would be as arrogant for the Christian to insist that Jews are stubborn and blind for their refusal to accept Jesus as the Messiah, as it would be for the Jew to refuse to acknowledge the glory and holiness evident in so many Christian lives down through the centuries. Both must hearken to the words of the Psalmist: "The Lord is near to all who call upon Him, to all who call upon Him in truth" (Ps 145:18).[49]

Heschel underscores in a clear and simple fashion how much Jew and Christian need one another, how much they can learn from one another. We live in an era when Jew and Christian meet no longer to refute one another, but to assist one another, to cooperate both in ventures of the highest academic and scholarly level and in the search within their common tradition for those treasures of devotion and prayer, for those insights into justice and mercy, which would be of benefit to all people.

Both Christian and Jew, along with every person of good will, can learn much from the patient tolerance, the scholarly wisdom, and the thoughtful sensitivity of Abraham Heschel. Having examined some of the more pertinent themes of his spirituality, I shall attempt to synthesize them in a manner which, I hope, will reflect with fidelity the thrust of Heschel's thought and at the same time speak to the needs of our age.

NOTES

1. *God in Search of Man*, pp. 200–201, 416, 421–22, 425.
2. *Insecurity of Freedom*, pp. 202, 205, 215, 218; *Israel*, pp. 94, 132–33.
3. *The Prophets*, I 32–33; *God in Search of Man*, pp. 425–26.

4. *The Prophets*, I 53, 153, 156–57.

5. *God in Search of Man*, p. 214; see above, chap. 3, pp. 89ff.

6. *The Prophets*, I 32; *Man Is Not Alone*, pp. 241–42.

7. *The Prophets*, I 71–73, 78.

8. Ibid., 60.

9. *God in Search of Man*, pp. 215–17, 426.

10. *Man Is Not Alone*, pp. 266, 271; *God in Search of Man*, p. 49; *Man's Quest for God*, p. 132; *Israel*, p. 145.

11. *Man's Quest for God*, pp. 109, 111; *God in Search of Man*, pp. 293–94.

12. *God in Search of Man*, pp. 281–87; *Man's Quest for God*, p. 104.

13. *God in Search of Man*, pp. 287–92, 361–62, 378; *Man's Quest for God*, p. 68.

14. *God in Search of Man*, pp. 295–300.

15. Ibid., pp. 300, 306–10.

16. Ibid., pp. 310–15, 320–28.

17. Ibid., pp. 336–39.

18. Ibid., pp. 339–40; *Man's Quest for God*, p. 68.

19. *God in Search of Man*, pp. 340–41. Heschel touches here on an area which is critical not only for Judaism but for Christianity as well and which is found throughout the history of religion: namely, what is often called the "coincidence of opposites." See the fine synthesis by Ewert Cousins in *Bonaventure and the Coincidence of Opposites* (Chicago: Franciscan Herald Press, 1978), esp. chap. 1.

20. *God in Search of Man*, pp. 345, 403–406; *Insecurity of Freedom*, pp. 141–42.

21. *Man's Quest for God*, pp. 106–107. Heschel admits that the insistence on a fixed pattern and regularity does tend to stifle spontaneity; Judaism's "greatest problem" is how to avoid this. The conflict between fidelity to order and the requirements of kavanah will always be a dilemma for the pious Jew. Cf. ibid., pp. 35, 65.

22. *God in Search of Man*, pp. 350–59, 375; *Man Is Not Alone*, p. 270; *Man's Quest for God*, p. 114.

23. *Man's Quest for God*, pp. 21, 124–35. It is precisely at this point that one may question Heschel's understanding of God's revelation to Israel, for there seems to be some ambivalence in his writings. For an earlier treatment of Heschel's thought on revelation, cf. above, pp. 66–75. To what extent does a mitsvah directly reflect the revelation of God's will, and to what extent does it reflect our human attempt, guided by God's grace, to understand and to express the revelation of God's will? Heschel does not provide a fully structured theology of revelation. His thought on this subject is found primarily in the second volume of *The Prophets* and in

chap. 27 of *God in Search of Man*. Heschel speaks of the Bible as "the word of God *and* man, a record of both revelation and response" (*God in Search of Man*, p. 260), yet in dealing with the mitsvoth he comes closer to what Catholic theologians would call a "propositional" view of revelation, a view that today is considered to have more weaknesses than strengths. For a concise view of Catholic thought on this matter, cf. Dermot Lane, *The Experience of God* (New York: Paulist, 1981) and Avery Dulles, s.j., *Models of Revelation* (Garden City, N.Y.: Doubleday, 1983).

24. *Man's Quest for God*, pp. 135–37; *God in Search of Man*, p. 407.

25. *Man's Quest for God*, pp. 141–44.

26. Letter of July 5, 1924; the correspondence of Buber and Rosenzweig is found in *On Jewish Learning*, ed. Nahum Glatzer (New York: Schocken, 1955), pp. 109ff. See also Martin Buber, "Replies to My Critics," in *The Philosophy of Martin Buber*, edd. Paul A. Schilpp and Maurice Friedman (LaSalle, Ill.: Open Court, 1967), p. 724; and especially Maurice Friedman, *Martin Buber's Life and Work: The Middle Years, 1923–1945* (New York: Dutton, 1983), chap. 3.

27. Cf. *God in Search of Man*, pp. 273–74.

28. *The Sabbath*, pp. 8–15, 29–31, 101.

29. Ibid., pp. 28–29, 48, 89.

30. Ibid., pp. 51–54, 60, 80.

31. Ibid., pp. 89–91; *God in Search of Man*, 418–19.

32. *The Sabbath*, pp. 96–100. Although the terminology is different, it is at this point that Heschel's thought most closely parallels that of Martin Buber. Where Heschel opposes a world of space and temporality to a world of time, Buber opposes space and time to presence. Heschel's "time" and Buber's "presence" are almost identical. For example, Buber writes: "Presence is not what is evanescent and passes but what confronts us, waiting and enduring" (*I and Thou*, ed. and trans. Walter Kaufmann [New York: Scribner's, 1970], p. 64).

33. *The Sabbath*, pp. 100–101.

34. *God in Search of Man*, pp. 313, 379–80; *Insecurity of Freedom*, pp. 138–39.

35. *Insecurity of Freedom*, pp. 134–35, 145–46; *Passion for Truth*, p. 300.

36. *Israel*, pp. 155–59.

37. *Man's Quest for God*, p. 151.

38. *Israel*, pp. 100–104, 119–21, 147–49.

39. Ibid., pp. 55–59, 94–97, 139–41.

40. Ibid., pp. 59–67.

41. Ibid., pp. 178, 182–86, 211–25.

42. "Protestant Renewal: A Jewish View," *The Christian Century*, 80,

No. 49 (December 4, 1963), 1501–24 (repr. in *Insecurity of Freedom,* pp. 168–78).

43. *Insecurity of Freedom,* pp. 168–70.

44. Ibid., pp. 170–75.

45. "No Religion Is an Island," 117–31, and "From Mission to Dialogue?" *Conservative Judaism,* 21, No. 3 (Spring 1967), 1–11.

46. "No Religion Is an Island," 120–22; "From Mission to Dialogue?" 4–6.

47. "No Religion Is an Island," 123–26; "From Mission to Dialogue?" 7–8.

48. "No Religion Is an Island," 126–31; "From Mission to Dialogue?" 9–10.

49. "No Religion Is an Island," 129; "From Mission to Dialogue?" 10.

6

Holiness
Through Humanness

THE SPIRITUAL VISION that Abraham Heschel has left us is one that in many aspects can be shared by all men and women of good will, but especially by both Jews and Christians. Speaking and writing from the context of his own prayerful relationship with God and his intense experience of the human condition, Rabbi Heschel reaches across the religious boundaries that so often divide men and women and reveals a common ground that can be trod by all. His insights into prayer, faith, and the Bible are relevant to anyone who seeks to live on a level that is at once authentically human and authentically spiritual, for he has demonstrated, as have few others of this era, how the human and the holy are so essentially interrelated.

There is clearly a prophetic ring both in Heschel's writings and in his life. He himself admitted that the many years given to his study on the prophets, both in the earlier German version and more importantly in the expanded English version, were years that changed his life. "I've learned from the prophets that I have to be involved in the affairs of man, in the affairs of suffering man."[1] Throughout the 1960s until his death in 1972 Heschel became increasingly active in many of the key social and political movements of the time, from participation in civil rights marches and presidential campaigns to Viet Nam protests and concern for the problems of the aging. It was as though he underwent in his own life the same metamorphosis as, in one of his earliest publications, he had traced in the life of the great twelfth-century Jewish philosopher, Maimonides. In the last years of a life that had been so deeply immersed in intellectual pursuits, Maimonides underwent a transformation, turning from metaphysics to medicine, from contemplation to action, from speculation about God to imitation of God. Heschel attributes the change in Maimonides to the pull within him of the prophetic ideal to actualize moral and religious ideals through one's deeds. Instead of defining human perfection as purely intellectual, Maimonides saw the ultimate end of humankind as *"the imitation of God's ways* and actions, namely, kindness, justice, righteousness." Only in his last years was Maimonides finally able to unify contemplation of God with service to others.[2] This is an ideal that is often described in Christian spirituality as "contemplation in action" or "finding God in all things"; one becomes more deeply united with God through all that one does. This is also the ideal that permeates much of what Heschel has to say about spirituality.

I shall begin with Heschel's understanding of "the pious man" as found in the last section of *Man Is Not Alone*. This is an attempt to picture the spiritual person who is not dependent upon any specific religious commitment. To this I shall add some ideas from a specifically prophetic or biblical spirituality as found both in *Man Is Not Alone* and especially in *God in Search of Man*. Then I shall look at two divergent views of this prophetic spirituality as found in the lives of Rabbi Israel ben Eliezer of Mezbizh, the Baal Shem Tov, and Rabbi Menahem Mendl of Kotzk, the Kotzker, as found primarily in Heschel's last major work, *A Passion for Truth*. I shall then point out some of the principal characteristics of the community that for Heschel represented an ideal of Jewish spirituality, the Ashkenazi Jews of Eastern Europe, the community into which Heschel himself was born and in whose tradition he stood. Obviously there are many similar traits in each of these perspectives, but I shall try to focus on those characteristics that might contribute to an overall understanding of the spirituality which Heschel bequeaths to us.

THE PIOUS MAN

When Heschel examines piety apart from the vantage point of any specific faith-commitment, he sees it as a "spiritual way of thinking and living" which points to something beyond itself. It refers us to something that transcends the human, that goes beyond what is visibly at hand; it is a "perpetual inner attitude" that permeates the whole of oneself and the whole of what one does, one's deeds and words and thoughts. It is a quality of life that reveals itself in one's character and in one's actions. Piety brings with it the realization that the horizon of reality reaches beyond the span of one's own life or nation or era. The pious person perceives something of ultimate significance in the common and the simple, the "stillness of the eternal" in the rush of the passing moment. Piety brings one to compliance with destiny, the only course of life worth living. Piety for Heschel is "faith translated into life," focusing one's concern on the concern of God; this then becomes the controlling factor of the whole of one's life.

Piety is directly opposed to selfishness; it seeks to bring all our insatiable and egoistic inner forces under the control of God. The pious person moves toward "self forgetfulness and an inner anonymity of service," making no claim to a reward. Piety certainly involves self-control and self-denial, but its essence consists simply in "regard for the transcendent" and in "devotion to God." The pious one attempts to lift the human to the level of the spiritual by allowing the self to be actuated by the sacred and by striving to be identified with every movement in the world which tends toward the divine. Piety aims at realizing and verifying the transcendent in human life, not merely encountering the divine, but abiding by God, agreeing with His will, echoing His words, responding to His voice. As an attitude toward God and the world, toward persons and things, toward life and destiny, piety discloses the purest elements in our human venture and reveals what is most delicate in the human soul.[3]

Piety may be identified with a deep awareness of the "presence and nearness of God." Always and everywhere the pious person lives as though in God's sight. The pious person is immersed in the presence of God, a presence that is, as it were, unavoidable and inescapable and that is recognized as a never-ending source of tranquillity and mercy and compassion. No special communication from God is necessary in order to become aware of His presence; no crisis is necessary to validate the meaningfulness of that presence. Each simple occurrence brings with it a hint or reminder of the divine. Piety is described by Heschel as simply "a life compatible with God's presence."[4]

In society today utilization has so often become the measure of all things; we value things and people by the work they can do, by the profit they render, by the pleasure they confer. We rob things and people of their real dignity; we desecrate them by placing them in the service of our own vested interests. By enslaving others we plunge ourselves into slavery; by treating others as instruments, we ourselves become cogs in the system we have created. Piety rejects this prevailing mentality, for it alerts us to the spiritual value and dignity of the whole of creation; it is a choice of appreciation over manipulation. The pious person approaches reality with reverence, recognizing that in every event "there is something sacred at stake." Piety is alert to the preciousness and value of all things, to the trace of the divine that can never be completely concealed; it is rooted, therefore, in the attitude of wonder and awe, so essential to Heschel's concept of the human and of the holy as discussed earlier in this study.

The pious person makes no claim to anything and seeks no personal advantage from anything, and so there is a genuine peace with life; suffering or anguish or failure is seen as part of the totality of life, each bearing a spiritual potential. This does not betoken complacency or fatalism; on the contrary, there is a keen sensitivity to pain and suffering and adversity both in one's own life and in the lives of others. Compassion is a greater response than grief, and because of its farsightedness one does not overestimate momentary misfortune. Thus gloom has no place in the outlook of the pious person, for gloom implies that one has a right to something more suitable and more pleasing; it implies a rejection of reality instead of an appreciation of reality. The gloomy person perceives hostility everywhere and hence has no awareness of how illegitimate his complaints are.[5]

Piety means then that we can never take life for granted, that life is a challenge from which we can never be free; it is a reminder that we can never discharge this responsibility for the whole of life by fleeing into some type of spiritual realm. We meet this responsibility by our life and by our deeds, which either implement or impede God's concern for our world. All of life and all of nature belong to God, so the pious person does not grumble or despair when calamity strikes, for the whole of reality comes from God and is a concern of God. Piety leads one to view whatever is at one's disposal as gift and not as possession. Possession implies an exclusion of others; to insist on possession is to embark on a path of isolation and loneliness. Gift, on the other hand, implies the love of the giver; in looking upon all that comes one's way as gift, one experiences the love of God again and again intervening in one's life.

Heschel views piety as bringing us to the point where, for the sake of God and others, we deprive ourselves of things that are precious and desirable. Such sacrifice is a form of thanksgiving, returning to God what we have received by employing it in His service. The purpose of sacrifice is not to render oneself poor; poverty of itself is not a good. Rather in yielding all to God, we create space for Him in our hearts.[6]

Piety, finally, implies a resolve to follow the will of God. Life becomes a mandate, a task, a command, presenting an ongoing flow of opportunity for service. Every experience represents an appeal, a clue to a new duty, a means of renewing one's devotion. The will to serve shapes one's entire conduct; the great desire is to place one's whole life at the disposal of God. For Heschel this is the heart of piety and the very meaning of human living. Life is enhanced in value when one is engaged in fulfilling purposes that lead one beyond oneself, meeting a concern of God, revering the spirit of God, fulfilling the will of God. It is God's will and God's service that matter, not one's own perfection or salvation. To know that one's destiny is to serve is to achieve the deepest wisdom. When one lives one's life as an answer to God's concern, death becomes a "homecoming." For eternity does not imply a perpetual future but a perpetual presence. "The world to come is not only a hereafter but also a *herenow*." For the pious person the meaning of death is "ultimate self-dedication to the divine." Death should not be distorted by a craving for immortality; rather it ought to be one's act of reciprocity to God for the gift of life. For the pious person "it is a privilege to die."[7]

What Heschel has written in this section of *Man Is Not Alone* is indeed the outline of a spirituality that could be followed by persons of all faiths. We will examine now those aspects of a more prophetic or biblically oriented spirituality that might add to the general framework already given.

A PROPHETIC SPIRITUALITY

Any explanation of a prophetic or biblical spirituality must spring from that which Heschel calls the "cardinal attitude" of the religious Jew, namely, awe. The attitude that is basic to human living, that is basic to faith, is precisely the attitude so central to a biblical understanding of creation and to the prophetic spirit. Awe precedes faith and is the basis for faith. Only when guided by awe can we be worthy of faith; it is a prerequisite for wisdom. "Forfeit your sense of awe, let your conceit diminish your ability to revere, and the universe becomes a market place for you." We would no longer be responding to the presence which confronts us. Awe is evoked as one moves into harmony with the mystery of reality; thus a moment of awe is a "moment of self-consecration." It is the moment of our greatest insight, the moment of our becoming aware of transcendent meaning and hence of transcendent demand.[8]

Thus awe is closely allied with another primary thrust of a prophetic spirituality, namely, the demand to overcome complacency. If one should attempt to list those attitudes that have no place in the soul of a prophet, Heschel writes, "contentment would be mentioned first." Self-satisfaction is the abyss the prophets consistently warn us about. Prophetic spirituality demands that we constantly strive to be more than what we already are. All creativity springs from this seed of "endless discontent." Yearning for what is ultimately unattainable, one should never be content with the world as it is or with the self that one is. Any awareness of God brings with it an end to self-righteousness and to a smug satisfaction with our achievements. Thus Heschel sees the aim of prophetic spirituality as the fomenting of a discontent with present goals and achievements, the fomenting of a "craving that knows no satisfaction." It plants within us a seed of "endless yearning," teaching us to be restless, to strive continually for the utmost, to be content with what we have but never with what we are. In Heschel's mind one *is* what one yearns for, and the great authentic yearning imbedded in the human spirit is the yearning to praise and to serve. Unfortunately, such ultimate yearnings are often crowded out by our vested self-interests. Our authentic goals thus remain unvoiced or unappreciated. Religion must articulate what is unvoiced. And since the person who is self-satisfied has never known true yearning, prophetic piety seeks to bring about a genuine "dissatisfaction with the self."[9]

The yearning and ability to transcend or surpass the self play an important role in Heschel's prophetic spirituality. They are essential to the uniqueness of the human person, to the basis of religion, and to the heart of spirituality. The power to rise above one's needs and desires, to transcend selfish motives, is unique to humankind. In order to be human, one must be more than human. Heschel repeats this point frequently in his writings. It would be a grave mistake to assume that our destiny is simply to be human, for the human person is one who is "called upon to be more than he is." The task given to us is to move continually beyond the status quo; we must never stand still. If we ignore this tension between the self as it is and the "beyond-the-self," we doom ourselves to a fool's paradise. If we despair of this ability to transcend the self, we become mired in cynicism. The prophets demand that we love God wholeheartedly with a love that transcends all self-interest; such a love then must be possible for us.

Yet there are no simple answers and no easy solutions for achieving this prophetic ideal. The well-trod ways "lead into swamps." What comes to us easily "is not worth a straw." Both psychologically and experientially this prophetic ideal seems to be impossible. Can we ever love God wholeheartedly? Can we ever do the good for its own sake with no thought of reward or personal gain? It is so difficult to free ourselves from selfish interests; any serious self-reflection reveals self-love present "in every cell of our brain." Our vested interests are "more numerous than locusts." Even if we begin to act out of a purely selfless motive, we so easily fall prey to the vanity and pride of directing an act solely toward God. Seemingly our best efforts are doomed to be tinged with some degree of selfishness. The people of the Bible were greatly concerned over the question of integrity, so much so that an entire book, the Book of Job, was given over to this question. Job stands forth as the person truly capable of a selfless piety, but only after undergoing dreadful suffering. The ordeal of Job underscores, for Heschel, how basic and serious this problem of integrity was for Israel.[10]

The art of living spiritually is the art of dealing with one's needs and thus transcending them. Character is shaped by the way one deals with one's passions and desires. The human person has the capacity to convert and to modify needs according to the goals of his own choosing. The freer we are the more we regard our lives as oriented toward chosen goals, not as imprisoned by fixed needs. Selfish persons simply adjust their goals to meet their needs; they are ever ready to conform to their needs. Free persons weigh and compare their needs and will choose to satisfy those that contribute to the enrichment of higher values; their motto is not "needs justify the ends" but rather "ends justify the needs." In order to forgo the gratification of one need for the sake of another or for the sake of a moral goal, free persons must be to some extent persons who are independent of needs. The more we ignore higher or ultimate goals, the more we will tend to pursue selfish or vested interests, weaving a web of needs out of thoughtless habits and selfish desires. A prophetic spirituality does not necessarily demand the elimination of needs and satisfaction. For Judaism the carnal is not evil, something to be annihilated, but something to be surpassed. The enemy is not in human flesh but in the human heart. We are not required to abandon this life and turn our back on this world. There is no conflict between the divine and the secular, between the holy and the human. If we could glimpse the eternal in our everyday deeds, we would recognize that the "road to the sacred leads through the secular."

Heschel is quick to point out that elimination of the self "is in itself no virtue." If such were the case, suicide would be the apex of moral living. Yet obviously discipline and sacrifice are needed, and the value of sacrifice is measured not so much by what is "given up" as by the goal one is striving for. In Hebrew, Heschel reminds us, sacrifice means to draw near, to approach. Our human task, therefore, is not to renounce life but to bring life closer to God. This is accomplished especially through our relationships to other persons as images of God. We strive not for self-denial but for the affirmation of others as selves and for the capacity to perceive their needs and problems. This does not imply a self-effacing attitude; what is effaced is our own callousness.

The beginning, then, of growth in prophetic piety lies in establishing a "concern for the non-self." Our spiritual dignity consists in our attachment to goals that lie not within but beyond ourselves. Regard for the self is not evil, but it becomes evil when self is set up as the ultimate goal, when one's personal interests are enhanced at the expense of others. In such cases we must recognize our inner enslavement to the ego and our consequent lack of concern for others and then try to rise beyond the level of self-interest again and again. Self-transcendence is never achieved once for all. We must indeed strive, in the words of Micah, "to act justly, to love tenderly and to walk humbly" with our God, but we do this with the awareness that we are so often incapable of real disentanglement from the self. This should not lead to discouragement. Rather we should heed Heschel's words: "To be contrite at our failures is holier than to be complacent in perfection." Hence his insistence that the way to pure intention, to transcendence of self-interest, is paved with good deeds. Prophetic spirituality, as with prophetic faith, is achieved by a "leap of action." We do what we can with the firm assurance that the rest is completed by God.[11]

Heschel's teaching on the value of deeds is primarily given in the context of the Jewish law. The Jew is called to follow not only the voice of conscience but also the demand of the law. The fulfillment of the law is seen by the Jew as his response to the demands of God. Through the law the life of the religious Jew becomes one of service through agreement with God's will. The faith of the Jew leads to an acceptance of an order that "determines all of life." Thus no time is ever wasted. Life may be running out, but the law "takes us by the hand and leads us home to an order of eternity." Heschel's deeds, then, are basically the fulfillment of the mitzvah.

Nevertheless, there is a much broader interpretation of the meaning of good deeds apart from a particular faith-commitment, as noted above. The deed may be viewed as fulfillment of one's concern for God's ends or purposes in this world, as one's response to God's demands upon one's life, as one's recognition of being a need of God, as one's yearning to live a life of service. It is through deeds that one transcends self and expresses concern for other selves. We achieve fullness of being through fellowship, through our care for others. The index of our humanity is precisely the degree to which we transcend ourselves and become sensitive to the sufferings and needs of others. In other words, Heschel is reminding us that the good deed, even for the Jew, is not limited to the fulfillment of the mitzvah.[12] Christian readers will see this very much in line with the teaching of Jesus as found, for example, in his parable of the Last Judgment (Mt 25:31–46):

> Then the king will say "Come, you blessed of my Father. . . . For when I was hungry, you gave me food; when thirsty, you gave me drink; when I was a stranger, you took me in. . . ." Then the righteous will reply, "Lord, when was it that we saw you hungry and fed you, or thirsty and gave you drink, a stranger and took you home . . . ?" And the king will answer, "I tell you, whenever you did this for one of my brothers here, however humble, you did it for me."

Christian spirituality too demands Heschel's "leap of action" in order to transcend self and to grow in the concern for others.

The "grand premise" of all religion, in Heschel's view, is that we are able to surpass ourselves and our self-interest, and this ability is the "essence of freedom." Freedom does not consist simply in being what we want to be, for what we want to be is frequently determined by forces outside of ourselves. Nor does it consist simply in our will's deciding our actions, for again the will is often determined by forces beyond its control. To affirm freedom is to affirm that a person can act in a way not determined by antecedent factors. The truly free person is a "partisan of the self-surpassing." Freedom is the capacity for "going out of self" and rising to a "higher level of existence," and thus it is an act of "spiritual ecstasy" implying the power "to live spiritually." The free person is one who is not enslaved by self or by circumstances but who can creatively transcend both. That is why one of the tasks of prophetic religion is to challenge our accepted values and to overcome our complacency. It seeks to awaken and to foster within us the will to be more than what we are; it reminds us that humanity and religion are unfinished tasks.

Although we all are endowed with freedom, we actuate our freedom only in "rare creative moments." Freedom is found in the act of transcending the self when one no longer regards the self as one's own end. Freedom is "an act of self-engagement to the spirit"; it is, therefore, a "spiritual event." Thus, spirituality and freedom are closely intertwined in Heschel's thought.[13]

The spiritual person understands the continuing demands of religion and humanity. Religious existence represents a challenge rather than a catalogue of ready-made answers. The grave error of any religious teaching is a claim to finality, as if the whole truth of God could be captured once for all, as if God had nothing more to say to us. We need the outburst of prophetic demand lest our lives become fossilized. The prophetic spirit remains critical of all complacency. It foments discontent and smashes idols. It began with Abraham's saying "No" to life as it had been and breaking away. It encourages us to say "No" to all that pretends to be triumphant or final or ultimate. The ultimate, writes Heschel, is a challenge, not an assertion. We must accept the challenge and become involved ever again in transcending self and in bringing our lives closer to God.[14]

There is a certain dynamism and concreteness which permeates Heschel's prophetic spirituality and which blends in well with what he has set down about the "pious man" in *Man Is Not Alone*. There is an added emphasis here which, while based on Heschel's understanding of Judaism, remains accessible to all who share a respect for the Hebrew Bible as a privileged locus of God's dealings with humankind. Obviously there will be diverse ways of spelling out this spirituality in our own lives, depending both upon the circumstances in which we live and upon the degree of importance which we give to certain aspects of this spirituality. Heschel was keenly aware of this diversity because of his own close relationship with the two sharply contrasting figures of the Hasidic movement mentioned above, the Baal Shem Tov and the Kotzker.

THE BAAL SHEM AND THE KOTZKER

In his Introduction to *A Passion for Truth* Heschel tells of his grandfather Reb Abraham Joshua Heschel, the great rabbi of the Hasidim in Mezbizh in the Ukraine. So faithfully did his grandfather echo the joyful enthusiasm of Hasidism's founder, the Baal Shem Tov, who had died in 1760, that many believed the Baal Shem had come back to life in him. In his childhood imaginations, Heschel often journeyed to this ancestral region of Mezbizh, for this is where he felt so much at home.

Yet at an early age another Hasidic force entered Heschel's life, one vastly different from that of his grandfather or of the Baal Shem. It was the stern and somber teachings of Reb Menahem Mendl of Kotzk, the "Kotzker." Unwittingly at first, Heschel allowed these two forces to struggle for domination in his life. "Both spoke convincingly," Heschel writes, "and each proved right on one level yet questionable on another." Although at ease with the Baal Shem's teachings, he was "driven" by the Kotzker's. The Baal Shem stood for joy and wonder and exaltation; the Kotzker represented anxiety, consternation, dismay. Heschel could not escape from either approach and respected them both. If his heart was in Mezbizh, it is obvious that his mind was enthralled by the Kotzker. The Baal Shem uncovered immense depths of meaning in the world, while the Kotzker uncovered deep-seated absurdities. The Baal Shem was wont to worship in song; the Kotzker, in silence. The Baal Shem illuminated the dark hours of life, while the Kotzker warned of approaching darkness. The Baal Shem emphasized the mystery of life, the power of love and compassion to heal brokenness; the Kotzker underscored the hollowness of life and the ever-present temptation to abandon one's authenticity. While the Baal Shem dispelled gloom, the Kotzker deepened it.

Heschel saw clearly the advantages and disadvantages of each of these approaches to spiritual living. The way of the Kotzker, uncompromising in its search for honesty and integrity, could be destructive of oneself and of others. The way of the Baal Shem, with its enthusiastic outburst of joy and fervor, could blind one to the tragic aspects of reality and lead to a utopian unrealism. To deny the valid insights of either approach is to court disaster; each deserves further elaboration.[15]

When the Baal Shem rose to prominence among the Jews of Eastern Europe during the first half of the eighteenth century, Judaism was in a state of decline and despair. The Baal Shem attacked the despair by teaching Jews to cherish all that is. To deprecate the world is to deprecate its Creator. All creation is endowed with dignity and meaning. There is a divine spark at the core of all that exists, and it is Judaism's task to redeem this hidden radiance. God is everywhere, and thus the divine radiance might be experienced at any time in any place.

The Baal Shem combined a deep reverence for God with a genuine affection for all men and women. Love was the basis of his lifestyle. The power of love, the recognition of the uniqueness and worth of each individual, a concern for the problems of the common people whom one is to treat as equals—all were part of the Baal Shem's message, which was aimed at the Jewish masses. He wanted them to serve God with zeal and joy, to recognize the rich potential of existence, and to release the joy and song that all too often are stifled in day-to-day living. He intended his message for all Jews, rich and poor, great and small, the celebrated and the obscure. Each person, whether learned or ignorant, had the dignity of being created in the image of God. The ordinary untutored Jew was no less dear in the eyes of God than the clever scholar.

The Baal Shem was consumed with the awareness of God's presence within the world. While recognizing both the transcendence and the immanence of God, it was more often God's immanence that he extolled. He brought heaven nearer to earth; the nearness of God was the most important point for his disciples to remember;

creation was infused with the divine. The Baal Shem moved people to wonder and joy, awe and exultation; good can be achieved in all circumstances, at all times. Evil represents a yet-hidden good, just as the profane represents the not-yet-hallowed. What is evil must be transformed into what is good, the unholy into the holy. Basically the Baal Shem considered evil to be a mirage; the good is the real, and non-good implies non-existence.[16]

What is central to the Baal Shem's teaching is the striving to live in attachment to God. Thus contrary to the mainstream of Jewish thought, which places emphasis upon the deed, the Baal Shem proclaimed that it is the intention which is essential, that the intention is at the core of Jewish living. Hence the stress on love rather than truth; for the Baal Shem love ought to be the prime motivating factor in our deeds, and our relationship to God ought to be perceived as a romance. Too much of life is given over to empty ritual; thus the Baal Shem sought to stir the fervor that lay buried in the ashes of routine. His inspiration resulted in a stream of enthusiasm among the Jews of Eastern Europe. A people of suffering and tears were remade into a people of exultation and joy.

The Baal Shem's teaching led to a new style of living for the Jews of Eastern Europe. The Hasidim prayed, studied, and lived in exultation. Their joy and fervor was reflected in every aspect of their lives; an inspiring word could bring them to a state of ecstasy. For the Baal Shem joy is the essence of faith and the very heart of religious life. Heschel reminds us that the frequent admonitions against melancholy and gloom by the Baal Shem and his early followers are indicative of the widespread depression and malaise that had settled upon the Jewish community due to generations of exile and persecution. An important ingredient of Jewish faith had been lost—a sense of humor. The people must recognize once again that it is a delight to be a Jew and banish all melancholy from the soul. The God of Israel is not only the Creator of heaven and earth but also the Creator of "delight and joy." Evil frequently can be more adequately overcome through joy and ecstasy than through fasting and mortification.[17]

Another strong Jewish tradition challenged by the Baal Shem was the emphasis on study as the most rewarding occupation. Knowledge, he insisted, should not be an end in itself; learning does not necessarily make one better than others. Study of itself was not enough, for it too often led to arrogance and snobbery. The Baal Shem detested smug and self-satisfied intellectuals who cared little for the problems of the poor. Awe was more important than learning and required an equally great effort to achieve. Hence the disciples of the Baal Shem were concerned lest their knowledge exceed their deeds; new insights were to be followed quickly by new deeds.

The Baal Shem refused to follow the long-held assumption that scholars were to be treated with deference, while those unschooled could be readily ignored. Scholars could also be scoundrels, while the deeds of the lowly could maintain the existence of the world. The Baal Shem treated all as his equal. There was a unique preciousness in every human being; the glory of being human enthralled him, and so he generated a new appreciation and love for the people. In contrast to the accepted view that love of the Torah should precede love of Israel and of the people, the Baal Shem insisted that love of Israel should take precedence: the Torah was created for the sake of the people. The real test of love is how one relates to the evildoer; this is the area where one is truly called to witness to God's love for all men and women. The Baal Shem's success in this is attested by the saying of one of his disciples, Reb Aaron of Karlin: "I should like to love the greatest tzaddic as God loves the lowliest villain."[18]

It is little wonder, then, that the Jews of Eastern Europe recognized in the Baal Shem Tov one who was preparing them for the coming of the Messiah. Other teachers had spoken of God's message, of His goodness; they sang His praises, but only the Baal Shem, in Heschel's words, "brought God Himself to the people."[19] And the people responded with enthusiastic fervor.

Nevertheless, some fifty years after the Baal Shem's death, a small group of Hasidic leaders began to express concern about the movement. Hasidism was becoming ritualized, habitual; it stood in need of renewal. This concern reached its climax in Reb Menahem Mendl of Kotzk, who died in 1859 at the age of 72. Heschel views the Hasidic movement begun by the Baal Shem as reaching its "climax and its antithesis" in the Kotzker.

In place of love as the pre-eminent virtue, the Kotzker put in its stead truth. To achieve truth one must be ready to sacrifice everything and to do away with habit and emotion. True worship of God consisted not in finding the truth but in searching for the truth; it was a quest that demanded total abandonment of self. The Kotzker also recognized how far we are from truth; he was indignant that we dare mention God's name, for a gaping chasm separates us from God.[20]

We live for the most part in a world of evasion and pretense; the world becomes simply a projection of ourselves, and we become prisoners of our own deceptions. Pretense becomes truth, deception becomes certainty, and we are soon entangled in madness. It is this to which the Kotzker reacted, impelled by his passionate ardor for truth.

Falsehood and hypocrisy distort the basis of human living, leading one to inhabit a world of self-delusion, a world that simply does not exist, a phantom world with no substance, a world where truth has no home. One of humankind's strongest inclinations appears to be self-deception.[21]

Thus, while the Baal Shem recognized the closeness of God to this world, the Kotzker saw the deception and corruption that prevails in the world. Alienated from the world, his outlook was somber and critical. He was appalled at the Baal Shem's teaching that the world was infused with God's presence. If God were near the world, He would destroy it because of its malice. Reb Mendl believed a great chasm separated humankind from God because of our estrangement from truth. There is a fundamental disparity between God and humankind, between the divine and the mundane. Furthermore, the Kotzker tended to overestimate the capacities of his disciples, making exalted demands because he believed that they could make the necessary prodigious effort if they would only will to do so. We too easily allow our aptitude for good to become dissipated.

The teachings of the Kotzker were never aimed at comforting or calming the heart; they demanded sober and severe self-reflection. Truth in the area of self-knowledge is so difficult to achieve, because nothing is so easy as self-deception. The more sophisticated we become, the greater the tendency to deceive ourselves. Is it truly God we are worshipping or is it simply some projection of our ego? Religious commitment can tolerate no compromise. It is blasphemous if, as often happens, God becomes a mere pretext for self-indulgence. The disciples of the Kotzker took great care to avoid self-deception; they were not to dwell in tranquillity; they must be one with each word spoken and with each deed performed. Yet they were to avoid a rigid pattern of religious behavior, for no piety can sustain the tedium of unlimited repetition. If one is to maintain the intensity of one's original faith-commitment, then surprise, adventure, and new appreciation are needed, not merely obedience. To act as a Jew, or to act with any religious commitment, demands that one "make a new start upon the old road." Stagnation endangers all traditional religion. Whatever becomes settled and established easily falls into routine; creed replaces faith, repetition replaces spontaneity. Heschel thus considers the challenge to Judaism and the criticism of Judaism by the Kotzker as "acts of liberation." This confrontation within Judaism, which Heschel details in *A Passion for Truth*, played an important role in Heschel's own spirituality.[22]

The Kotzker scorned any show of piety. The human heart is so deceitful, making piety a mere show of pretense. How could we ever presume to strive for attachment to God, the source of all truth? As long as falsehood maintains such a strong grip on us, our love and goodness will be mere hypocrisy. Piety must thus be kept secret. The flame of religious yearning should be kept burning fully and steadily, but it should be deeply concealed.

Melancholy, not ecstasy, was the mark of the Kotzker's disciples, for they were to be above all restless souls seeking to come to terms with the human condition. Joy too easily leads to complacency and indifference. Mindful of this, Heschel notes, the Kotzker wrapped himself in gloom.

While for the most part Jewish scholars concentrated upon the law and upon its correct interpretation, the Kotzker was preoccupied with the "I," with the religious believer's interior life. The cry for purity of heart reverberates in biblical teachings, but religion no longer seemed sufficiently concerned with this quest. Self-love, of itself, is not wrong, but when it leads to callousness toward the needs of others and increasing isolation from others, it can bring about self-destruction. There is a constant temptation here to depose God and to remake the world in one's own image. The choice between love of God and love of self is ever before us; the only way to meet the choice, in the Kotzker's mind, is to live in militant opposition to the self.[23]

The Kotzker wanted to end the illusion that one is serving God when in reality one is simply pleasing the ego. This is the major evil: falsehood, mendacity, perversion of heart. Falsehood scarcely remains a private affair; it expands and affects an ever-widening circle; it is pernicious. Yet we want to live in deception. In the public sphere we give lip service to honesty, but privately we pursue our own deceitful desires. The vast majority of men and women, whose lives are shaped by compromise and evasion, cannot live without deception; it is a goal beyond their reach. They must mask their selfishness and vanity. Thus the Kotzker's challenge appeared to the majority as threatening and inimical, and it brought about his estrangement from the community.

In his insistence on truth as the main concern of Judaism, the Kotzker had in mind the living of truth or, better, living in confrontation with God. Truth implies fidelity to the will of God, and this is a never-ending pursuit; one is always in the position of having to strive for greater truth. In Heschel's words, the Kotzker's "passionate striving for Truth was a hunger and thirst after the Lord." [24]

Clearly the demands of the Kotzker were excessive. He manifested little compassion for the limitations of the human condition, and in this respect he went beyond Jewish tradition, which respects the demand for normal living and does not insist on perpetual heroism; martyrdom would be expected only in rare instances. Yet the Kotzker was merciless in his demand for self-sacrifice, in his rejection of mediocrity and compromise, in his insistence on a total honesty that cuts through all pretension. His teaching seems incompatible with either love or compassion. Common sense calls for moderation, but the Kotzker called for constant self-denial and self-examination. Common sense labels the excessive as unwise and unhealthy, yet the Kotzker called for perpetual self-renewal and self-transcendence. All repetition is a forgery and a surrender to routine. Religion should condemn complacency and habit and compromise; it demands a strong life lived *in extremis*. For the Kotzker, then, authentic faith was a rare commodity, the yoke of a gifted few who would bear it for the whole of humankind. Only through the few would the many be uplifted. The Kotzker concerned himself with the elite, the chosen few, and not with the masses, who were considered to be unable or uninterested in fulfilling the demands of religious faith. Most people enjoy the moral and spiritual tranquillity that comes from unchallenged assumptions. The ordinary person is content to follow without question, to worship and practice routinely. Hence the Kotzker's continual effort to unsettle and disturb his hearers, to jolt them out of their complacency. The authentic faithful must free themselves from the crowd and ignore public opinion; they must regard their vocation as unique. They are continually called upon to transcend themselves and to bring their lives into complete conformity to God's will. In other words, the authentic faithful are called upon to live the truth.[25]

What is perhaps the most crucial point in the Kotzker's whole approach to a life of faith is his understanding of the incompatibility of God's ways with human ways, an incompatibility that belongs to the very essence of human existence. This incompatibility undercuts all our human effort to discover ultimate meaning in our lives. This is the teaching of the Kotzker which Heschel appears to have found most challenging. Carried to its extreme, it implies that the passion for truth reduces the human situation to one of absurdity; it hints that all our human efforts are in the final analysis fruitless. Only when one reaches this point of despair, however, does one understand the full meaning of faith.

To illustrate his point, the Kotzker used the story of the king who ordered his laborers to fill with water barrels that were punctured with holes. The foolish laborer sees this as a hopeless task and does nothing. The wise laborer, recognizing the absurdity, goes ahead with the task, convinced that "my obedience is important to the king." The real truth, he argued, is not to fill the barrels; it is to fulfill the command of the king. As with the myth of Sisyphus, the parable points to the absurdity of human existence. The Kotzker wanted to emphasize that all our efforts to discover meaning are overshadowed by the fundamental Jewish reality: "to live is to obey." We have all experienced the futility of our endeavors, our helplessness, along with the triumph of brute force and mindless greed. Is it not a self-deception to indulge in hopefulness? The Kotzker would lead us to the brutal discovery that the meaning and purpose that *we* have placed on our lives may be utterly absurd. The greatest absurdity would be to deceive ourselves into thinking that we have succeeded with our life's project. This brings us to the need of transcending *our* sense of values and *our* sense of meaning and of accepting in faith a meaning beyond absurdity, a meaning that our reason cannot grasp. For the Kotzker the highest point to which reason can bring us is to a sense of being commanded, and the supreme response to this is obedience.

Yet, lest one arrive too easily at such a "faith solution," Heschel asks: Perhaps we misunderstand the king's assignment and should be busy repairing the barrels rather than futilely filling them with water; where does the truth lie? Does the king, who demands audacity and defiance, ultimately insist on surrender and submission? The barrels were full of holes. Is the whole human enterprise to be considered absurd? [26]

The essential point of the Kotzker's parable is that the laborers were aware that they were hired and would be compensated, and thus the enterprise had significance in the king's eyes. It points to a meaning that transcends our understanding. In the midst of absurdity, we recognize our lives as a response to an expectation. What gives meaning to our lives is in recalling the One who has engaged us.

Our inability to comprehend the ultimate meaning of God's ways does not invalidate that meaning. On the other hand, our anguish is not silenced because of the certainty that the ultimate answer lies with God. When meaning is absent from our lives, the anxiety is real because something of vital significance is missing; there is a deep-seated expectation that meaning must be somewhere. If God's ways are beyond our ways, a point crucial for the Kotzker, then it follows that it is impossible for us to comprehend His ways, and hence impossible to discover an answer to humanity's ultimate question. For Heschel our goal is not to discover ultimate solutions but to recognize ourselves as part of a context of meaning. Twice in the final pages of A *Passion for Truth* Heschel states his response to the challenge posed by the Kotzker: "We are not the final arbiter of meaning. What looks absurd within the limit of time may be luminous within the scope of eternity." [27]

Yet again Heschel does not propose this response as a panacea for the anguish that grips humankind. We would be wrong to assume that the Kotzker wrestled with the problem of truth and evil in order to discover an intelligible answer. No answer could soothe the terrible agony in which the world is writhing. And Heschel was aware that no answer could obviate the agony that Judaism endured in this century; it would be blasphemous to deem that any answer is possible. "Life in our times has been a nightmare for many of us, tranquillity an interlude, happiness a fake."

The biblical response recognizes that when humankind is in anguish, so also is God. "In all their affliction, He was afflicted" (Is 63:9). God needs those who are faithful in times of distress, both His and our own. He needs those who, come what may, will continue to trust in His goodness. The query may rise to a crescendo, the search for an answer may leave one speechless. One may be required to bid farewell to comfort and tranquillity. Faith, Heschel insists, begins with compassion, a compassion for God. At that moment when we are "bursting with God's sighs," we come to the realization that beyond all absurdity there lie meaning and truth and love. And we are reminded that by each sacred deed we perform and each prayer we utter, we help to reduce distress, advance redemption, and bring about the coming of that messianic age when falsehood will be buried and truth resurrected. Meanwhile, although many of our efforts may lead to absurdity, there are others that prove to be rich in meaning. Yet for the Kotzker, truth will continue to be concealed, a concealment that is necessary for our greatest adventure, the striving for truth. If truth were not concealed, there would be no need to choose and to search, and that in turn would mark an end to humankind whose very essence is "to choose and to search." [28]

Our efforts to embody the truth will always be inadequate; the key point is to recognize this inadequacy, for otherwise there is the danger of complacency and mediocrity. For the Kotzker the fundamental concern of religion must be the uprooting of mediocrity. His was a religious radicalism that shuns all moderation. He was convinced that only this radical approach to religion could help bring about self-transcendence.

One of the great failures of religion in Western society is the tendency to equate religion with self-interest. In Judaism that self-interest goes under the guise of "survival of the people," while in Christianity self-interest is expressed as "personal salvation." If we were attuned to the mystery and marvel of living, Heschel argues, or if we would only listen to the cries of anguish and misery that rise up from so many areas of the globe, we would recognize the shamefulness of a life lived within the confines of a narrow self-interest. Going beyond self is exceedingly difficult. It requires a constant effort on our part along with divine assistance. This is where the radical approach of the Kotzker is so important: we must never be content with our achievements before God. Something more is always demanded; the easy, mediocre life is not worth living. The teaching of the Kotzker shatters our satisfaction with the status quo. To accept the established order is to accommodate ourselves to evil, for it implies an acceptance of all the callousness and corruption that are inherent in our world; more subtly, it implies a repudiation of messianic hope. Yet those wedded to ease and moderation, to the *status quo*, will continue to insist that the Kotzker's ideals are simply unrealistic.[29]

While others may look upon God primarily as a source of security and prosperity and easy forgiveness, anyone who falls under the Kotzker's influence would never be at ease with such conventional religious notions. Heschel sees the Kotzker as the one tolling the end of "spiritual nonchalance"; to confront his challenge is to become aware of our spiritual stagnation, ashamed at our peace of mind, revolted at our ever-present dishonesty. In the world of the Kotzker it is not beauty or love that should reign but truth, and truth does away with comfort and ease and moderation. Those who hear the voice of the Kotzker today recognize in it the call to shed our masks, our pretensions, and our mediocrity. It is a reminder that truth is alive and that all humankind is needed to bring about its liberation.[30]

It is evident from all this that both the Baal Shem and the Kotzker had a profound influence on Heschel and on his spirituality, on his understanding of the role of the human person before God. The one gave him wings; the other encircled him with chains. Whether or not it was wise or helpful to live torn between exaltation and dismay, Heschel does not say; he simply tells us: "I had no choice." He could not deny either master, yet in the light of his thought as expressed in his writings, it would seem that he identified more closely with the Baal Shem. All his major works, especially *Man Is Not Alone*, *God in Search of Man*, and *The Prophets*, emphasize the love and compassion of the God of Israel and the awe and wonder which they evoke in humankind. Heschel's great contribution may well be the keeping alive of these two opposing traditions and his recognition of the need to maintain a tension between them by uniting them in his own person.[31] As additional evidence that the attitude of the Baal Shem was closer to Heschel personally, we look now at a final example from his works of a "lived spirituality."

The Jewish Community in Eastern Europe

Another area of Heschel's concern which helps to reveal dimensions of his own personal spiritual outlook lies in his treatment of the Jews of Eastern Europe as found above all in his slim volume *The Earth Is the Lord's*. This community of Ashkenazi Jews, extending roughly from the Middle Ages into the present century, represented for Heschel "the golden period" of Jewish history, a period of deep inwardness and intense devotion. While the Sephardic Jews of the Iberian peninsula tended to blend their Jewish culture with that of their neighbors, emphasizing the common elements between Judaism and Western thought, the Askenazi Jews lived in an isolated manner from their European neighbors and hence tended to emphasize much more their own Jewish roots and tradition. They borrowed nothing from other cultures, but instead they developed their own culture out of what was for them most deeply and most personally Jewish. As a result the Ashkenazi community was an uncompromisingly Jewish community.

In contrast to the Sephardic ideal of prudence and practicality, the Ashkenazis maintained a passion for the unlimited, for the infinite, always striving to transcend the present. Instead of harmony and order, they stressed spontaneity and creativity. Rather than a logical and systematic approach to reality, the Ashkenazic approach was much more fervent and personal, "praying and learning without limit or end."[32]

Under the influence of the mystical teachings of the Kabbalah, the Ashkenazis stressed attachment to the "hidden worlds," those spiritual worlds built by power of devotion invested in deeds. Thus the actions of the pious Jew have an effect, they believed, both on this world and on the hidden worlds, so that each Jew to some extent may be the Messiah. Redemption is not considered to be a single event occurring at the end of time but a continual ongoing process taking place at each moment of time. All good deeds play a role in this "long drama of redemption." Each one is called to perfect the universe, to redeem the hidden divine sparks scattered throughout creation. Thus the deliverance of this world is dependent upon each person. At the same time Jews must also recall how near the power of evil is. Every sin unleashes a demonic force in the world that enhances the power of evil and endangers us all. Our world becomes crowded with "malicious beings" created by our evil deeds. We live in the midst of a hostility that we ourselves have engendered. Both rapture and sadness, then, marked the life of the Ashkenazic community; these Jews recognized the infinite beauty and nearness of heaven along with the darkness and gloom spread by the presence of evil. The influence of the Baal Shem and of the Kotzker on the Jews of Eastern Europe served to accentuate this twofold attitude and the tension that follows from this and from all coincidence of opposites that marks the religious situation of humankind.

What Heschel seems to emphasize above all in his analysis of the Ashkenazi Jews is the essential humanness that is found in their tradition. They emphasized the earnestness of life; life was too serious to be wasted on trivia; rest and relaxation were rarities. The good does not come about automatically; Jews do not achieve God's goals merely by living. Goals must be constantly addressed; life is to be lived with intensity. Joy and celebration were certainly present, but always for solid and serious reasons, and always with a touch of sadness. The hardship and suffering of life were never kept at a distance, but despite this, as Heschel points out, "the Jews all sang," whether studying or mending or preaching or cleaning. They recognized that the family table could become a consecrated altar, that the single deed of one person could determine the fate of all. Their piety was simple and unassuming, modeled no doubt after that of the thirty-six just men of each generation for whose sake God continues to show mercy to our world, who live in our midst as poor laborers, and whose holiness is unknown even to their closest friends.[33]

Heschel recalls the story of Rabbi Isaac Meir Alter of Ger who had written a commentary on the Jewish Civil Code and who asked his master, the Kotzker, for his opinion of the work. After studying the manuscript, the Kotzker told Rabbi Isaac: "'It is a work of genius. When published, the classical commentaries . . . will become obsolete. I am only grieved at the thought of the displeasure which this will cause to the souls of the saintly commentators.' It was a winter evening. Fire was burning in the stove. Rabbi Isaac Meir took the manuscript from the table and threw it into the flames." Self-abnegation and sacrifice were essential aspects of Ashkenazic piety; these are the traits that make the human person superior to the angels. This spirit of sacrifice was especially evident in efforts made to study the Torah. The people might have empty stomachs and barren quarters, but their minds were "crammed with the riches of Torah." Parents would go to any extreme to cover the cost of tuition for their children. If a father were poorly educated, he would be determined that his children become scholars. Wives would work endlessly in order that their husbands might devote their lives to study. If the people themselves were too poor to set aside time for study, they would somehow help support students. Their humble homes were always open to itinerant students. Poverty and worries might abound, but when Jews found a few moments of leisure, they would use them to read through pages of one of the holy books or to join in a study group. For these Jews knowledge was not considered a source of power but the way to maintain their tradition and to unite themselves to their God. It would be a desecration to study simply for the sake of scholarship.[34]

This Jewish faith touched every aspect of life. Sanctity was not an excursion into a spiritual world; rather it was an ennobling of the common. Holiness was found in all one's deeds, not just in specific acts; it involved one's whole lifestyle but was expressed especially in "loving kindness," in responding to the needs of others, in sensitivity to their problems and anxieties. Holiness endowed material things with a heavenly beauty. For the pious Jew life was a task to be accomplished, a responsibility entrusted to each person, and never the occasion for mere indulgence or gratification. Each Jew by fulfilling the Torah is to restore wholeness to the universe by serving the world for the sake of God.

No one is far from the brink of chaos. There is a need for a permanent vigilance against the temptations of the evil one. One must be continually watchful to maintain order and direction in life; for the Jew this implies continual submission to the guidance of the law. Some are horrified at the very thought of subjecting themselves to a spiritual authority, and in their insistence on absolute freedom they become prisoners of their own whims and desires. Only the spiritually free person can recognize that self-restraint does not imply loss of self. Yet for the pious Jew observance of the law is not really self-restraint, but an exercise rich in spiritual significance. To the point is Heschel's story of a mother who was distressed because her sons had abandoned religious observance, although they remained good young men and would inherit a share in the world to come. "But I feel distressed at the fact that they do not enjoy the pleasures of this world as well, the pleasures of observing the Jewish law." [35]

For such Jews, especially those under the influence of the Baal Shem, there was the joy of recognizing God's presence in the world, the joy of perceiving His glory in all of creation. They might be plagued by persecution, but they carried within the vision of God's redeeming power. The Torah was always close to their hearts, evoking "an infinite world of inwardness." The sufferings of the past and of the present never departed from their souls, yet their delight in being Jews never wavered. They experienced the truth of the words of the Bratslav rebbe, Rabbi Nahman: "Do not fear. . . . God is with you, in you, around you." In the holiness of their fellow-Jews could be glimpsed the light of the Messiah. But Heschel reminds us also that there is a price to be paid for being a Jew. To be human the Jew must be more than human; to be a people Jews must be more than a people. [36] The world at large is determined to judge its Jewish brothers and sisters by stricter norms and ever more stringent expectations.

Not surprisingly, the Jews of Eastern Europe, who experienced so much harassment and persecution, put little trust in the secular world with its power politics and boastful pride. Neither the world's scorn nor the world's praise was of any consequence for them. Social status and technical accomplishments were not nearly so important for them as houses of worship and halls of study. Life without the Torah was meaningless and absurd. They were living in exile in a world that was unredeemed, full of dangers and trials, yet their lives were centered on the service of God, and within them the light of God's likeness was never extinguished. The holiness of the Sabbath permeated each day of the week; a glimpse of the eternal could be had in each passing moment. They may not have constructed magnificent edifices, but they did build bridges "leading from the heart to God." For Heschel these Jews realized in their own way the truth of Israel. Their self-effacement, their concern for one another, their inner strength and devotion, their simplicity and patience in the midst of poverty and suffering tell a story which will never be fully known, but which continues to offer silent testimony to the meaning of Judaism and of Jewish faith.

The forces of enlightenment and modernity wrought many changes in the Jews of Eastern Europe, but Heschel sees the zeal and fervor and vitality of this tradition maintained in a variety of Jewish movements. No matter how stridently these Jews moved into the twentieth century, the majority of them continued to experience the powerful urge for redemption and often passed up fame and wealth and career in order to stand by the community and to work for its healing. Unlike in other communities emancipation was not accompanied by abandonment of faith. With the determination molded by a tradition enduring for three millenia, these Jews mastered the new sciences and social disciplines; the depth of their inward life produced men and women of extraordinary artistic talent. Their discipline and devotion to study often led to bold and creative scientific research. Their religious faith blended well and meaningfully with the challenges of modernity.[37]

Heschel laments the fact that in more recent times something of this faith and vision has been eclipsed. "We have helped to extinguish the light our fathers had kindled." It is incumbent upon Jews today to remember and to recapture the legacy that is theirs from Eastern Europe. Judaism, Heschel reminds us, is "spiritual life." The greatest service Jews can render humanity is by living Judaism authentically, giving witness to that endless striving that is at the core of all human and religious living. Judaism cannot be converted into something else; there is no substitute for Judaism; any alternative way of life is for the Jew spiritual suicide. Jews have been summoned to play a role in history that transcends all vested political interests; there is a divine earnestness associated with Judaism that confers upon each Jew the dignity of representing something far greater than oneself. The worst thing a Jew might do is to forget what he or she represents, namely, "God's stake in human history." The coming of God's kingdom may be quite distant, but the task of Judaism is to continue to maintain its share in God, despite the cost, by battling against all the forces that incessantly seek to dehumanize society and by witnessing to the presence of the ultimate in the ordinary, to the presence of God in our daily living.[38] Thus one of the key responsibilities of Judaism in Heschel's eyes is to recapture and maintain the inner beauty and wisdom and holiness of the

Ashkenazi Jews of Eastern Europe, for theirs is a tradition that is enriching not only for Jews but for all who recognize the inter-relatedness of the human and the holy.

THE ROLE OF EDUCATION

Crucial to the preservation of such a tradition is the role of education. Heschel touched on this point a number of times in the last dozen years of his life, dating primarily from his participation in a 1960 White House Conference on Children and Youth.[39] Heschel noted there the many obstacles that thwart the educational process in the United States. Chief among these is the craze for efficiency; ours is an age of "instrumentalization" of the world, of persons, of values. Concern for the transcendent or for morality or for reverence has a very low priority. There is no sense of indebtedness either to God or to society; on the contrary, many believe that the world and society are indebted to them. We act as though the universe were created to satisfy our needs and interests. Young people are sheltered from the dark side of life; they have little experience of the bitterness and grief, the anxiety and agony which afflict so many human lives. The "good" life of privilege and comfort, of pleasure and self-indulgence dulls their moral awareness and responsibility. Security and success provide no exaltation, no demand for self-sacrifice, no sense of the need for adoration, no concern for what is ultimately precious. For all intents and purposes we have liquidated the inner person, consigning the inner life to oblivion. Our educational system fails completely to cultivate a sensitivity to wonder, to mystery, to the ineffable; it is too busy calculating and explaining and classifying. Science and technology convey enormous information about the cosmos and the history of humankind, but we must not pretend that such information gives a complete understanding of the human person or provides solutions to the ultimate questions of life and death and meaning.

What Heschel calls the "cardinal sin" of educational theory in the United States is its failure to make sufficient demands of students. We ask too little, as though young people are incapable of sacrifice and self-denial; their enormous potential remains untapped. A life with no demands on mind and heart and soul spells the doom of both the individual and the culture. This attitude manifests itself in an education that presents religion as a tranquil-izer, as a diversion or a hobby, omitting entirely the spiritual power and audacity young people crave. Tradition is considered irrelevant; our religious heritage is no longer thought capable of shedding light on the personal problems each person must confront. In our class-rooms we no longer deal with the fundamental issues of human-kind, with life and death and suffering, or how to handle jealousy or loneliness or violence, or the importance of honesty and fidelity.

Even religious education cannot bring about any change if it is limited to norms and principles and "timeless ideas," if it bypasses the concrete world of our everyday living. Religious education must be aimed at the mind and the heart of this unique individual; to be effective it must emphasize both a content and a moment. Not only is there the content or the subject matter to be grasped, but there is the moment of "insight and appreciation" which pupil and teacher must share together; this, however, occurs all too rarely. Instead we are raising generations of young people who are "spiritually stunted" and who do not know how to relate to the classical sources of their tradition. We prepare them for the job market, but we often fail to teach them how to be persons, how to probe for what is of lasting value in human existence, how to relate to ultimate meaning, or how to resist conformity and to grow inwardly. We develop the outer person but often at the neglect of the inner person; we fail to stress the role of stillness and of self-restraint. Of what value are knowledge and ability and success when commitment and compas-sion are lacking? Why take pride in a high standard of living that does not demand in return a high standard of behavior and concern? Each of us must work to put an end to this "trivialization" of human living, but it is especially incumbent upon our teachers to demon-strate the earnestness of life, the possibilities for spiritual and moral exaltation, the capacity for love and sacrifice.[40]

In Heschel's mind the highest priority of education today ought to be to teach young people how to revere. Our schools must insist on proficiency, but even more on reverence; they must be sources of information, but even more of appreciation. Reverence is the basis for sensitivity, for compassion, and for responsibility. For Judaism the very purpose of education is not so much to comprehend as to revere and to indicate how one may live in a way compatible with the mystery of human existence. Education for reverence is crucial

for recovering a sense of awe and mystery, for developing an awareness that something is being demanded of us, and for the preservation of freedom. It calls for the cultivation of a "total sensitivity," an
empathy for the grandeur and mystery of being and for the dimension of the holy in human living. Reverence helps one to recognize
that life is not only a scientific fact but also a dramatic opportunity,
that being created in God's image is not only a doctrine to be believed but a truth to be lived. Reverence alters the way I look at this
paper and pen, at this desk and lamp, at everything in creation; it
helps me to be sensitive to the wonder and mystery of this moment;
it helps me to maintain a sense of awe and amazement for the gift of
life and not to be overly infatuated with our technological achievements. Reverence for study helps students to view their work as
prayer, as an act of worship, rather than an ordeal or a step toward
self-aggrandizement. Without education for reverence religion is
isolated from life, a useless appendage, and God becomes simply an
idea, a substitute for genuine faith.[41]

Education for reverence is closely allied in Heschel's mind with
education for service; reverence for God demands reverence for humankind. Perhaps the most important characteristic of reverence is
sensitivity to the needs of the poor and to the situation of the poor.
We do not live in isolation. It is essential to teach young people by
word and example that the goal of human living is to be of service
and help to others. Mastery is to be acquired for the sake of service.
There must be a personal involvement with the sufferings of the
poor and with the relief of this suffering. We should educate our
youth to confront the callousness of a society that is indifferent to
the wretched of the earth and that squanders so much of its material
resources on personal luxuries in a world where famine and misery
stalk billions of people each day; we must help them to ask what
should one *do* with talent and power, with abundance and compe-
tence, in such a world. A radical revision of attitudes is called for,
and Heschel has no doubt that this revision can be achieved. Young
people possess greater hidden talents than we can imagine. If they
are inspired, they will act; if they are challenged, they will respond.[42]

Some of Heschel's most pertinent remarks on the role and purpose of education were given at the close of an hour-long interview
that was videotaped just three days before his death. It was only at
the end of this program that Heschel was given the opportunity to

speak to what he had earlier requested: a message for young people in our society. Indirectly, he was also addressing a message to educators. His advice was simple and incisive. It is important for young people to recognize that every deed counts, that every word has power, and that every one of us can share in redeeming this world despite the absurdities and frustrations and disappointments that we encounter. Above all, each one should view his or her life as a "work of art" and start working on this "great work of art" which is the life given to each of us. To accomplish this task Heschel set down three norms: (a) the importance of self-discipline, (b) the study of the great sources of wisdom, and (c) the recognition of life as a celebration. "There's much entertainment in our life. And entertainment is destroying much of our initiative and weakens our imagination. What's really important is life as a celebration." One of the most vital tasks we have, Heschel concluded, is to teach the world "how to celebrate."[43] These remarks of Heschel, given at the close of his life, comprise in a sense his "last will and testament" not only for young people, but for all people. In addition, they are an eloquent witness to so much of what was central to his own life and of what has been central to this study: the interrelatedness of the human and the holy.

A Universality of Concern

From a Jewish perspective few scholars in recent history, as Samuel Dresner testifies, have demonstrated such mastery of so many key aspects of Judaism as Rabbi Heschel. His appeal within Judaism extends from Reform and Conservative Jews to the Orthodox and Hasidic Jews. Likewise, his appeal to Christians of various persuasions and to a wide variety of men and women of good will underscores the universality of his concern and of his scholarship. Heschel, in Dresner's view, stands as a *Nasi*, a prince of his people, a man held in high esteem, but not only by his fellow-Jews; Catholics, Protestants, and Muslims all looked to Heschel as a man of integrity and wisdom. He earned recognition as a spokesman for the poor, the aged, the blacks, for the victims of the Holocaust, and for Russian Jewry.[44]

This universality of concern is perhaps even more evident in Heschel's approach to humankind and to the world. He does not close his eyes to the dark side of history or to the brutalizing tendencies within humanity; rather he demonstrates an acute awareness not only of the greatness and nobility of human existence but also of its enormous capacity for evil and depravity.

From one vantage point, as Heschel notes in a 1957 address, "Sacred Images of Man," one might read history as humankind drenched in blood, dominated by wars, victories or defeats, and more wars, with so many dead and maimed, so many in mourning and tears. Ever since God expelled Adam and Eve from Paradise, the human race has attempted to build its own Paradise from which it has expelled God, and the Paradise we have built may well prove to be nothing but a vast extermination camp. There is a stigma, a shame in being a member of the human race. Instead of conveying a sense of God's presence and of God's image, humanity too often conveys a sense of arrogance and of false sovereignty that rightly fills the world with terror; instead of being a pointer, a symbol of the divine, humanity makes of itself an idol. We have imprisoned God in synagogue and church; we have reduced God to a mere slogan; we no longer speak His word.[45]

Again in a 1970 article, "On Prayer," Heschel points to the "spiritual blackout, a blackout of God" that dominates our age; what we experience is not only the dark night of the soul but the dark night of society. We have driven God out of our hearts and minds. "The spiritual blackout is increasing daily. . . . We no longer know how to resist the vulgar, how to say no in the name of a higher yes. . . . We have lost the sense of the holy." Our world is aflame with arrogant atrocities and naked terrorism. Our scandalous desecration of the world cries out to the heavens. And as we grow aware of and face up to this evil, we either become "callous participants" or remain "indifferent onlookers." The relentless pursuit of our own selfish interests so often makes us oblivious to what is going on around us, and so nothing counts unless it can be turned to our own advantage in the service of our self-interests. "Dark is the world to me," laments Heschel; the glitter of its cities and the glimmer of its stars provide no relief to the darkness. "If not for my faith that God . . . still listens to a cry, who could stand such agony?"[46]

Heschel writes of humankind torn between "the good urge" and "the evil urge," swinging like a pendulum between what is godly and what is beastly, between the pull toward the divine and the pull toward the selfish, between what is more than human and what is

less than human. We live in anguish in an affluent society, an anguish that threatens to make a mockery of our boasts. We insist on
high standards of living but are satisfied with "vulgar standards of
thinking"; we are seemingly helpless to block the "spiritual liquidation" of humankind; we fear that humanity may become obsolete.
We turn blessing into curse, converting the healing power of God's
word into a deadly poison. Our power for corruption manifests itself again and again in our destruction of God's designs. So humankind is immersed in what is brutal, callous, and cruel. Our self-
righteousness impedes the search for truth. We prefer to close the
shutters and to lock the doors so that no light might enter and no
sound might disturb our complacency; in such surroundings we are
the master, and all else is a void. Thus we become the opposite of
what we are called to be, and, as Heschel often reminds us, the opposite of the human is not the animal but the demonic. As a Jew,
Heschel recoils from belief in the demonic; the salvation wrought
by God through Moses and the prophets entailed the elimination of
demons and demigods from the consciousness of the people. Yet
humanity has the "uncanny ability" to create or revive demons.
Our very worship of power has brought forth the demon of power.
Auschwitz and Hiroshima have turned the world into a "spiritual
no-man's land." Perplexed and misguided, we have distorted God's
word and wisdom; we have abused His gift of power.[47]

Our social life and our educational system combine to corrode
our sensitivity. We do not respond with a feeling of outrage even
when confronted with acts of mindless violence; we become accustomed to evil in its many forms, calling it, in our surrender, "inevi-
table." The Bible urges us to choose life, but again and again we
choose death under the guise of despair or arrogance or blindness or
helplessness. "I am not optimistic"; Heschel confesses, "we are getting poorer by the day." He fears that we are losing our vision and
our wisdom, our insight and our commitment; we no longer have
the capacity for self-sacrifice. If power is the ultimate goal, then
humankind has indeed come of age; if meaningful existence is the
ultimate goal, then humankind has descended to a new nadir.

Heschel constantly balances this bleak view of our past and present
history both by his deep faith in the abiding goodness and care of
God and through those insights he derived from his study of the
Kotzker. Even in the face of defeat, continued courage was essential
to the Kotzker; he was repelled by submissive and docile "yes-men."

Even before God one ought not to be servile, but stand erect and hold one's head high. All the more is this true when one confronts the brutal arrogance and cruel violence that mark so much of human history. History is not a blind alley; the present darkness is neither complete nor final; we must recognize in it "a challenge and a passageway." Over the depth of darkness lies the vision of a new dawn. Our power lies, as always, in prayer, in prayer that will pierce the darkness and discover moments "full of God's grace and radiance." We are called to preserve such moments, to "keep them alive in our lives, to defy absurdity and despair, and to wait for God to say again: Let there be light." God has entered our spiritual agony and dwells in our perplexities; beyond all doubts and frustrations, beyond all dogmas and doctrines, stands the living God, God in quest, God in waiting, "God in search of man." Deeper than all our knowledge and understanding, writes Heschel, is "our bold certainty that God is with us in distress, hiding in the scandal of our ambiguities."[48]

To achieve this awareness of God's presence in the midst of chaos and despair, Heschel urges that we recall the dimension of depth present in the human situation within which can be seen the basic issues of human existence in a way compatible with the "grandeur of the human condition." In other words the more deeply one is attuned to the human situation, the more readily one can sense the nearness of God. This is the task of Heschel's "depth theology," which plays such an important role in his whole spiritual outlook. Depth theology examines the "pretheological situation," that is, the total lived situation of persons, including their attitude toward life and toward the world, including especially those experiences that are the antecedents of religious faith and religious commitment, the prerequisites for being sensitive to God. Heschel's God, we must remember, is never the product of reflective thought, but "an outcry wrung from heart and mind," an outcry uttered when our body is seized by tremors and "our whole being bursts into shudders," uttered only in fear and astonishment and always challenging our stance in life. Heschel is speaking here, not of a feeling or emotion but of "a power, a marvel beyond us, tearing the world apart." One comes to this experience only through the reverence and awe, the openness to the mystery that surrounds us, so essential to authentic human living. When we detach "doctrine from devotion" or "reason from reverence," when we divorce faith and creed from the specific lived experiences that give rise to them, we reduce God to a "logical hypothesis, theoretically important, but not overwhelmingly urgent."[49] Needless to say, such a "God" would have no relevance for Rabbi Heschel.

Heschel insists that there is something divine at stake in human existence. We are not innocent bystanders in the cosmic drama; we are instead a concern of God, an object of His love and care, called to act in the likeness of God. What Heschel says of Israel, he says also of all men and women of biblical faith. If God is to be present to our world, we must be His witnesses. Without a people of faithful witness, the Bible is mere literature, making no demands, evoking no response. And being a witness implies involvement and responsibility. We are endowed with "God's dreams and designs," sharing God's dreams of a world redeemed, of a world in which all humankind truly images God by imaging His wisdom and justice and compassion. We are called to be co-participants with God in the continuous drama of creation. Each action of our lives either furthers the process of redemption, diminishing the power of evil, or it frustrates the process of redemption, enhancing the power of evil. Indeed there is something of divine consequence in every human life; each human life is sacred.

For Heschel, if we are to live humanly, we must be sensitive to the sanctity of life and to all that is sacred. This implies a recognition that there are certain aspects of creation that are not at our disposal, that *all* things are not subject to our power and manipulation. The sacred is what is ultimately precious; thus sensitivity to the sacred implies sensitivity to "what is dear to God." This is simply another way of asserting what is so central to this study of Heschel's spirituality, namely, that our religious commitment, our openness to God, is no mere adjunct to our existence, but is at the very heart and core of our being human. Human life is holy because human life is lived in partnership with God. The deeper this partnership and the deeper one's sensitivity to the divine, the more deeply human one becomes.

The problem which confronts humankind at all times, and which makes our age particularly perilous, is the gradual erosion of this sensitivity to God because we are no longer aware of the ineffable. Throughout history men and women lived authentic human lives by combining manipulation with appreciation, utilization with celebration. These two approaches to reality were harmoniously combined in most cultures and societies. Today the situation is clearly different. Ours is an age that to a great extent has lost the ability to appreciate. The tragedy, in Heschel's view, is that we have moved "out of the realm of God's creation into the realm of man's manipulation." We have become so familiar with, and knowledgeable of, the world around us. Heschel does not denigrate familiarity and knowledge as such, but ours is a familiarity that breeds apathy and a knowledge that breeds arrogance. Being alive no longer bespeaks mystery; radical amazement has yielded to indifference; celebration has been replaced by entertainment. Celebration is an expression of reverence, a recognition of the transcendent dimension of human living. Through his stress on humankind's pretheological situation, Heschel would lead us to that profound inner appreciation which recognizes the sublime gift, the solemn mystery, that is human life, and which ultimately celebrates the invocation of God's presence "concealed in His absence." Our very existence as human beings, our living deeply the human condition which is ours, is of itself an assistance to the divine, a witness to the divine. "For the divine to be done," writes Heschel, "the human part must be present." [50] God comes to His world only through us, and only when we are living in an authentically human way. For Heschel one's holiness is to be measured by one's humanness.

An Unfinished Task

Heschel's spiritual legacy represents an unfinished task, just as humanity and religion are unfinished tasks. Clearly it must be so. His very understanding of the term "spiritual" is that of a "never ending process," an upward movement of being as it were, the "reference to the transcendent" that is found in all human existence. The spiritual is that which turns all arrivals into new pilgrimages and new ventures; it is "the ecstatic force that stirs all our goals"; it keeps us from transforming values into ends in themselves. We can never own the spiritual, but we may share in it; we can never possess the spiritual, but we may be possessed by it. Spirit, for Heschel, is ultimately a direction, "the turning of all things to God: *theotropism*. It is always more than—and superior to—what we are and know."

It is the presence of this spirit in humankind, this spirit breathed into humankind by God at creation, that makes of all human enterprises an unfinished task. It is the spirit, the spiritual dimension of human existence, that is the source of the endless discontent that is so crucial to Heschel's understanding of religion. It is the same spirit which ensures that no person can ever arrive at a stage of final completion and which makes humanity and finality mutually exclusive terms for Heschel. That is why he insists that being human means "being on the way, striving, waiting, hoping."

Heschel describes this predicament of humankind in terms of each soul descending from heaven to earth by means of a ladder. The ladder is then taken away, and each soul is called from heaven to return; it is a call that is issued time and again. The souls keep looking for the ladder, but it cannot be found. Then wisdom dictates that there must be another way of returning. Thus we must face the challenge and act; we must commit ourselves; we must leap "until God, in His mercy, makes exultation come about." This religious commitment is "the heart and core of being human." The human person is called to live in solidarity with God. That is why Heschel insists so often that "to be human, one must be more than human." We can never stand still; no two moments should ever be alike; we must always be more than we are.[51]

Heschel was keenly sensitive to this call to live in solidarity with God; it guided the whole of his life. "My life is shaped by many loyalties," he tells us; but each loyalty has its basis in one ultimate relationship, namely, in "loyalty to God, the loyalty of all my loyalties." And loyalty to God, for Rabbi Heschel, can never be separated from loyalty to the community of Israel. "For us Jews there can be no fellowship with God without the fellowship with the people of Israel." To abandon Israel would be to abandon God. What Jews achieve as individuals is trivial; what Jews achieve as Israel causes them "to grow into the infinite." Heschel stood squarely within the tradition of his people. He saw this as an essential characteristic of all those who strive to spiritualize this world, to turn all things toward God, namely, that they recognize that they belong to a tradition, that they are part of an historical process, that they are "neither an end nor a beginning but a link between the ages," that they bear within themselves both a memory and an expectation. One cannot isolate the present moment, denying its involvement in both the past and the future. Every movement represents a new beginning, but always within the continuum of history. The task of spiritualizing our world can be carried out only by those who recognize the importance of tradition. Only one "who is an heir," writes Heschel, "is qualified to be a pioneer."

Community with Israel must ultimately extend to community and fellowship with all. Fellowship implies communality of concern, sharing together sorrows and joys and anxieties. This care for the security and well-being of every person is "a concern that we must cultivate all the time without qualification." This concern and compassion is obviously an integral aspect of moving toward solidarity with God, of turning all things toward God. Wherever in this world one person is harmed, "we are all hurt." On the other hand, wherever one is ardently and actively caring for another, one enters a way "of worshipping God, a way of loving God." In Heschel's mind, it is precisely such "love without cause" that will save Israel and all of humankind.[52]

Abraham Heschel embodied this love without cause and exposed the richness of his own spiritual tradition as few others have. More and more Christians, it is hoped, will come to recognize the rich beauty of that tradition which they share in common with Rabbi Heschel. Unfortunately, the majority of Christians have not fully grasped the truth expressed, for example, in the 1975 statement of the American Catholic Bishops: "Christians have not fully appreciated their Jewish roots. . . . Most essential concepts in the Christian creed grew at first in Jewish soil. Uprooted from that soil, these basic concepts cannot be perfectly understood." Too easily do we Christians forget the teaching of St. Paul that the Christian community represents a wild branch grafted into the olive tree in order to share in its life. "Remember that you do not support the root: it is the root that supports you" (Rm 11:18). Rabbi Heschel stands as one of many witnesses to the validity of the bishops' statement that postbiblical Judaism is "rich in religious values and worthy of our sincere respect and esteem."[53]

These same points were echoed more recently by Pope John Paul II in his talk at the Jewish synagogue in Rome in April 1986. "'The Jews are beloved of God,'" John Paul emphasized, and God has called them with "'an irrevocable calling.'" Christians must come to a better understanding of Judaism because Judaism is "'intrinsic'" to Christianity. Christianity has a relationship with Judaism, John

Paul added, which it does not share with any other religion. "'You are our dearly beloved brothers, and, in a certain way, it could be said that you are our elder brothers.'" There is a critical need, then, "'to deepen dialogue in loyalty and friendship, in respect for one another's intimate convictions taking as a fundamental basis the elements of the revelation which we have in common as a great spiritual patrimony.'" This visit and talk of the pope's testify remarkably to the prophetic insight of Rabbi Heschel's written twenty years earlier: "Jewish–Christian relations have improved beautifully. There is certainly a new atmosphere and increasing mutual esteem. . . . Christians are discovering that there is a religious voice and a human voice in the Jew."[54]

This area of Jewish–Christian relations is perhaps one of the most important of the unfinished tasks that Heschel's spiritual legacy has bequeathed to us. He himself recognized that, following the advances of Vatican II, where for the first time in dealing with Judaism, the Church, in response to Heschel's intercession, avoided any notion of a "mission to the Jews," there is "a receptivity in the Christian world to Jewish insights, to Jewish awareness of God and His demands, to Jewish understanding of Scripture and existence." This receptivity represents a unique responsibility and a unique opportunity. "Such occasions rarely come twice." In increasing numbers Jewish and Christian scholars have devoted themselves to this ever-unfinished task, seizing the opportunity described by Heschel "for studying together on the highest academic level in an honest search for mutual understanding and for ways to lead us out of the moral and spiritual predicament affecting all of humanity."[55]

In his 1967 article "What We Might Do Together," Heschel underscored the urgency of this opportunity confronting Jews and Christians by reminding both: "The world is too small for anything but mutual care and deep respect; the world is too great for anything but responsibility for one another." It is morally incumbent upon Christian and Jew to strive for "*a full awareness and appreciation*" of each other's spiritual commitments. What unites us is "the awe and fear of God" which we share in common. This may be difficult to communicate to one another, but whenever and wherever people truly attune their lives to the sacred, to what is precious in God's eyes, they cannot fail to meet "in the presence of Him whose glory fills the hearts and transcends the minds." In this meeting, moreover, Jew and Christian will realize that their purpose is neither to flatter nor to refute one another but to help one another, to share both insight and learning, and "to search in the wilderness for well-springs of devotion, for treasures of stillness, for the power of love and care" for all humankind. Jew and Christian are to cooperate "in trying to bring about a resurrection of sensitivity, a revival of conscience, . . . reverence for the words of the prophets, and faithfulness to the Living God."

Referring to the unfinished task of the Jewish–Christian dialogue, Heschel recounts a personal episode when he was just seven years old, reading about the sacrifice of Isaac. He sobbed out of pity for Isaac, and out of fright his heart froze within him as Abraham lifted the knife. As the voice of the angel was heard, the seven-year-old Heschel broke out in tears and wept aloud. The rabbi tried to comfort him: "'You know that Isaac was not killed.'" "But Rabbi," the weeping child asked, "'supposing the angel had came a second too late?'" The rabbi comforted and calmed him with the words: "'An angel cannot come late.'" Heschel concludes this personal reflection: "An angel cannot be late, but man, made of flesh and blood, may be late." [56]

The opportunity is evident; the responsibility belongs to all Christians and Jews, indeed to all who recognize the interrelationship of the human and the holy; the task is unique and urgent. May we not be late in striving for its fulfillment, faithful to the legacy left to us by Abraham Joshua Heschel.

NOTES

1. "Conversation with Doctor Abraham Joshua Heschel," p. 6.

2. *Insecurity of Freedom*, pp. 289–91; *Maimonides*, trans. Joachim Neugroschel (New York: Farrar, Straus & Giroux, 1982), pp. 243–44.

3. *Man Is Not Alone*, pp. 275–82.

4. Ibid., pp. 282–84.

5. Ibid., pp. 285–87.

6. Ibid., pp. 288–93.

7. Ibid., pp. 294–96.

8. *God in Search of Man*, pp. 77–78, 106.

9. *Man Is Not Alone*, pp. 254–61.

10. *God in Search of Man*, pp. 387–90, 397; *Who Is Man?* p. 40; "On Prayer," 10. It is quite understandable that for the Christian reader of Heschel the exemplar, *par excellence*, of such wholehearted love of God is

Jesus. The Gospel of Saint John stresses the complete gift of Jesus to the Father; his is clearly a love of God unto death. Though Martin Buber sees in the Johannine picture of Jesus a clear example of unconditional relation, or of wholehearted love, Heschel never speaks of Jesus in this manner.

11. *God in Search of Man*, pp. 397–403, 406; *Man Is Not Alone*, pp. 220–21, 264–66.

12. *God in Search of Man*, pp. 298–300, 331; cf. *Who Is Man?* pp. 46–47.

13. *God in Search of Man*, pp. 409–12; *Man Is Not Alone*, p. 251.

14. "What We Might Do Together," 137, 140; "On Prayer," 9–10.

15. *Passion for Truth*, pp. xiii–xv.

16. Ibid., pp. 24–40.

17. Ibid., pp. 42–43, 47–48, 52.

18. Ibid., pp. 61–63, 66–68.

19. Ibid., p. 7.

20. Ibid., pp. 10–11, 17.

21. Ibid., pp. 20–22.

22. Ibid., pp. 25–26, 30–37, 87, 92–95.

23. Ibid., pp. 49–54, 96–107.

24. Ibid., pp. 158–60, 164.

25. Ibid., pp. 138–44, 167–69, 308–15.

26. Ibid., pp. 286–90, 295.

27. Ibid., pp. 290, 293–95, 301.

28. Ibid., pp. 296–301.

29. Ibid., pp. 312–17.

30. Ibid., pp. 319–23.

31. Ibid., pp. xiv–xv. Cf. Harold Kasimow, *Divine–Human Encounter: A Study of Abraham Joshua Heschel* (Washington, D.C.: University Press of America, 1979), esp. pp. 13ff. The conflict of these two opposing spiritual outlooks and the consequent tension for Heschel in accepting them both is a good example of the coincidence of opposites which Mircea Eliade and other historians of religion view as the very core of religious experience. Martin Buber characterizes the religious situation of humankind as "essential and indissoluble antimony." Its significance lies in the fact that this coincidence of opposites is confronted and lived, "nothing but lived, continually, ever anew, without foresight, without forethought, without prescription, in the totality of its antinomy" (*I and Thou*, trans. Ronald Gregor Smith [New York: Scribner's, 1958], p. 95). Buber's words capture so well what appears to have been Heschel's experience as he accepted both the Kotzker and the Baal Shem into his life. See above, chap. 5, note 19.

32. *The Earth Is the Lord's: The Inner World of the Jew in Eastern*

Europe (New York: Schumann, 1950; repr. New York: Farrar, Straus & Giroux, 1978), pp. 10, 25–26, 34.

33. Ibid., pp. 16–19, 71–74, 89.

34. Ibid., pp. 43–49, 93–94.

35. Ibid., pp. 20–21, 61–64.

36. Ibid., pp. 64, 90–93.

37. Ibid., pp. 98–105.

38. Ibid., pp. 105–109.

39. Cf. "Children and Youth," *Insecurity of Freedom*, pp. 39–51, and Heschel's talk on religious education, "Idols in the Temples," given before the Rabbinical Assembly of America in 1962, ibid., pp. 52–69.

40. Ibid., pp. 43–51, 62.

41. Ibid., pp. 21, 39–41, 59.

42. Ibid., pp. 51, 66.

43. "Conversation with Doctor Abraham Joshua Heschel," p. 21.

44. Cf. his "Introduction" to Heschel's *The Circle of the Baal Shem Tov: Studies in Hasidism*, ed. Samuel H. Dresner (Chicago: The University of Chicago Press, 1985), pp. viiff., and his "Heschel the Man."

45. *Insecurity of Freedom*, pp. 164–65.

46. "On Prayer," 11–12.

47. *Insecurity of Freedom*, p. 164; *Who Is Man?* pp. 92–93, 101–102; "What We Might Do Together," 133–36; "Choose Life!" 37–38.

48. *Passion for Truth*, pp. 269–70; "On Prayer," 11–12; "What We Might Do Together," 135.

49. *Man Is Not Alone*, p. 78; "What We Might Do Together," 137. Cf. also "Depth Theology," *Insecurity of Freedom*, pp. 115–26. For an excellent critical analysis of the whole pretheological situation in Heschel's thought, cf. Merkle's *Genesis of Faith*.

50. *Insecurity of Freedom*, pp. 125, 160, 281; *Who Is Man?* pp. 48–49, 76, 116–19.

51. *God in Search of Man*, p. 416; *Who Is Man?* p. 41; "On Prayer," 10.

52. "No Religion Is an Island," 129; *God in Search of Man*, p. 423; *Israel*, pp. 211–12; *Who Is Man?* p. 99.

53. National Conference of Catholic Bishops, "1975 Statement on Catholic–Jewish Relations," in *Faith Without Prejudice*, ed. Eugene Fisher (New York: Paulist, 1977), pp. 159–68.

54. *The New York Times*, April 14, 1986, p. 4; "Choose Life!" 38.

55. "From Mission to Dialogue?" 11.

56. "What We Might Do Together," 139–40.

BIBLIOGRAPHY

Bennett, John C. "Agent of God's Compassion." *America*, 128, No. 9 (March 10, 1973), 205–206.

Brown, Robert McAfee. "Abraham Heschel: A Passion for Sincerity." *Christianity and Crisis*, 33, No. 21 (December 10, 1973), 256–59.

Buber, Martin. *I and Thou*. Trans. Ronald Gregor Smith. New York: Scribner's, 1958.

——. *I and Thou*. Rev. ed. Ed and trans. Walter Kaufmann. New York: Scribner's, 1970.

——. "Replies to My Critics." In *The Philosophy of Martin Buber*. Edd. Paul A. Schilpp and Maurice Friedman. LaSalle, Ill.: Open Court, 1967. Pp. 689–744.

Campion, Donald, s.j. "Of Many Things." *America*, 128, No. 9 (March 10, 1973), 200.

"Contemporary Judaism and the Christian." *America*, 128, No. 9 (March 10, 1973), 202.

"Conversation of Cardinal Bea with Jewish Scholars and Theologians." March 31, 1973. American Jewish Congress Archives. New York City.

"A Conversation with Doctor Abraham Joshua Heschel." December 20, 1972. National Broadcasting Company transcript.

Cousins, Ewert. *Bonaventure and the Coincidence of Opposites*. Chicago: Franciscan Herald Press, 1978.

Dresner, Samuel H. "Heschel the Man." In *Abraham Joshua Heschel: Exploring His Life and Thought*. Ed. John C. Merkle. New York: Macmillan, 1985. Pp. 3–27.

——. "Introduction." In Abraham Joshua Heschel. *The Circle of the Baal Shem Tov: Studies in Hasidism*. Ed. Samuel H. Dresner. Chicago: The University of Chicago Press, 1985. Pp. viiff.

——. "Remembering Abraham Heschel." *America*, 146, No. 21 (May 29, 1982), 414–15.

Dulles, Avery, s.j. *Models of Revelation*. Garden City, N.Y.: Doubleday, 1983.

Friedman, Maurice. *Martin Buber's Life and Work: The Middle Years, 1923–1945*. New York: Dutton, 1983.

Heschel, Abraham Joshua. "Children and Youth." *The Insecurity of Freedom: Essays on Human Existence*. New York: Schocken, 1972. Pp. 39–51.

——. "Choose Life!" *Jubilee*, 13, No. 9 (January 1966), 36–39.

——. *The Circle of the Baal Shem Tov: Studies in Hasidism*. Ed. Samuel H. Dresner. Chicago: The University of Chicago Press, 1985.

——. "Depth-Theology." *Cross Currents*, 10, No. 4 (Fall 1960), 317–25. Repr. "Depth Theology." In *The Insecurity of Freedom: Essays on Human Existence*. New York: Schocken, 1972. Pp. 115–26.

——. *The Earth Is the Lord's: The Inner World of the Jew in Eastern Europe*. New York: Schumann, 1950. Repr. New York: Farrar, Straus & Giroux, 1978.

——. "The Ecumenical Movement." *The Insecurity of Freedom: Essays on Human Existence*. New York: Schocken, 1972. Pp. 179–83.

——. "From Mission to Dialogue?" *Conservative Judaism*, 21, No. 3 (Spring 1967), 1–11.

——. *God in Search of Man: A Philosophy of Judaism*. New York: Farrar, Straus and Cudahy, 1955. Repr. New York: Farrar, Straus & Giroux, 1977.

——. "Idols in the Temples." *The Insecurity of Freedom: Essays on Human Existence*. New York: Schocken, 1972. Pp. 52–69.

——. *The Insecurity of Freedom: Essays on Human Existence*. New York: Schocken, 1972.

——. *Israel: An Echo of Eternity*. New York: Farrar, Straus & Giroux, 1969. Repr. 1977.

——. Letter to Augustin Cardinal Bea. May 22, 1962. American Jewish Committee Archives. New York City.

——. *Maimonides*. Trans. Joachim Neugroschel. New York: Farrar, Straus & Giroux, 1982.

——. *Man Is Not Alone: A Philosophy of Religion*. New York: Farrar, Straus and Young, 1951. Repr. New York: Farrar, Straus & Giroux, 1977.

——. *Man's Quest for God: Studies in Prayer and Symbolism*. New York: Scribner's, 1954.

——. "No Religion Is an Island." *Union Seminary Quarterly Review*, 21, No. 2 (January 1966), 117–31.

——. "On Improving Catholic–Jewish Relations." Memorandum to Augustin Cardinal Bea. May 22, 1962. American Jewish Committee Archives. New York City.

——. "On Prayer." *Conservative Judaism*, 25, No. 1 (Fall 1970), 1–14.

——. *A Passion for Truth*. New York: Farrar, Straus & Giroux, 1973.

——. *The Prophets*. 2 vols. Philadelphia: Jewish Publication Society of America; New York: Harper & Row, 1962. Repr. New York: Harper Torchbooks, 1969, 1971.

——. "Protestant Renewal: A Jewish View." *The Christian Century*, 80, No. 49 (December 4, 1963), 1501–24. Repr. in *The Insecurity of*

Freedom: Essays on Human Existence. New York: Schocken, 1972. Pp. 168–78.

———. *The Sabbath: Its Meaning for Modern Man*. New York: Farrar, Straus and Young, 1951. Rev. ed. New York: Farrar, Straus and Co., 1963. Repr. New York: Farrar, Straus & Giroux, 1979.

———. Statement. September 3, 1964. American Jewish Committee Archives. New York City.

———. "The Vocation of the Cantor." *The Insecurity of Freedom: Essays on Human Existence*. New York: Schocken, 1972. Pp. 242–53.

———. "What We Might Do Together." *Religious Education*, 52, No. 2 (March–April 1967), 133–40.

———. *Who Is Man?* Stanford: Stanford University Press, 1965.

Kasimow, Harold. *Divine–Human Encounter: A Study of Abraham Joshua Heschel*. Washington, D.C.: University Press of America, 1979.

Lane, Dermot. *The Experience of God*. New York: Paulist, 1981.

Merkle, John C. *The Genesis of Faith: The Depth Theology of Abraham Joshua Heschel*. New York: Macmillan, 1985.

Minutes of the Meeting with Augustin Cardinal Bea (English translation). March 31, 1963. American Jewish Committee Archives. New York City.

National Conference of Catholic Bishops. "1975 Statement on Catholic–Jewish Relations." In *Faith Without Prejudice*. Ed. Eugene Fisher. New York: Paulist, 1977. Pp. 159–68.

On Jewish Learning. Ed. Nahum Glatzer. New York: Schocken, 1955.

"Questions to Be Submitted to Cardinal Bea at the Meeting with Jewish Scholars." March 7, 1963. American Jewish Committee Archives. New York City.

Stransky, Thomas. "The Catholic–Jewish Dialogue: Twenty Years After *Nostra Aetate*." *America*, 154, No. 5 (February 8, 1986), 92–97.

Tanenbaum, Marc. "Heschel and Vatican II—Jewish–Christian Relations." Unpubl. lecture. The Jewish Theological Seminary of America. February 1, 1983.

Vatican Commission for Religious Relations with the Jews. "Guidelines and Suggestions for Implementing the Conciliar Declaration *Nostra Aetate* (n. 4)." In *Stepping Stones to Further Jewish–Christian Relations*. Ed. Helga Croner. New York: Stimulus, 1977. Pp. 11–16.

Vatican Council II. "Declaration on the Relation of the Church to Non-Christian Religions [*Nostra Aetate*, October 28, 1965]." In *Vatican Council II: The Conciliar and Post Conciliar Documents*. Ed. Austin Flannery, O.P. Collegeville, Minn.: Liturgical Press, 1975. Pp. 738–42.